THE GLOBAL MIND

AND THE RISE OF

CIVILIZATION

THE PARADIGM SHIFT TRILOGY, VOL. 1:

THE
GLOBAL MIND
AND THE RISE OF
CIVILIZATION

A NOVEL THEORY OF OUR ORIGINS

CARL JOHAN CALLEMAN, PH.D.

Two Harbors Press
322 First Avenue N, 5th floor
Minneapolis, MN 55401
612.455.2293
www.TwoHarborsPress.com

ISBN-13: 978-1-62652-675-4
LCCN: 2014901800

Distributed by Itasca Books

Cover Design by Sophie Chi
Typeset by Steve Porter

Printed in the United States of America

What if human civilization is a product of an evolving

global mind field that we are all part of? What if this is a divine

mind that always influences the way we think?

THE PARADIGM SHIFT TRILOGY

VOLUME 1:
THE GLOBAL MIND AND THE RISE OF CIVILIZATION

CONTENTS

ACKNOWLEDGMENTS

My gratitude goes first to my wife Elaine, who has supported this book project and has contributed with very valuable advice regarding its content, and sometimes more detailed help. Suzzan and Craig Babcock have made a great and valuable contribution by helping me edit the book and providing good advice regarding its content. Great thanks go to Bengt Sundin, who has been my webmaster and provided critical help with the images for this book. I also want to thank Barbara Hand Clow for having gone through two revised versions of the manuscript and provided valuable feedback.

Preface by the Author

The current volume is the fourth I have written in the English language where the Mayan calendar provides the basic understanding of the fundamental structuring of evolutionary time. It has the distinction, compared to other ideas about the Mayan calendar, in that it looks upon this primarily as a description of the evolution of consciousness. I believe this way of structuring time remains just as powerful as ever for opening up different aspects of reality to a new and deeper understanding. My books based on this are:

1. *Solving the Greatest Mystery of Our Time: The Mayan Calendar* (Garev, 2001)

2. *The Mayan Calendar and the Transformation of Consciousness* (Inner Traditions, 2004),

3. *The Purposeful Universe: How Quantum Theory and Mayan Cosmology Explain the Origin and Evolution of Life* (Inner Traditions, 2009)

These are all relevant as backgrounds to the present book. Yet, even if these earlier books will facilitate the understanding of the present book, they are not in any sense prerequisites for reading it.

The book you are holding in your hand, *The Global Mind and the Rise of Civilization*, is the first volume in *The Paradigm Shift Trilogy*. This first volume presents a completely new and original perspective on our origins and the rise of the early civilizations on our planet. It outlines why there is a civilization here in the first place: Spiritual imprints, or if you like, mental holograms emanating from the Earth that have not previously been systematically studied, shape our minds and lie behind the course of history. The evolutionary process that results from our assimilation of such imprints is what has led up to how we currently live our lives. Since how we relate to our present reality, and its possible future transformation, very directly depends on how we look upon our own origins and our own minds, I invite you to explore this possibility with me in this book. As an alternative to the views of both mainstream and alternative historians, I will then argue that human civilization finds its origin in the mind, a global and collective mind of a divine origin that over time has changed in a predictable way. Even if this may sound like a conspiracy story, it is only so to the extent that we are unaware of how the mind works.

If the mind sounds like a trivial cause for the rise of civilization, I can assure the reader that it is not, and we will come to find on this journey that the mind has a different origin than most people believe. We will find that the conventional views of what the mind is, and how it has been created, are profoundly misleading and then also potentially disempowering regarding how we shape our future. The heart of the matter is that history cannot be understood without understanding the mind and vice versa. If through these new insights we now finally may arrive at a higher and more inclusive truth, then these insights will serve to create a new clarity regarding our own mental evolution. I especially invite those eager for fundamental scientific and philosophical novelties to evaluate this theory as a potential part of the paradigm shift that many others and I believe is now taking place. This is not likely to be a theory that anyone has heard before, either regarding the mind or in regards to history and archaeology. It seems only now these areas of study are being directly connected on a deeper level.

The development of the theory presented in this book took its beginning around October 28, 2011, the date I had concluded based on my studies of the ancient Maya and human history in general would be the actual "shift date" of the Mayan calendar. To experience this shift of the ages, I decided to go to a mountain area between Sweden and Norway, located at the 12th longitude East, in order to have as profound an experience of the shift as possible. This had the advantage of giving me relative seclusion from external influences in an important location at this particular time. While I was there, I had an authentic experience of the shift between October 28, 2011, and October 29, 2011, which gave me a sense of how the waves of creation would continue from then on. Equally importantly and unbeknownst to me, several other people I knew to have a genuine sensitivity to the Mayan calendar also experienced this shift. The shift we experienced was very real.

Nonetheless, in the days and weeks that followed upon this shift there were very few signs of anything dramatic happening pertaining to the world at large. The shift did not seem to manifest in the way that any of us had expected, and we did not witness any events of real consequence good or bad, at least not immediately afterwards. To provide context, we should then recall that ever since the activation of the the the so-called Ninth Wave of the Mayan calendar system on March 9, 2011, the world had become the stage for almost unprecedented protests against the established order, including not only the Arab Spring, but also the Occupy Movement. It was thus not a farfetched expectation that such movements would intensify to immediately transform the world in tangible ways. However, if anything, after the most important shift in my lifetime these movements tended to lose momentum. Yet, at least spiritually orientated people turned inwards to a new stillness that seemed to emanate from this shift in the Mayan calendar.

Naturally, because of this stillness, I started to wonder if I had been wrong about the end date and saw myself in a defensive position. Could the archaeologists who had told the world that the shift would take place on December 21, 2012, have been right? Most people already believed this, and then there were the many stories, films, and such that purportedly substantiated this date. I still very much doubt this, mostly because I had actually experienced the shift on October 28, but also because I saw no reason to trust the archaeologists on this particular point. As the reader of the current book will find, I have a deep respect and trust in how professional archaeologists carry out their fact-finding missions. Yet, an archaeologist is not someone I would go to in order to find out when there would be an "energy" shift. This is because they are not trained to address such a question, and many of them would probably dismiss such a notion altogether.

Moreover, I had been able to make some very precise predictions based on the shift date I had embraced, such as the beginning of the economic downturn in late 2007 that I had made ten years in advance. I had also precisely pinpointed when the Ninth Wave of the Mayan calendar system, expected to result in a very evident frequency increase would begin. Two days after the activation of this wave, this increase seemed to be confirmed with the large earthquake in Japan, followed by its nuclear crisis at about the same time as the wars in Libya and Syria began. *Newsweek Magazine*, in fact, wrote "Apocalypse Now" on its cover the following week, since to its editors it seemed that an extraordinary number of dramatic events were then happening at the very same time. This is exactly what you would expect from a frequency increase, and using the Mayan calendar system I had been able to tell exactly when this would be expected based on the October 28 "end date."

However, even if the October date was correct and some of us had actually experienced it on an inner plane, the fading of the drama of 2011, the Year of the Protester, was not what we had expected. Thus, doubts remained if it was a real shift. In retrospect, however, I should have realized that a real paradigm shift is never exactly what anyone expects beforehand. It will not confirm the worldview anyone of us already embraces. Instead, a shift in consciousness alters the human beings in a way that we cannot experience in advance, and the emerging paradigm is never fully visible before such a shift. Shifting the consciousness brings us to a new mental place, which allows us to see connections and a unity of things that was not possible prior to the shift. A thought that came to mind regarding this unpredictability of evolution is something I had heard in Mexico; the Plumed Serpent (which, as we will see, is a metaphor of divine creation) sometimes molts its skin and moves in an unexpected direction. Shifts, in other words, do not take place in accordance with what we mortals may expect or want, but according to a plan conceived at a higher level.

Regardless, soon after returning to the United States in late 2011, I started to write a book I thought would be about the continuation of the Mayan calendar. Enough material for a book, somewhat defensively written, manifested in a fairly short period of time. However, I thought that I also needed to present some new historical angles on the Long Count in this by providing background to this wave of 5,125 years. After all, this wave was what had partly generated the shift and that so many people had been talking about. Then, as I started to write about the Egyptian pyramids and the human mind, it suddenly clicked; I saw a connection between the pyramids' straight lines and the mind that I had not seen before. I recognized this insight as coming from the particular shift I had experienced on October 28, 2011.

A new path opened up and I felt the book no longer "wanted" to be written in the way I had originally envisioned. After about half a year, this new mental opening had created so much new material that I decided to make a trilogy from it, leaving only the first volume to be about the rise of civilization and the basic outline of the mind. Hence, with the turn this book took, the present volume does not have a focus on predicting the future course of history. It is instead about the roots of humanity and the origin of civilization. Yet, if we are to create a new future it is imperative to understand the past and our own origin. Since then, I have explored this new theme for over a year, which took me in many different directions. In this sense the current book, connecting the rise of civilization with the dawn of the mind, is a direct product of the significant shift of the ages all of us have recently gone through, whether knowingly or not. It represents an attempt to formulate a new paradigm for the future and, as befits a result of such a shift in consciousness, it is wholly original.

Here we will ask who we really are and what factors determine how we experience and create our reality. It touches upon and covers a very wide range of disciplines traditionally considered separate, but which are now studied in the same context. Using such a multidisciplinary approach, involving history and its many specialties, archaeology, neurology, linguistics, psychology, and geophysics, it aspires to answer two significant questions: 1) "What is the origin of human civilization?", and 2) "What is the relationship between mind and brain?" For both of these problems, new and original solutions will be proposed.

Scientific theories are ultimately evaluated based on the accuracy of the predictions they give rise to, and it is only fair if such criteria be applied to my work. Chapter five of the present book then describes what may be the most compelling verification of a prediction made to date based on the Mayan calendar. It is a verification that implies there is a solid new basis for understanding the mind and its relationship to the brain. Fundamentally, everything is connected to everything else, and it is my hope that such a perspective, based on a wide range of disciplines will now create a deeper level of understanding of the unity of our existence.

An overview of this book reads as follows: chapter one begins with the dawning of the human mind and the rise of civilization. This establishes a relationship between the two that we will explore from many different angles throughout the book. Essentially, this study of the early civilizations becomes a means of studying our minds, and what our origins truly are. The second and third chapters summarize the background for studying the evolution of the mind in the Mayan calendar system and some of what this tells us about human history. In chapter four, we return to what human beings were like before civilization dawned; we will look at the mental transition that prepared them for it. In chapter five, we will explore the nature of consciousness and especially the earthly foundations of the global mind. In chapter six, I go through, one by one, some significant phenomena associated with the rise of civilization, and explore how the dimensions of space and time of the emerging global mind can explain these. Chapter seven, brings some of the pieces together and outlines the perspective that we may gain from this new understanding of our origins. There are also two appendices, one with a focus on the current shift, and another on biological evolution. Finally, there is a summary of conclusions, and afterword. Spirituality, altered states of consciousness and the future of the Mayan calendar will only be discussed in depth in the later volumes.

Since the paradigm shift I am proposing is so radical it is my intention to base this trilogy only on what is considered today as established fact by the scientific community. I think this is fairly well reflected in Wikipedia and so a majority of my notes will be references to particular articles on this site, because it is easily accessible to most people and allow for everyone to research the underlying basis. For certain specific topics, it has been necessary to use other web sources or some very important articles in the specialized scientific literature that may require library resources.

Although naturally the value of the proposed paradigm shift will depend on the response of the readers, I feel very privileged to have assimilated this shift and to be able to present a new way of looking at our history. This is a perspective where we are all part of a larger scenario, which means both greater responsibilities and opportunities for everyone. If fully assimilated, we may participate in the current shift to unity consciousness on a daily basis. In this, no one is powerless and everyone is able to contribute.

Seattle, January 1, 2014

CHAPTER 1:
The Dawn of the Human Mind

WHERE DOES THE HUMAN MIND COME FROM?

The mind is very powerful, and if we set our minds to something we can move mountains. We never seem to doubt the importance of the mind, and we often view it as a prized personal possession. Yet, do we really know where it comes from, what it is or why it is so powerful? Since the mind lacks physical substance and is not something we can smell, taste, or see, how do we even know, as many assume, that it comes from the brain? Even though philosophers and psychologists have been discussing the nature of the mind for a long time, the exact location and nature of the mind, and even whether it exists at all, is still debated.

The main dividing line in this philosophical debate has been drawn between "materialists" and "idealists." The materialists, the school dominating official science and the current educational system, assert that the mind does not exist as an independent entity and our thoughts can be reduced to, and understood as brain chemistry. Idealists, on the other hand, maintain the mind is all that exists and hold physical reality to be merely an illusion. These are the two extreme positions in this discussion. In general, most people will probably adhere to a so-called dualistic point of view, where the mind is connected to the brain and yet is something independent. This view would, for instance, be held by many religions believing in the existence of a nonmaterial reality and in a soul.

An unresolved problem thus seems to exist very close to home when it comes to the origin of the mind and what the mind is in the first place. Since the mind means much for how we think about the world, the intentions we have, and the decisions we make, it decidedly plays an important role in our lives. It is the purpose of this book to bring clarity to what the mind is and while doing so, bring an understanding of what caused the rise of civilization on our planet. The main source material will here then not be abstract philosophical concepts or introspection. In this case, I feel we would risk going around in a circle since the mind cannot really provide an objective analysis of itself. To me, what instead seems the most meaningful inroad for a scientific exploration of the mind is to study how it has evolved historically. Since the mind is a phenomenon that is nonphysical, we will then need some means of studying its emergence and evolution indirectly. This we may find by following certain particular historical processes. Some of the metaphysical concepts of the ancient peoples of our planet will then also be critical for understanding the origin of the mind and how it can play such a significant role in our lives.

THE GREAT PYRAMID

We will begin our studies of the mind in ancient Egypt, in a civilization whose independent existence spanned about three thousand years and underwent major fluctuations in this period. The most mysterious era in Egypt's history for us who live today is however the early dynastic period about five thousand years ago, when this civilization dawned. It was at this time works on an enormous scale were undertaken. Since then the pyramids, particularly the Great Pyramid of the Giza Plateau (Fig 1), have been seen as one of the grand mysteries of humanity, attesting to very advanced capabilities appearing already at the dawn of human civilization (It is believed to have been completed in 2560 BCE). The construction of this, and other pyramids, is haunting to us because we are not quite able to grasp what motivated those who built them.

Figure 1. The pyramids at Giza.

Why build such a pyramid? Even if it is a tomb, it is not immediately obvious to a modern person why it had to be built in this particular shape and, above all, on such a colossal scale. After all, for more than four thousand years this was the tallest building in the world, built as it was from an amazing mass of 5.9 million tons of stones. Attesting to its geometric precision are the facts that the ratio of the perimeter to its height is equal to 2π with an error less than 0.05%, and the four sides of the base have an average error of only 58 millimeters in length.[1] The architectural scope and geometrical accuracy of this pyramid is thus, by all standards, astounding. In antiquity, the Great Pyramid was already counted as one of the Seven Wonders of the World, and it is, unlike the others, still standing today. It serves as a constant reminder that there is something about the dawn of human civilization we have yet to learn.

The Great Pyramid thus begs answers to the questions: "How and by whom was it built?" and "Why was it built on the scale and with the geometric precision that it was?" That the Egyptians indeed built the pyramids themselves seems clear from the little known fact that on the Red Pyramid, usually seen as a kind of practice construction for the Great Pyramid, there are at different levels names inscribed by the teams of workers who built it.[2] Moreover, at these levels, along with the names are inscribed dates in the reign of Pharaoh Sneferu, which show that this whole pyramid took them about seventeen years to build. The Great Pyramid would then arguably also have been built by Egyptians in the early dynastic era and have been completed within a similar time frame. Nevertheless, the fact that they built the pyramids themselves makes their dedication even more stunning, pointing out that we have not quite understood what motivated them.

I will here only partly focus on the techniques that were used to build these pyramids. While this is an interesting question,[3] I do not think it is the most important for understanding the message the pyramids hold for us today. In my view, the more important question is: "For what purpose were the pyramids built?" For answering this, a good start is to go directly to the sources. According to the ancient Egyptian creation myths, the pyramids were built as reflections of the so-called Benben, the original primordial mound from which the Earth was created.[4] The pyramid shape was believed to be that of this primordial mound, which had brought order out of chaos as it emerged from the vast expanse of waters.[4] Yet, if this is so, how do we make sense of it based on our modern knowledge of the world? What is this primordial mound, and why would anyone build such a huge monument to it?

The present book will answer this in a way that is original, and so probably also quite surprising, but also gives a fundamental message about what makes the human being human and explains the nature of the mind. The primary focus will then be on what the minds of the pyramid builders were like and whether these were different from those that came before or after them, including ourselves. As an approach to this problem, my own extensive background in the Mayan calendar has pointed to a significant factor that seems to have been lost in the debate over the purpose of the Egyptian pyramids. This factor is the conspicuous timing of their construction and how this relates to the Mayan calendar. Our point of entry to the inquiry into the reason for building the pyramids will thus be this timing and of course since we will be studying the rise of civilization everywhere there will also be ample cross-referencing to other ancient cultures.

WORLDWIDE PYRAMID BUILDING AS RELATED TO THE MAYAN LONG COUNT

In the understanding of the Classical Maya, whose high culture rose about three thousand years after the first Egyptian pyramids were built, different deities, gods, and goddesses ruled different time periods. When a new such deity was "seated," a shift took place in life on Earth. In chapters two and three we will see that in actual fact it is possible to understand human evolution as a process taking place over time based on the shifts symbolized by these deities. This calendar may thus provide a timeline of shifting mental states and it is because the human mind is reorganized at such shift points that civilizations will rise and fall. In this view, *it is not the evolution of civilization that has created the mind, but the evolution of the mind that has created civilization.* This goes directly counter to the materialist viewpoint and would at first sight seem difficult to prove. Yet, while such mental shifts may not be directly measurable by physical instruments, it is certainly possible to observe their effects and this is why they can still be studied with a scientific method.

Based on such studies, I assert we will be able to understand, among many other things, that the emergence of human civilization, including the building of pyramids, was based on a mental shift. It is then because our own minds have evolved since then through a series of shifts that we no longer experience the world in the same way as the ancients did and do not endeavor to build pyramids of this size ourselves. The actual message to us from the pyramids would thus more than anything else be about the nature of our minds. If we are able to grasp this message, as I suggest is possible, we will gain a deeper insight into what it means to be a human being and what may be in store for us in the future.

If indeed the Mayan view that there are "preset" consciousness shifts along the time line of history is correct, then it seems that in order to understand the enigma of the Egyptian pyramids (and incidentally all other events in history as well) we will need first to study the timing of their appearance. To provide a background to this, Figure 2 shows how the building of significant pyramids in different parts of the world is related to the Long Count of the Maya (which is the calendar that begins in 3115 BCE[5] in the middle of the time line) and especially to its very beginning.

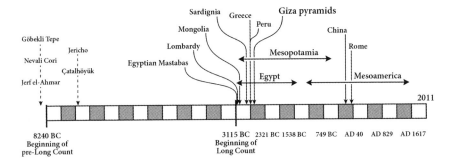

Figure 2. Important examples of pyramid building in the thirteen first baktuns of the Long Count[6] in different parts of the world. The broken lines at the beginning of the pre-Long Count show some of the world's oldest rectangular structures.[7, 8, 9, 10]

This Long Count calendar (that was famously supposed to end in 2012) primarily consists of a series of time periods called baktuns, each of a duration of 400 periods of 360 days (so-called tuns), translating into 394.3 common solar years. Thirteen baktuns of this time period thus amounts to a total time of 5,125 years, which is the time-span that recently was completed. As mentioned, the qualities of these different time periods vary, and in the figure the baktuns are marked either as white or gray, depending on whether they are periods of creative light (in the following called DAYS; described by small caps to distinguish them from regular days) or resting periods of darkness (NIGHTS), respectively. The alternations between such DAYS and NIGHTS provide the background to the fact that the Mayan Long Count is a wave movement, something we will describe and explain in chapters two and three.

When it comes to the Egyptian pyramids most archeologists base their ages on king lists and have dated Pharaoh Djoser's pyramid in Saqqara, the oldest of them, to around 2600 BCE. The Giza pyramids have been given a slightly lower age, and this is where these have been placed in the diagram. It should be noted, however, that, based on carbon-14 datings, samples of wood from these monuments have been estimated to be about two hundred[11] or even four hundred years[12] older. Regardless of this uncertainty, it is clear the Egyptians began to build small pyramid-like platforms called mastabas[13] close to the beginning date of the Mayan Long Count. A question that is immediately raised from Figure 2 is then why no pyramids were built in the world before this date and a reasonable hypothesis seems to be that pyramid building was related to and somehow triggered at the beginning point of this calendar. Interestingly, this date is also very close to the time (3100 BCE) when Menes unified Upper and Lower Egypt,[14] a unification into one nation that at the time was looked upon as a creation by "the gods."[15] This was the event that started the long line of Pharaonic dynasties and the establishment of this monarchy can rightly be looked upon as the dawn of human civilization. For those, like myself, who adhere to the time-line of events generally accepted by historians this synchronicity is quite remarkable.

Naturally, if the Long Count calendar took its beginning at the dawn of civilization, this would indicate it has something to tell us about what caused this. This is all the more so as also to the much later Maya, this particular time marked the beginning of a "new creation" by the gods,[16] and it was for this reason their Long Count took its beginning then. The Maya would use this calendar as a basis for knowing when to erect their own pyramids and altars at significant shift points, (included in the Mesoamerican time span in Fig 2).[17] Therefore, in a larger perspective their pyramid building may be looked upon as a continuation of a process of creation that had started earlier with the Egyptians.

Although the Giza pyramids may be the most awe-inspiring ever built, they are, as is evident from Figure 2, far from the only ones. Several pyramids, such as those in current-day Iran,[18] Greece,[19] Peru,[20] and Sardinia[21] in Italy, were also built at the time of the beginning of the Long Count. Recently, an increasing number of large hills that may be pyramids, even if they are not built from the bottom up by stones, such as in Lombardy in Italy,[22] and Mongolia,[23] have also been found from the same time. Based on these facts it is hard to dispute that this particular time was special when it comes to pyramid building on our planet.

Later, over the millennia very large pyramids have been erected in different parts of the Americas,[24] as well as smaller ones, for instance in Rome, Nubia, Canary Islands and elsewhere. Typically, the building of pyramids seems to coincide with the founding, or centralizing stages of different civilizations or nations. In China, the so-called First Emperor, Qin Shi Huang, for instance, built them as tombs around the time of the unification of this nation in 221 BCE. The last pyramid in the world built with the explicit purpose of reflecting a connection to divine creation is probably the seventh version of the Temple Mayor in the Aztec capital of Tenochtitlan, built shortly before the conquest of this by Hernan Cortes in 1521 CE. Based on such observations, it seems we would risk missing the point if we looked upon the pyramids as a product of each civilization by itself. Rather, what makes sense is to study pyramids in the overall context of their relationship to the emergence and evolution of civilization.

Naturally, many pyramids may also have disappeared or still remain hidden. If we include platforms, pagodas, and a variety of related structures our planet harbor many such monuments. Even if they are not pyramids in a strict sense, they may still have had a similar purpose. These monuments then also include, for instance, the famous megalithic sites on the British Isles—Stonehenge, Avebury, and Newgrange—that I will discuss in chapter four. According to the best datings of modern archaeologists, the construction of these began around 3100 BCE,[25] or, in other words, again simultaneously with the beginning of the Mayan Long

Count. Yet it seems archaeologists, at least so far, have not been able to explain why so much happened in widely different parts of the world at the beginning of the Mayan Long Count. Maybe there is then something fundamentally amiss in how we have understood history. Maybe modern archaeological research is so fragmented into various specialties—Egyptology, Mayanism, Neolithic Europe, etc.—that the obvious synchronicities at the dawn of history have escaped the entire profession or at least not attracted sufficient attention.

In addition to the pyramids in Fig 2, there are a number of others[26] whose authenticity is disputed. The so-called Bosnian Pyramid of the Sun is one such, which is 213 meters high—about 50 percent higher than the Great Pyramid in Egypt—and has an overall pyramidal shape, which is well aligned with the north-south direction.[27] However, the idea that the Bosnian pyramids are manmade is rejected by most professional geologists, who look upon them as natural emanations of the Bosnian geology. The extraordinary evidence that would be required to support the extraordinary claim that they are manmade thus appears to be missing.[28] Regardless, it is clear that pyramids have been built in many different parts of the world and not only in Egypt. Rather than being an Egyptian peculiarity, pyramid building seems to have emanated from an ancient mind held in common all over the world.

To find the common roots of the phenomenon of civilization, and pyramid building in particular, I suggest that we take as our point of departure the relationship this might have had with the human mind. We will then focus especially on the geometry of the mind and the perpendicular structures this may have given rise to in the first pyramids about 5000 years ago. We should also look at how these were related to the very oldest sites with their rudimentary geometries. For this reason, also the first known rectangular structures created by humans have been pointed out in Fig 2 with broken lines. Rooms with perpendicular corners have for instance been found from 8800-8000 BCE[29] at Göbekli Tepe in today's Turkey (see Fig 33).[30] As it turns out, rectangular rooms thus first appear around the beginning of what in the Figure goes by the name of the pre-Long Count. This pre-Long Count, beginning in 8240 BCE was the period of 5,125 years (thirteen baktuns) that preceded the Long Count calendar and ended as this started in 3115 BCE. It then becomes natural to ask if there is some connection between the appearance of rectangular rooms and pyramids, and the respective beginning points of these two Mayan calendars. Could the advent of agriculture and the rise of civilization be linked to changes in the geometry of the human mind that are expressed in such constructions?

The first rectangular structures discovered slightly precede the advent of agriculture, which as will be discussed in chapter four, only began to be practiced around 8,500 BCE,[31] Göbekli Tepe, for instance, which is considered as the world's oldest temple site then actually precedes agriculture. This has been quite unequivocally shown by the German archaeologist Klaus Schmidt, who has excavated this site with its T-shaped steles (Fig 33). Based on the high number of bones of wild game found there,[32] it has become clear that it was erected by hunter-gatherers. That hunter-gatherers built temples at this early time, before agriculture and also much before civilization, however turns many of the established notions of the pre-history of humanity upside down. This order of events implies that a geometric change in the human mind (expressed in rectangular rooms) may have been at the root not only of the first larger megalithic monuments, but also of agriculture.

To make the claim that Göbekli Tepe was not built by a civilization however means that the word civilization needs to be clearly defined. The word *civilization* is derived from the Latin word *civitas*, meaning city, and in this book I will use it in its original sense of a culture organized around cities. For reasons that will be clear in chapter six I also consider it a requirement that a civilization has a written language. Consequently, since non-settled hunter-gatherers built the first temples, these were not created by a civilization. Rather the insight that is emerging from Göbekli Tepe is that the existence of a civilization is not required for human beings to build large monuments.

The use of the term civilization may however be complicated by the fact that to many people it is associated with a value judgment, where "civilized" means "good". This is not how it is used here, where it is merely a technical term.

To be civilized simply means being part of a culture organized around cities and even if "civilized" may sometimes mean sophisticated, we may also remind ourselves that civilized people have caused considerably more damage to nature than non-civilized.

THE DRAMATIC EVENT ACTIVATING THE GLOBAL MIND

The situation at the beginning of the Long Count was somewhat similar to at the beginning of the pre-Long Count described above. At the beginning of the former, pyramid building, with considerably more advanced geometries than the perpendicular corners made earlier, emerges simultaneously in several places in the world. True civilizations appear only simultaneously with this new architecture and have continued to develop ever since. Therefore we can conclude the beginning times of the pre-Long Count and the Long Count, were not only reflected in the step-wise more sharp perpendicular geometries of the buildings, but also in the beginnings of large-scale transformations of life from hunting and gathering to agriculture and city life, respectively.

Civilization is known to have appeared quite suddenly around 3100 BCE. In the words of the English Egyptologist Toby Wilkinson, who studied rock carvings in pre-dynastic Egypt "there is still a major gap in the record, still a 'missing link.' So many of the aspects that distinguish pharaonic culture seem to have come into being quite suddenly, without any discernible predecessors."[33] Therefore, anyone who contemplates for instance Egyptian civilization will have to face up to the fact that its most spectacular creations emerged soon after the institution of its first dynasty, rather than at its height or end. To get a sense of how early the pyramids were in Egyptian history we may consider that Cleopatra (69-30 BCE), the last pharaoh of Egypt, was closer to our own time than she was to the erection of the Great Pyramid.

With this knowledge as a background—that the construction of the Egyptian pyramids marks the approximate starting point of civilization—we may now return to the question: "Why were these pyramids built?" Our most important hint is then that they were built at the time of beginning of the Long

Count calendar. Another, related hint is that they had been preceded by the world's oldest rectangular structures that derive from the time of activation of the pre-Long Count (Fig 2). This implies that these two calendars may mark shifts in the evolution of geometric structures. Maybe then, if we understand why the Maya set the beginnings of these two creations to the years 8240 and 3115 BCE, respectively, we may also understand why rectangular buildings and pyramids start to appear around these particular times. We will then of course have to take their calendar system seriously and explore if there is a reality to what they called "creations" and their relationship to the geometry of what humans created. If these calendars then turn out to reflect new creations and waves of evolution, bringing new frames of mind into existence, the enigma of the pyramids would be resolved if we only knew how the minds were altered—and by what.

For this we are in a fortunate position, since the Maya did indeed provide an explanation as to why their Long Count calendar began at the time it did. According to the late Linda Schele at the University of Texas, who has played a significant role in deciphering Mayan glyphs, it is inscribed at the Tablet of the Cross at the site of Palenque that at the beginning of this calendar, "the First Father erected the World Tree," so that "the light could enter."[34] To understand this at first enigmatic description, we need to be aware that according to the Maya, the World Tree (what most other cultures refer to as the Tree of Life) was the origin of the four directions. The inscription in Palenque then continues: "it was made proper, the Raised-up Sky-Place, the Eight-House-Partition, is its holy name, the House in the North." In the Mayan account this event is what initiated the Long Count. From this inscription, it seems clear they looked upon this event as a form of divine intervention by the First Father and we may ask if this event, described by the Maya more than three thousand years afterwards, could explain why the Egyptians built the pyramids at the particular time they did.

To address this, we should first note that the Tree of Life, mentioned at the center of this event, was in no way limited to Mayan culture. Instead, the Tree of Life may be regarded as the most widely spread "myth" of the ancient world, which was worshipped almost everywhere. What is of special interest here is that the three oldest civilizations of our planet, which arose around the time the Mayan inscription stipulates, those of Egypt, Sumer, and the Indus Valley worshipped the sycamore-fig tree (Hathor's tree), the Huluppu tree, and the Pipal (later to become the Bhodi) tree, respectively as sacred.[35] This means that the same symbol the ancient Maya described above, the Tree of Life, was also meaningful to those people who lived at the time when this according to the Mayan account should have been erected, and by implication the four directions created with it.

Several other symbols seem to have been associated with this Tree of Life. Serpents, Shiva linga, Axis Mundi, winged disks, and what in light of the Mayan inscription is most relevant here, the eight-petaled flower or rosette, were often shown with it on reliefs. Therefore, these early civilizations seem to have known the very reality that this calendar was based upon and which defined its starting point. The ancient idea that civilization was a creation, a gift from the gods, and emanated from the Tree of Life, is however essentially ignored in our modern world, both by mainstream and alternative historians. Nevertheless, I will here present the radically new, and yet obviously very old idea of the ancients that their civilizations were gifts from "the gods." To grasp this will require that we recognize a spiritual dimension of reality and at least temporarily change our perspective accordingly.

Already from this Mayan inscription it is clear that they looked upon the initiating event at the beginning of the Long Count as metaphysical, as it was described as a creation by one of their gods, the First Father. Notably, this view of the initiating event as metaphysical also coincides with the earlier mentioned view of the ancient Egyptians, who looked upon the unification of Upper and Lower Egypt taking place at the same time as a creation by the gods. It was at the time of the beginning of the Long Count that the god Horus was incarnated as a pharaoh for the first time. Rather than dismissing their own notions, I suggest that we incorporate the ancient view of gods, or spiritual influences, as having brought about the dawn of civilization in a modern theory about its origin.

THE WORLDVIEW MAPS OF THE MAYA AND THE AZTECS

To make sense of the above Mayan inscription, I propose that the World Tree in this event energetically partitioned the world in eight segments as viewed from the North Pole (the eight-house-partitioning). Such an eight-partitioning, shown for instance in the Mayan worldview map in Fig 3a, has a T-shaped pillar in the center as a symbol of the Tree of Life. Here this coincides with the polar axis at the North Pole. The partitioning lines marked in this "cosmogram" are thus not the four directions, as we normally know them, since such directions have no meaning if you are standing at the North Pole from which they emanate.

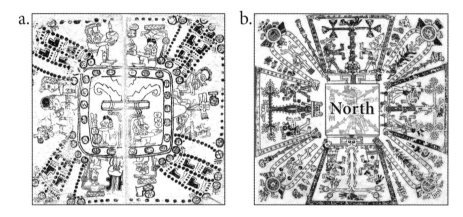

Figure 3. Worldview maps showing the eight-partitioning. (a) Mayan cosmogram from the Codex Madrid. In the center is the Tree of Life, the polar axis, which is surrounded by four pairs of deities and various calendrical signs defining their spiritual qualities. (b) Aztec cosmogram from Codex Fejervary-Mayer with a central deity in the north from which Trees of Life are projected in different directions thus separating four pairs of deities.

To illustrate this, in the Aztec worldview map (Fig 3b) showing the same partitioning the central deity (presumably corresponding to the First Father) has been marked with "North." Consequently, these worldview maps have the North Pole at their centers ("the House in the North"). The vertical and horizontal lines in these cosmograms are then cross sections of planes that cut through the Earth creating four major (plus four minor) segments from the perspective of the North Pole. In the periphery, on both sides of the vertical and horizontal lines, we also see four pairs of deities (making them eight altogether) representing different qualities.

The inscription in Palenque, which reflects the original view of the Maya, together with these worldview maps, then tell us something very significant about the shift that took place when the Long Count began. This is that a metaphysical Tree of Life, here coinciding with the polar axis, "was erected" in the north. As a result, the Earth was partitioned into eight energies symbolized by eight deities organized in pairs thus creating a grid of perpendicular lines separating different energies. What we may conclude is that with the manifestation of this tree, projected in eight directions from the polar axis, human beings in resonance with it would for the first time have become aware not only of the power of the four geographical directions, but also of the existence of straight lines. Again, in the Mayan view, the World Tree is what generates the four directions. These were created all over the planet because of the eight-partitioning lines emanating from the North Pole, and it is the resulting grid that their worldview maps describe. Based on this shift, the minds of people became part of a global structure with metaphysical boundaries originating in the Tree of Life. To use a somewhat more modern terminology, the eight-partitioning of the Earth created a hologram that the human beings downloaded through resonance. *This hologram, or spiritual imprint, is what we call the mind.* Consequently, before this event humans had no mind, or at least, as we will see in chapter four, it was much less developed than after the event. If this metaphysical shift actually happened, and much evidence will be provided in this book to support this, it may have given rise to an extraordinary experience of the four directions and, as we will see, resulted in a new mental order on a global scale.

This is my understanding of how the shift at the beginning of the Long Count actually happened. For the first time directional lines became part not only of the Earth, but also through resonance with the minds of the ancients. As a fact we know that at the time the Maya pinpointed for this event, the

Egyptians started to build very straight pyramids aligned with the four directions. The eight-partitioning then presumably meant that the whole Earth for the first time became covered with a grid that allowed people to orientate themselves geographically, and through resonance with this grid, became aware of the three dimensions of space. *People in other words began to organize their world mentally in relation to straight lines.* The eight-partitioning set an end to the earlier experience of life as chaotic or floating, expressed for instance in widespread myths of a "flood". For those that came after, the men living in this previous state of floating chaos came to be described in dreamlike terms as being beyond measure, as giants, demi-gods or patriarchs living for thousands of years.

In modern times people have looked at such legendary stories either as literally true, or as mere lies or fairy tales. Here we will explore a third alternative, which is that a grid emanating from the "eight-partitioned house" in the North then would come to cover the Earth. From this global grid a new mind would emerge resulting in an altered state of consciousness in the human beings. Over a period of a few hundred years (short in this context) life became radically more structured and measurable than before and reality perceived in a new way. From this new state of mind civilization arose, which indeed is what we know happened at the time the Long Count began (Fig 2). It was because the ancients experienced the origin of the eight-partitioning as metaphysical that they came to look upon civilization as a gift by the gods. As a global mind emanating from the polar axis came into existence everywhere on Earth, the mental shift might have been experienced as very powerful for people who had never before been aware of boundaries. Although it may seem naïve to take this ancient Mayan inscription at face value this is what I have done and I ask the reader to bear with me and explore where it will take us.

THE SIGNIFICANCE OF STRAIGHT AND PERPENDICULAR LINES

Nowadays, we take the existence of straight lines, and lines perpendicular to them, so much for granted that it may be hard to understand how dramatic the initial emergence of such lines might have been. Straight perpendicular lines are now so much a part of modern civilized life that we hardly give their origin a second thought. We see such lines everywhere around us; in our houses and streets and in American cities the latter are often even aligned with the four geographical directions as indeed many ancient monuments are. Yet, everything has a beginning. At the start of the Long Count the phenomenon of straight lines, and what might have been the downloading of a linearly organized mind, was almost a complete novelty. Hence, while to us the Star of Inanna at the beginning of this chapter may seem just like another symbol, to the ancients this geometric structure, emerging from a non-physical realm implied a real power that influenced their lives and must have been very mysterious.

In fact, such perpendicular lines *are* a mystery. To see this, I recommend that the reader here pauses a moment and reflects on the origin of straight lines and recognizes that except for some crystals, which are in general very difficult to find, there are no straight, not to mention perpendicular, lines anywhere in nature. Straight and perpendicular lines are instead hallmarks of civilization, and as people begin to build square houses rather than round or oval they become civilized.

Where then do these straight and perpendicular lines come from, and how did all civilizations come to incorporate them in their designs and architecture? This enigma is compounded by the fact that no straight lines are part of the cells of the human central nervous system.[36] No straight lines can be found in our brains on the molecular level either, and so we must seriously ask how such lines that we are creating in buildings or streets could be projections of the human brain. Modern brain research assumes that organized thinking is a product of the brain, but if this is so, how can it be that straight and perpendicular lines can be seen everywhere in the civilized world but are completely absent in the brain? How can a brain come up with something that is so much unlike itself as a perpendicular line? Maybe then there is something seriously amiss in the modern understanding of how the mind is related to the brain, which is also directly related to the rise of civilization. What I am proposing is that straight lines find their origin in the global grid and not in the brain.

Since the straight line is an abstract concept that is not originally present in physical reality, I suggest that it is manifested through the human beings as a result of their exposure to the new mental hologram with straight lines and angles activated at the beginning of the Mayan Long Count. The origin of this hologram is described in the Mayan creation story as the eight-partitioning of the Earth. This, as we will see in future chapters has had enormous concrete repercussions throughout the evolution of human civilization as it has been downloaded by our brains. A significant fact about the pyramids, for instance, is that they are the first large-scale straight lines ever to have manifested on our planet. They were also erected at the very time the Maya pinpointed for the eight-partitioning, when straight lines initiating their Long Count calendar "were made proper" as recorded in the Palenque inscription above.

What I assert is that the pyramids were built when straight eight-partitioning boundaries were first integrated in the human mind. Straight and perpendicular lines are in fact what civilization—houses, roads, machines, and, more recently, computers—is organized in relation to, and they serve much as blueprints for all of its designs. Without straight lines there would be no civilized order and if we would look for civilized life on a distant planet they would be its clearest signs. As we will see, the emergence of straight lines belonging to this grid is why civilization first arose on our planet. In this reasoning, history is based on the principle of "As inside the humans—so outside in the world," which will be a theme throughout this book.

ANCIENT REFLECTIONS OF THE EIGHT-PARTITIONING

What immediately adds credibility to this background to the rise of civilization in the "eight-partitioning" of the world is the little noted fact that the Great

Pyramid of Giza actually has eight sides. This is rarely visible from the ground, but is quite clear from satellite photos (see cover and Fig 4). The indentation producing this eight-sidedness is so slight that any practical function has been difficult to imagine. To build a pyramid with eight sides is also considerably more difficult than to build it with four,[37] and for this reason we have to assume that this was a significant aspect of a conscious design. Aside from the technical construction argument that this eight-sidedness was intentional, we may note that the Red Pyramid, again usually seen as a practice construction for the Great Pyramid, shows the same concavity. We may thus conclude that the Egyptians built the Great Pyramid, the most spectacular of their pyramids, with eight sides shortly after the mind of our planet according to the Mayan inscription had become eight-partitioned and organized along straight lines. This may then be a crucial part of the explanation to why the Great Pyramid was built in the first place and designed in the way it was. The eight-partitioning is also consistent with the Egyptian origin of the word pyramid: *"Pir E Mit"*, meaning "division of number" or "division of perfection."[38]

Figure 4. Satellite photo of the Great Pyramid of Giza showing that it is eight-sided. From the ground this eight-sidedness is only visible at equinoxes.

There is also a significant parallel to the eight deities of the Maya and the Aztecs in the oldest creation myths of Egypt. These came from the city the Greeks called Hermopolis, and whose name in the Old Kingdom was Khmun, meaning "eight-town".[39] A variety of these myths involved the Ogdoad, eight different deities forming four female/male pairs: Naunet and Nu, Amaunet and Amun, Kauket and Kuk, and Hauhet and Huh. These deities were all associated with the watery mass of directionless chaos from which the primeval mound would emerge. We have every reason to believe that the Great Pyramid in fact symbolized how the primordial mound was created by this Ogdoad since this mythology is from the era when this was built. The eight-sidedness of this pyramid would then be symbolic of the eight-partitioning of the Ogdoad, which set an end to the directionless chaos.[40] Although I have not been able to find evidence that these deities were directly linked to the eight geographic directions I presume that they in their essence are identical with the Mayan and Aztec four couples of deities. Seen in this light there seems to be an amazing correspondence between the Mayan and Egyptian creation mythologies, which may be good to keep in mind if someone doubts the relevance of using the Mayan calendar to study the Egyptian pyramids. Naturally, the fact that the creation stories seem so similar also indicates that they indeed are real.

To find further evidence that civilization on our planet began with an eight-partitioning, giving rise to straight lines on the mental plane, we should go to a culture contemporary with the early Egyptian, the Sumerian, located in present-day Iraq and meaning "the land of the civilized kings."[41] There, an eight-partitioning very notably served as a symbol for An (Fig 5a), which was their name for "heaven" or the foremost of their gods, "the god of heaven." From this sign, we can assume also the Sumerians saw the heavens as eight-partitioned. This eight-partitioning symbol, called Dingir, was in fact so important in the civilization that arose in Mesopotamia that all its gods would come to have this symbol attached to their names.[42] Through this, we can gather that in the Mesopotamian worldview eight-partitioning was synonymous with divine.

Figure 5a. Sumerian cuneiform sign called Dingir, symbolic of heaven, or An, the eight-partitioned god of heaven. This sign was placed next to the names of Mesopotamian gods to signify their divinity.

Representations of the eight-partitioning structure are quite common among other symbols from Sumer and other early civilizations, sometimes in so-called winged discs. To me at least, this provides compelling evidence that the Sumerians associated the eight-partitioning with a divine order as indeed the Maya did. Like the Egyptians, the Sumerians around the time of the beginning of the Long Count also began to build pyramid-like structures called ziggurats. It is well known that the Sumerians, and Mesopotamians in general, built these with the purpose of connecting heaven and Earth.[43] Since they built their temples as perpendicular structures we can conclude that they also saw the heavens as perpendicular (Figs 5a) and this would be another sign that the heavens would have introduced the straight lines. (If they built them just in order to come closer, physically speaking, to the heavens, as sometimes has been suggested, the Sumerians could have climbed a mountain instead. They did not do so, as a mountain would not have the perpendicular layout of the heavens.)

Among the major ancient civilizations of the Near East are also counted the Hittites in Anatolia.[44] Its population may not have been as large as those of Egypt and Mesopotamia, but it is known that their kings were recognized as Great Kings and then actually looked upon as their equals. We know considerably less about Hittite mythology than we know about the other two. Yet, they have left behind a religious standard from the third millennium BCE (Fig 5b), which is believed to symbolize the universe. While the Maya, Aztec, Egyptians and

Sumerians left behind symbols of eight directions, the Hittites then actually left behind a whole eight-partitioned grid decorated with some more common four-partitioned sun-wheels. The eight-partitioning was thus a theme among all the major civilizations in the ancient world in the Near East, even if there was some variation between them. In the Indus Valley, another major civilization from this time that we know considerably less about because its writing has not been deciphered, the eight-partitioning was predominantly symbolized by the swastika,[45] which also has straight lines in eight different directions. It would probably be easy to fill a book of ancient reflections of the eight-partitioning, including for instance, also the Dendera Zodiac[46] or the Aztec Calendar Stone.[47] Arguably, some of the most prominent symbols from the ancient civilizations hold a common message about the new grid. It is only modern people that look upon these eight perpendicular lines as natural and then fail to see that they are enigmatic.

Figure 5b. Standard from the Hittite Kingdom in Anatolia believed to symbolize the universe (third millennium BCE [44]).

When we further look at the relief from Babylon in Fig 6, showing the sun god Shamash, it is hard to avoid the impression that this portrays exactly the same creation event that the inscription in Palenque describes. The sun god, who presumably is what the Maya called the First Father, is shown there with the eight-partitioning as this became visible after the erection of the Tree of Life. (Incidentally, there is much to indicate that the eight-partitioning is only the most basic division of the mind and much ancient symbolism indicates that on top of this it is divided into 16, 32, 64 etc compartments as can also be seen in this Figure.) What is especially important about this relief is that the Babylonians in the 20th century BCE were quite recent inheritors of the Sumerians, who had dominated Mesopotamia at the time when the initial eight-partitioning took place. This image is thus close to a live report of what happened.

In modern times such representations of eight- or sixteen-partitionings have sometimes been interpreted as stars or planets.[48] Yet, this does not seem to be consistent with the view of the ancients. To the Sumerians, An meant heaven, and in the Mayan creation inscription this is spelled out even more clearly. There, it is said that a heaven that previously had been "lying down" became visible as the "Raised-up Sky-Place" at the beginning of the Long Count. This appears to have meant that a new metaphysical imprint then emerged, which, as I will explain in the next chapter, also sometimes came to be associated with the sun. But the eight-partitioning by itself was metaphysical. Heaven in the sense it is used here has the meaning of

Figure 6. The Babylonian sun god Shamash with the Tree of Life and an eight- (or sixteen)-partitioned sun.

a global hologram of a mental order, although many who live today and have not experienced the emergence of a such may not know what to relate it to. How and from where this heaven had arisen, I will only explain in chapter five. Our minds may actually be so much the products of this eight-partitioned mental hologram that we are now unable to see this as something separate from ourselves.

Taken together, these observations tell us that the civilizations in the Near East that emerged around the beginning of the Long Count had actually experienced exactly what the Mayan inscription would later say: "It was made proper, the Raised-up Sky-Place, the Eight-House-Partition, is its holy name, the House in the North." Not only the Egyptians and the Sumerians, but also civilizations that more widely began to flourish at the beginning of the Long Count, created very significant symbols of this eight-partitioning.

That the eight-partitioning event must have been very powerful we may also gather from the fact that the Maya 2,500 years later made it the starting point of their calendar. Maybe it is then not so surprising that the people living when this event actually took place, struck by awe and amazement from the downloading of a new mental organization, built huge pyramids, ziggurats, or similar perpendicular structures as a reflection of this. People always love novelty, especially if it holds the promise of a new divine creation. This new order of the eight-partitioning brought civilization to our planet for the first time and this was perceived as a gift. Thus, it seems only natural that any culture aspiring to become a true civilization would build huge constructions placed in their midst to mirror the heavens and facilitate this.

The purpose of these monuments was then to connect heaven and Earth and to honor the gods, the Tree of Life, and in Egypt the Benben, which were behind the emergence of the eight-partitioned grid. The very project of erecting such buildings would then also be a means of fully assimilating the new mental reality organized by the eight-house partition. Maybe then it was in response to this new heavenly order of precise perpendicular lines that the base of the Great Pyramid was made horizontal and flat to within ±15 millimeters, and the sides of the square base very closely aligned with the four cardinal compass points (within four minutes of arc).[1]

MATHEMATICAL AND PHYSICAL CONSTANTS EMBEDDED IN THE GREAT PYRAMID

In the perspective developed here a pyramid is a whole new mental order cut in stone emanating from a metaphysical grid. Such a mental order has many different aspects and influences the lives of human beings in many different ways. As we will see, this new mental order for instance, played a key role for developing the organized social relationships of civilization, including its systems of governance. Before going on to a discussion of this I would like to address the relationship between the Great Pyramid of Giza and various measurements that are part of its design. This pyramid in fact appears to have been the most important of the pyramids of the Egyptians and many have suspected that it holds a number of "secrets" in how its dimensions are designed. If nothing else, its geometric precision, expressed for instance in the near identical lengths of its four sides and its flatness[1] has for good reason astounded many modern visitors. How could it be that it has certain properties that we most likely would not be able to reproduce today?

In addition to the abovementioned obvious examples of geometric precision, the idea that this pyramid, its location at the Giza Plateau and the King's Chamber would incorporate also many other geometric and mathematical relationships has been around since the 1800's. A large number of frequencies, constants of nature or geographic and astronomical distances known to us from modern measurements have then been proposed to be embedded in its design; the circumference of the Earth's equator, the so-called Schumann frequency related to the Earth's circumference, the sizes of the planets, the distance to the moon, the gravitational constant and astronomical alignments, are among those suggested. Academic Egyptologists on the other hand have often countered, based on what is known about the relatively low level of mathematics and physics in Egypt at the time, they could not possibly have known such constants of nature or geodesic measurements that require very sophisticated modern instrumentation to measure.

While not all of the numerical relationships proposed are necessarily grounded in reality, some of them obviously are and I think to make the point it is enough to stay with those that are generally acknowledged. The Great Pyramid is, for instance, directed towards the direction of the north (not electromagnetic north we should note, but true north as consistent with the Mayan inscription about the Tree of Life) with an error of only 4 minutes of arc (4/60th of a degree), an absolutely astounding accuracy. Therefore, at least in one respect – the alignment of the Giza Pyramids to the four cardinal directions – these constructions do reflect a geodesic measurement of very high precision. Moreover, the Great Pyramid has been built horizontally flat to within ± 15 mm.[1] We also know that the Great Pyramid reflects a mathematical constant, π, which was built into the pyramid through the relationship between its height and circumference.

Based on this we may conclude there is nothing inherently apart or unrealistic with the idea that the Great Pyramid may reflect other mathematical constants, geographical distances or constants of nature as well. Even if the present is not meant to be a book to discuss which ones of the proposed numerical relationships that may be real, we have already every reason to believe that some of them indeed are, especially basic mathematical constants like π and Φ and distances related to the Earth. Among these the proposal that the circumference of the pyramid should be related to the equator of the Earth is especially interesting since the relationship of this to its height is 2π as if it were a circle. It has then for instance been measured that the square base circumference of the Great Pyramid is 921,455[49] meter as compared to 921,452 meter, which is the distance estimated by modern measurements to correspond to half a minute of arc on the equator of the Earth.

Together with the number π, this correspondence to the Earth determines the exact lengths of the sides and the height that the Great Pyramid have been built in accordance with and shows that it was built with a very conscious design. This conscious design, as I have already suggested, thus exactly reflects the eight-partitioning of the whole Earth as it means that the circumference of the Earth is divided by the eight sides of the pyramid, which would be an exactly replica of the new mental order cut in stone. We have in this a perfect corroboration of the Mayan inscription, which actually could not be more clear and precise in mathematical terms. Hence, the Great Pyramid of Giza was built as an act of reverence to the eight-partitioning of the Earth that brought a new mind and civilization to the Egyptians.

There was then a reason that the sides of the Great Pyramid were given exactly the dimensions that they did and that they were so similar. We should then note that this is a confirmation of its purpose, which is not based on any modern units of measure, such as inches or grams, but only on the division of the circle into 360 degrees. To divide the circle into 360 degrees was a practice invented early on in Mesopotamia and may very well be based directly on their experience of the Earth's grid. It is also the number of days in a tun used in the Mayan Long Count and so may be considered to have a true metaphysical origin. Hence, it is not an arbitrary number.

This obviously is not the only explanation for building the Great Pyramid that has been suggested over the centuries, but in addition to many other strong points that will be developed in the following it is absolutely unique in being consistent with the Mayan description of the beginning of the Long Count. It is validated much more broadly than a narrow focus on the building itself in isolation. Naturally, if we accept the circumference of the pyramid was based on the circumference of the Earth, and given its accuracy this is hard to refute, we are confronted with a number of questions that have haunted especially non-academic pyramid researchers for decades: "How did the ancient Egyptians know such constants of nature or geodesic measurements only a limited number of generations after they had emerged from the Stone Age?" and "Why did they not write down any of this knowledge on paper?" We may also wonder where they got the technological proficiency of building the Great Pyramid with such precise distances along its horizontal and vertical lines?

Academic researchers tend to avoid such questions altogether. Many alternative researchers on the other hand merely sweep them under the rug by implying that extraterrestrials or a prior "lost civilization" provided the intelligence behind the construction of the Giza pyramids. After all we know the Egyptians built these themselves. Such suggestions seem more to be based on a need to fill in a gap in our own modern understanding of the mind than on actual evidence. Moreover, such proposals do not explain why the Great Pyramid is such a unique creation, in certain respects surpassing the geometric accuracy of most, if not all monuments erected both before and after it. If we miss this important point we risk missing to learn something from this about ourselves and the nature of our minds. To address the problem seriously we have to explain what the minds of the builders were like and why they were different from ours.

How then could the theory proposed here – the downloading of a new mind based on an eight-partitioned global grid – explain the accuracy with which the Great Pyramid was built and also some of the mathematical constants and geodesic measurements that seem to be embedded in it? Well, if we for instance consider how the size of the Great Pyramid is related to the Earth's circumference at the equator, we may easily understand that this circumference was directly related to, and actually part of the Earth's eight-partitioned grid emanating from the Tree of Life (polar axis). As the Great Pyramid was built in response to, and in order to honor and highlight the establishment of, the new mental order emanating from the eight-partitioned grid then *the circumference of the equator would actually automatically have been embedded in the design of the Great Pyramid.*

That the Great Pyramid, including the very accurate lengths of its sides, was primarily designed to reflect the eight-partitioning of the Earth, does not negate that a number of other geodesic measurements or physical constants may have been embedded in it as well. When the Egyptians downloaded the mental hologram in resonance with the newly established global grid, a number of such constants very likely would have come as an integral part of this, such as possibly the Schumann resonance or the speed of light. Since the eight-partitioning downloaded by the ancients was metaphysical in nature this may have included a number of mathematical and physical constants that pertain to the physics of the Earth and obviously there are precise relationships between these constants for the universe to function properly, whether we know about them or not. Through their new mind they would through resonance experience the world through a grid that had directly incorporated such constants. The tendency would then be for those that had downloaded the new mind to reproduce the corresponding mathematical and geodesic constants in various aspects of the design of the pyramid according to the principle of "As inside-So outside." The architects may not even have been conscious, or only partially so, of the meaning of the various constants that they embedded in the pyramids, which would explain why they did not write any of this knowledge down. They were busy creating a monument in stone reflecting the design of their new mind and quite possibly this was expressed in the design of the King's Chamber and sarcophagus as well.

Hence, the present theory explains why mathematical constants would be embedded in the Great Pyramid in the first place. The Egyptians who built it were simply in an advanced state of resonance with the Earth's metaphysical grid established according to the Mayan account at the beginning of the Long Count. The understanding of the origin of the human mind presented here thus for the first time provides a reasonable explanation to the apparent enigma as to why the Egyptians embedded constants and distances in the Great Pyramid and why it has such a geometric precision. Their brains were the same as ours, but their minds were very different and the fundamental message of this pyramid is, as I stated in the beginning, about the nature of the mind. It is also about how this, as we will see in the following, has evolved in relation to the brain under the influence of the eight-partitioned grid.

I believe it is only now, after the shift of the ages in the Mayan calendar of October 28, 2011 that we may fully appreciate why, when and with what design the Great Pyramid was built and also why it was built in the first place.

If, indeed, as the Maya and other ancient peoples were saying the Long Count began with the establishment of a new metaphysical grid, and hence a new global mind of our planet, then it seems only logical that also at the end of its thirteenth baktun there is a significant mental shift, when we leave many outdated notions behind and a new understanding opens up.

Two things that may increase our understanding of this phenomenon should be added to the discussion. Firstly, the hologram that was downloaded already five thousand years ago was the hologram of the civilized mind, which as we will see in the following is also what has profoundly contributed to the creation of civilization, and the measurements of constants and distances in our own time. So why would the same mind not already then have been able to access some of the constants that we know of today? Science, and especially its measurements, ancient as well as modern, are very much the products of the mind. Secondly, the Egyptians who built the Great Pyramid had access to the perpendicular hologram of the mind in a purer form than ever before or after (To see this the reader may take a sneak preview at Fig 8). This means that if they built the Great Pyramid in order to reproduce the cosmic order, which we know was their intention,[4] then the clarity of this hologram would help them build it so that divine creation was optimally reflected in its construction. From the acute state of resonance that was available with the eight-partitioned grid at this particular time, we may also understand why no building with a similar geometric precision has been built either before or after it.

The purity of the mind at the time of the building of the Great Pyramid (Fig 8) would also explain some of the technical advancement and the amazing geometric precision with which it was built. In modern times it is considered that laser technology would be needed to achieve the horizontal flatness to which the site of the Great Pyramid was leveled. My own view is then that the sharpness of the horizontal line of the new hologram (Fig 5a) that the Egyptians were in resonance with was instrumental for accomplishing this task. Similarly, aligning the building with true north would be accomplished through their heightened resonance with the Earth's grid, which we have now largely lost. I also believe the new vision that this perpendicular imprint gave by itself explains a large part of the remarkable symmetry the Egyptians displayed in many of their other buildings or when crafting stones such as obelisks, granite coffins etc.

At least a part of creating precisely is seeing precisely and if you had downloaded a hologram with sharp perpendicular lines this would have given exactly such a vision. The altered state of the mind that through the eight-partitioning emerged in the ancients, may then explain that the accuracy of their stonework and constructions sometimes surpass our own and led them to create for instance remarkably flat surfaces. I am not implying that a heightened resonance with a sharp perpendicular hologram would automatically solve all the technological problems involved in building a pyramid or creating a granite coffin. But I do believe that such heightened resonance would go a long way and that modern people (because of our blurred perception of horizontal and vertical lines (see Fig 8)) may have become overly reliant of machinery and technology, which was not needed at the time. For this reason, no machines, or signs of technology similar to modern, have been found among the pyramids, but only simple tools. The reason for this absence may then be that their precise vision organized by the new mind played a crucial role in their construction. What I am suggesting is that advanced technology is not everything and the quality of work will in the final analysis also depend on the mental state of an artist, architect or builder.

Because of the new grid the Egyptians, as well as their contemporaries in other cultures, may at this time seem to have become obsessed with straight lines and alignments and sought to establish such in a multitude of ways. One of the shafts in the Great Pyramid, for instance, pointed in the direction of the pole star in the time period 3000-2400 BCE,[50] which may be an expression of what the Maya referred to as "the House in the North" from which the eight-partitioning emanated. From how the Maya described the grid it is not surprising if the particular constellation of the three Giza pyramids finds its origin in the necessity of their architects to gain a clear view of north to align their sides with the four directions. This is part of how archaeologists have traditionally explained the way they were laid out.[50]

In addition to this earthly level, we will in the next chapter see that the eight-partitioning created a new order also on the levels of the heliosphere, galaxy and cosmos. It is therefore also possible that shafts in the Giza pyramids might have highlighted other alignments than the four directions, or that they were laid out as reflections of the belt of stars of Orion[51] or the constellation of Cygnus.[52] There are presumably many fascinating alignments and mathematical relationships in ancient constructions also with cosmic phenomena. Yet, I believe that if these are to help us understand early civilizations they should be looked upon in the context of the eight-partitioning of the human mind and how this gave rise to the various belief systems and institutions of the early civilizations. Only a mind that has integrated straight lines is able to see alignments and it was a mind partitioned by such, which was the true novelty at the dawn of human civilization.

That the ancient Egyptians and Sumerians in this way may have felt strongly compelled by a higher power to build their pyramids is consistent with the studies of Julian Jaynes of the ancient mentality. In *The Origin of Consciousness in the Breakdown of the Bicameral Mind*, he conveys how people in this early phase of history (what we know to be the first half of the Long Count) simply obeyed "the gods." For this reason, he described their relationships to the gods as "hallucinatory" in their subservience. For instance, as we know from the Old Testament of the Bible, Yahweh would often demand and receive absolute obedience, or at least the Jews then experienced it in this way. If Jaynes is right, the Egyptians and Sumerians would have had similar relationships to their gods, and presumably the influences of the metaphysical domain were experienced as much more compelling than at any point closer to our own time.

Yet, you may equally well call this inspiration from a higher source. If the pyramids were based on such a divinely inspired resonance, it is for instance not surprising that the quarters where the workers were living attest to good conditions of life[53] and that there is little to indicate they were slaves. If they built the pyramids to honor the gods that gave them civilization, the builders may have seen their work more as a sacred service than as forced labor. The purpose of building the Great Pyramid seems clear– to project heaven on earth– and this regardless of whether it was ever a tomb for Pharaoh Khufu or not.

ALIGNING SOCIETY WITH THE POWERS OF THE HEAVENS

Yet, civilizations are not only pyramids and temples, but first and foremost an organized society, a system of governance and city life. As mentioned earlier the Egyptian monarchy takes its beginning around 3100 BCE[14] and the world's oldest cities with diversified functions–palaces, temples, markets and living quarters–are from Mesopotamia and dated to about 3200 BCE.[54] What is then interesting to note is that the new system of rule and the diversification of city life are synchronized with the beginning of pyramid building and take their beginnings around the beginning of the Long Count and the eight-partitioning. The question that is now natural to ask is if also these phenomena would somehow be based on the activation of the eight-partitioned grid described earlier and this is what we will explore next.

If we begin by looking at the rise of the monarchy we may then note that the structures and maps the ancients made to symbolize the eight-partitioning very notably had a center, which for instance in the case of pyramidal capstones seems to have been very special. In fact, only at the time of the eight-partitioning a central authority in the form of a monarch emerged in some societies and the most plausible way of understanding this is that he was a reflection of the central point in the hologram where the different lines in the eight-partitioning was converging (Figs 3 and 5). Why else would the monarchies emerge at the very point in time that the Mayan Long Count began and why else would the ancient peoples of the early civilizations perceive the monarchs as representatives of the divine order or even as gods? In Egypt this center would come to be embodied by the pharaohs, and in Sumer by the civilized kings.

Accordingly, the institution of the monarchy was not necessarily just a result of a cynical quest for power, but something people believed in at the time because it actually mirrored the new heaven. The new mind that people then downloaded made the creation of a centrally organized nation around a pharaoh seem natural, and it was because of this that the unification of Upper and Lower Egypt was seen as a reflection of a new creation. The heavens, conferring the authority on the earthly center provided by a monarch, is what made people put up with and revere this institution for such a long time. The temples in different city-states and countries were then there for the populace to connect not only to the heavens, but also at the same time to the center of their nations, their kings.

We should also not ignore that the very organization of the pyramid construction projects may have contributed to the emergence of a centralized nation, as suggested by Kurt Mendehlsson.[55] Logistically, these projects are no small feats, and different members of society had to cooperate on a scale never seen before, serving to create an experience of a nation unified around a king at its center. In this sense, the early pyramid builders, early in the Long Count, were also nation builders organizing themselves around kings that were reflections of the metaphysical center in the heavens.

The monarchs, therefore, were very important aspects of the new mental order, and it was around their authority that the system of rule of the first nations were developed. If this earthly order was a reflection of the heavenly order, it is only natural that the pharaohs and priest kings at the center of this were seen as gods. It then also seems natural if such men at death were expected to return to the center of the divine order and so were sometimes buried in pyramids, whose central points symbolized the center of the eight-partitioning (or mostly the more basic partitioning of the four directions). Remains of human bodies have been found in some Egyptian pyramids,[56] while many others were most likely already robbed of their mummies in ancient times. This would be similar to how some Mayan and most Chinese pyramids served as tombs. On the other hand, if nothing else but for the simple reason that three different pyramids were built in Egypt within the reign of Pharaoh Sneferu, they apparently also had a larger purpose. These pyramids may have been practice pyramids for the larger project they were about to embark upon and it is doubtful if the Gizah pyramids ever served as tombs.

The early Egyptian pyramids, and monuments in other places as well, were then probably partially built to honor and reflect the straight and perpendicular lines of the new eight-partitioned heaven that created their respective civilizations and partially to honor the god-kings that were at the center of these. The more the pyramids would be connected to divine creation—and the sacred numbers that this was associated with—the more people would through them be connected to the heavens. The more people would be connected to the eight-partitioned heaven, the more their minds would develop to create a civilized order on Earth with a monarchy at its center. This presents a sufficient explanation as to why the early civilizations were organized the way they were and, more specifically, why some of them built pyramids.

From the beginning of the Long Count and onwards, different nations, each with its own center and ruler would then continue to emerge, with their temples playing chief roles for this new social organization. Indeed, throughout the Long Count the basic organization in different nation states has later spread across the whole world, where it has manifested in somewhat different forms, including with different languages. The reason that in previous books I have called the Long Count calendar the National Underworld is that the creation of nations is one of its predominant facets. The emergence of a nation is a result of people being drawn to and recognizing the same metaphysical center of their activities.

HOW THE NEW ORGANIZATION OF THE MIND CREATED CIVILIZATION

A theme that will be continuously expanded upon in the following of this book, and especially in chapter five, is how the resonance is created between our individual minds and the global mind-grid. The aforementioned Mayan inscription in Palenque notably refers to the eight-house-partitioning on the global level. We can however only explain why the shift at the beginning of the Long Count had such powerful effects if also the individual human minds were influenced by the same global event through what we might call holographic resonance. If such a resonance did not exist, I assert we have no reason to believe that the ancients would have participated in such immense construction projects. Hence, the existence of such a resonance between the global and individual minds is crucial when it comes to explaining how civilization in the sense of city life with different professions and functions came about.

In the view presented here our brains are not looked upon merely as isolated thinking machines. They are instead primarily receivers, molded by mental holograms operating according to the principle of "As above—So below." If, for instance, the heavens imprint perpendicular lines, people will begin to see things in relation to these and start to build houses and monuments that are perpendicular. Through their effects on the individual human brains, the downloading of such lines has been instrumental for the rise of human civilization. This has happened partly when people, as we have already seen, recreated these lines in their designs, but partly also, and probably much more importantly, when the same mental lines have created a compartmentalization of these brains.

In *The Mayan Calendar and the Transformation of Consciousness,*[57] I have already extensively discussed and exemplified how the two hemispheres of the brain serve as parallels to the Eastern and Western hemispheres of the Earth. Therefore, as the latter were separated on a global scale by the eight-partitioning they would also manifest as compartmentalized minds in the human beings in resonance with this. This led to the primary separation of the functions of the left and right brain halves and the localization of activities to at least eight different compartments of their brains. The four couples of deities in the Mayan/Aztec worldview maps symbolize the different qualities of these fundamental compartments. It deserves to be pointed out here that there is no inherent difference between the grey matter of the left and right hemispheres of the brain. Instead, it is the downloading of the eight-partitioning that has created such a separation and made the left hemisphere more analytical and the right more holistic in its functions.

The compartmentalization of the mind is, for instance, beneficial to persons, who use their minds in different ways at different times, and need to shift between integrative and analytical ways of thinking. As an example, if the accounting of a Sumerian merchant's sales of vegetables was localized to the left brain hemisphere, then this mathematical activity would not be taken over by his/her emotions, dreams, or entities from the spirit world, which by the eight-partitioning were localized to the right hemisphere. If, on the other hand, he/she participated in a ritual to the goddess Inanna, numbers and accounts could be kept in the left hemisphere so that his/her religious feelings could be allowed to flow. This illustrates the power of the compartmentalization brought by the eight-partitioning: The compartmentalization of different mental activities allows a human being to become deeply specialized in any one of them and through this she would even have a choice in the matter.

Therefore, the compartmentalization of the mind provides for a vastly increased versatility in the activities of human beings. This would be a factor instrumental for the rise of civilization as in the external world the specialization that the compartmentalization created would manifest in a diversification of labor where different individuals focused on different tasks. Prior to the beginning of the Long Count – and the activation of the eight-partitioning of the mind – almost everyone was a farmer, but after the separation of brain hemispheres and other compartments of the mind, people also became priests, soldiers, weavers, merchants, artists, metal and construction workers, scribes, kings, and a whole range of specialized professional roles as parts of the emerging cities. Certainly, it is for good reason many consider the diversification of labor a hallmark of civilization.

Or should we rather say that the diversification of labor *is* civilization? As soon as we have a diversification of labor we will also have cities with diversified functions, and this is what we know emerged in Mesopotamia at the time. The compartmentalization allowed not only for versatility in the activities of an individual, but also for the distribution of labor in civilized societies. Thus, if civilization is defined as city-life with diversified functions we can understand that the compartmentalization of the human mind directly created the rise of the early civilizations of our planet and why this occurred so close to the beginning of the Long Count. This gave rise to a new order; an order of a compartmentalized mind and after having downloaded this new partitioned mind the human beings would never again be the same. Civilization took over and the unity with nature was broken.

From this compartmentalization of the mind at the beginning of the Long Count, it is possible to explain what for so long has baffled historians, namely that the first civilizations of our planet appeared so suddenly and with so few preparatory forms. The compartmentalized mind generated by the new hologram in fact had a whole range of different consequences that generated the "package" of phenomena that we associate with the rise of civilization. As we have already seen, this package included straight constructions, monarchies, cities, diversification of labor and others are to be discussed later such as writing, calendars, money and the wheel. Historical research places their appearances to approximately the same time at the beginning of the Long Count. While the cause of this was simple—the downloading of a new eight-partitioned hologram at a specific point in time—the consequences were remarkably multi-faceted. Remarkably, all the gifts in the package of civilization seem to have resulted from the same inner change and projected into the outer reality according to the principle of As inside-So outside. Another point to realize is that if the cause of this would not have been global in nature, there would be no reason that these packages would appear at the same time in different areas.

THE TOWER OF BABEL AND THE FLOOD

I will present ample evidence to demonstrate that the eight-partitioned global mind influences the individual human minds in several different ways, and another example that may be brought up now is the influence the eight-partitioning seems to have had on the diversification of languages. Notably, the Biblical myth of the Tower of Babel implies some kind of event took place early in the history of the Near East that was experienced as a divine intervention leading to the diversification of languages. Although it does not specify an exact time for this the Bible thus provides another ancient source that a mental shift with a metaphysical origin indeed occurred.

It is in this context interesting to note that recent studies (2012) of the development of Indo-European languages by Quentin Atkinson at the University of Auckland— using computer simulations[58]—suggest that a diversification of these languages took place around the beginning of the Long Count (Fig 7). Even if we can see that this was not the only time estimated for such a diversification, it seems to have been very marked at the time of the eight-partitioning of the human mind, and then, like pyramid building, continued for a long time afterwards. Much like the diversification of labor, the diversification of languages thus seems to have been caused by the inner compartmentalization of the mind created by the eight-partitioning.

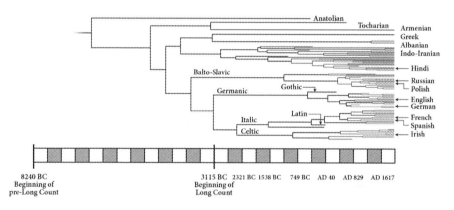

Figure 7. The emergence of the Indo-European languages[58] in Anatolia in the pre-Long Count and their later diversification in the Long Count.

Going further back in time, we can see in the figure that this group of spoken languages finds its origin around the time of the beginning of the pre-Long Count, in Anatolia. Not only is this the area where agriculture appeared very early, it is also where people first built perpendicular houses (Fig 2) indicative of an early compartmentalized mind. This is consistent with the Mayan inscriptions[59] implying that the pre-Long Count is similar in nature to the Long Count, which would mean that the former brought a rudimentary compartmentalization of the mind. When a rudimentary form of the compartmentalized mind was downloaded in Anatolia, so did the ability to isolate concepts and use them in what may have been the first real language. Then later, as the mind became fully eight-partitioned, this original language was however dramatically diversified at the beginning of the Long Count proper.

This later diversification of languages timewise paralleled the building of pyramids at the beginning of the Long Count (Fig 2). Since both phenomena, and also the diversification of labor, could easily be understood as reflections of the partitioning of the human mind, this is not very surprising. The observed separation of languages obviously also rings a bell of the Tower of Babel legend, since this indeed seems to have meant a splitting up of a previous more or less common language. There may have been parallels to this in Semitic or other groups of languages. So in this perspective, and based on this empirical evidence it seems very much to make sense that there was an event like the fall of the Tower of Babel, which was experienced as a divine intervention.

The Tower of Babel event described in the Bible as brought by Yahweh, resulting in the split-up of an earlier common language (Fig 7), is then in fact energetically identical with the eight-partitioning event described in Palenque as brought by Hun-Hunaphu, the First Father. This profound insight brings us to a new level of understanding. It now seems clear that, despite a culturally based variation, the ancient Jews, Egyptians, Mayans and Babylonians described the same divine presence – with the power to compartmentalize – as the source of these creation events. Its essence would be identical whether humans called this An, Yahweh, Amon-Ra, Hun-Hunaphu, Shamash or something else. These would simply be different names for the same being that was behind the eight-partitioning whether this was described at an inscription in Palenque or in the Book of Genesis. There is then little reason to look upon the five first books of the Bible, the so-called Pentateuch or Torah, as something apart from other ancient sources. Also this describes the initial downloading of the compartmentalized mind in a variety of myths, such as the Tower of Babel, the Expulsion from the Garden of Eden with its Tree of Life or the survival on Noah's Ark of four female/male couples from the Flood.

It is worth noting that the Biblical story about Noah's Ark and the Flood, which has variations in a large number of other cultures, in its essence is the same as the Egyptian creation myth about the Benben, the eight-sided primordial mound emerging from the expanse of waters. That the former is indeed a creation myth seems clear from the fact that in the Book of Genesis the Flood is presented as an intentional act of God. Hence, the Flood was not there described as an ordinary overflow, but as a new creation or an overthrow of the old creation. The boundary-free life was replaced by one organized by straight lines that could be measured and this was true to different degrees wherever on Earth people were living.

What from the perspective presented here is interesting about the Biblical Story about the Ark of Noah is that it eventually ends up in the "Mountains of Ararat." However, in early Christian, some Jewish and the Quranic tradition this location refers to Mount Judi on the Syrian-Turkish border. This means that at least according to these sources, the new creation, the rectilinear Ark beginning after the "Flood," landed very close to Göbekli Tepe and the other sites where people indeed according to modern archeology first built rectangular structures. This also meant that this landed where they first seem to have used a real language and began to practice agriculture, whose connection to the creation of the mind will be discussed in chapter four. The new creation after the Flood would then be identical with what the Maya called a new creation at the beginning of the pre-Long Count, the one with the first perpendicular lines. If the Flood did not indeed describe this creation, why would Yahweh have instructed Noah to build a vessel that had a rectangular shape?

It should now be clear that on my own part I do not think we should understand ancient myths as literal accounts of physical events. Yet, they are not mere fantasies either, but metaphors for what at the time actually happened on the level of consciousness. To understand their deeper meaning it is only now that we are fortunate to have empirical evidence from archeology (Fig 2) and linguistics (Fig 7) gather to show the common origin of many phenomena in the underlying reality of the dawning of the human mind. It is a curious fact that the Book of Genesis pinpointed the location where the early (pre-Long Count) mind first manifested, something which has only been known to us in the past few decades.

Hence, the above creation stories from the Bible fall into the same category as the Mayan and Egyptian creation stories and can also be seen as metaphors for the effects of the establishment of the rectilinear grid. As different as these creation stories at first may seem, the Eight-House-Partition, the Benben emerging from the expanse of waters, the Tower of Babel or Noah's Ark, they all reflect the same metaphysical event. We then have every reason to conclude that these creation stories reflect real processes originating from a divine source that actually transformed the consciousness of human beings. If so, it is not so difficult to appreciate the ancient view that civilization was a gift from the divine.

Going back to the Tower of Babel, the ziggurat called Etemenanki in Babylon, dedicated to Marduk in the 7th century BCE, has sometimes been suggested to be what this described physically. This building seems however too recent for this, since it is described in the first part of the Bible that is believed to have been written about a thousand years earlier. Since the word Babel means "confusion" in Hebrew, and does not have to refer to a city, it makes more sense if the physical correspondent of this myth refers to the ziggurat in Eridu, which according to Sumerian legend was the oldest city in the world. There are several arguments that this ziggurat, to which the goddess Inanna would go to receive the gifts of civilization, is the real origin of the myth of the Tower of Babel.[60] Another point we might add here is that Eridu was a mighty city of mud brick already in 2900 BCE, which would place it around the time when the original linguistic unity was broken as we may see from Fig 7.

The connection to the Tower of Babel myth again points to how immensely powerful the new global mind must have been experienced. In chapter six I will provide a detailed explanation as to why the eight-partitioning would have influenced languages in this way. For now, what there is to note is another effect of the mind that coincides roughly with the beginning of the Long Count.

THE LATER FATE OF THE HEAVENLY EIGHT-PARTITIONING

Yet, evidently the shift at the beginning of the Long Count did not manifest in an identical way everywhere. Pyramid-building civilizations with systems of writing initially only emerged in Egypt, Mesopotamia, and the region towards the Indus Valley, even though the eight-partitioned grid covered the whole Earth and people everywhere potentially could be in resonance with the new mind. However, depending on such factors as population size, type and intensity of agriculture and the natural environment, civilizations would only take hold in certain regions. After all, it takes a relatively large population of farmers to sustain the building of a pyramid or city life and it seems initially only the areas around fertile rivers would be able to do so.

As we will see in chapter five there are also differences inherent in the grid in how civilizations will evolve in different parts of the world and especially between East and West. In Egypt, it seems that a certain balance between men and women prevailed, and its art and texts attest to a relatively harmonious society. In Sumer and Mesopotamia, on the other hand, the myth of the male god Marduk killing Tiamat,[61] the earth mother, reflects a more conflictual relationship not only between men and women, but also between human beings and nature. An, the god of heaven, there came to be seen as a god of judgment, and certainly many of the later Babylonian and Assyrian kingdoms would become obsessed with war and conquest rather than with attaining harmony. Such differences between cultures would in ancient times have been attributed to the difference in quality of the various couples or twin pairs of the eight-partitioning (Fig 3), which over time as we will see in the next chapter, will have their upturns and downturns.

It is now however time to address why pyramid building, especially in Egypt, made a downturn and came to an end; this is as important for our understanding of the phenomenon as knowing why it began. To bring clarity to this we should again first go to ancient Mesopotamia. This is where early on, as mentioned, there were countless representations of Trees of Life and eight-partitioning symbols, sometimes with wings symbolizing divinity to reflect the influx of a new mind from the heavens. We have already seen how a cuneiform sign for heaven, the Dingir (Fig 5a), had been created there. What is then interesting to see from the work by Ana Maria Vazquez Hoys at the University of Madrid,[62] is that this particular sign has changed over time and so has had a history (Fig 8). Why would this be? On my own part, as I have stated before, I believe that this sign was a reflection of the heavenly hologram that brought the eight-partitioning. If this was so, the evolution of the Dingir would reflect the altered perception people in Mesopotamia had over time of the eight-partitioning that they were in resonance with. Apparently the people in Mesopotamia experienced the eight-partitioning of the heavens as undergoing change in a particular way.

Uruk	Jemdet Nasr		Sumer	Old Akkad	Old Assur	Old Babylon	New Assur	New Babylon
3200 BC	2900		2400	2200	1900	1700	700	600

Figure 8. The evolution of the Mesopotamian Dingir cuneiform (see Fig 5a) for god/heaven. (Based on the research of Dr Ana Maria Vazquez Hoys.)[62]

Based on Figure 8, it seems that at the beginning of the Long Count people were so blinded by the hologram that they could not see the lines as quite straight and orderly. The people in Egypt at this point in time were only able to build rather unsophisticated mastabas, which were more like elevated platforms, for burials of their kings. Yet, as we know the hologram was clear enough for a monarchy and a system of writing to emerge. It was however only as people could get a clear view of the eight-partitioning, reflected in the Dingir being represented as perfectly symmetrical (about 2600 BCE), that the Egyptians built the perfectly symmetrical eight-partitioned Khufu's pyramid. At about the same time, some other indisputable stone pyramids were built in Greece and in Peru and some other places as well (Fig 2) indicating that this hologram was recreated all over the planet.

As we may further see in Figure 8, the eight-partitioned Dingir is however later transformed into more of a yin-yang symbol until its origin as reflecting the eight-partitioning can no longer be discerned. Gradually, in parallel with what we should then interpret as the distortion of the original hologram, the Egyptians ceased to build pyramids. The last pyramid built by an Egyptian ruler was that of Pharaoh Ahmose (1550–1525 BCE), which was not on the same scale as previously. Later, as towards the midpoint of the Long Count around 550 BCE all resemblances of the eight-partitioning disappear, the Egyptian and Mesopotamian civilizations were both conquered by the Persians, who thus set an end to the continuity of the most ancient civilizations of our planet. The Dingir then had become just another sign, shortly before the cuneiform writing would go out of use completely.

Judging from the evolution of the Dingir, the Egyptian pyramids have thus been built according to the principle of "As above—So below," or if you like, "As in the metaphysical reality— So in the physical." From such a perspective it seems very reasonable that the eight-partitioned Great Pyramid at Giza in fact was built close to the time (2560 BCE), which is the consensus of most archaeologists. This is also the time when the Mesopotamian symbol of heaven had the clearest eight-partitioned nature and the calling of this heavenly hologram to recreate it on Earth should have been felt the most strongly. According to the Mayan calendar, it is reasonable if the resulting hologram was the most symmetric at the midpoint of the first NIGHT, 2523 BCE, which is reasonably close to both dates. Later, people would run into the problems associated with the yin-yang-duality of the mind, which in the continued evolution of the Dingir impairs its symmetry and causes the decline of some remarkable aspects of ancient technology. This yin-yang-duality will be described in chapter two and will be a major focus of volume two of this trilogy. With this development of the mind, humanity would gradually become oblivious to its origin in the primordial mound. In chapter seven I will however make an attempt at recreating this, but before this is possible, the relationship between mind and brain will have to be set straight in chapter five.

MIND OVER MATTER

It has long been obvious that the old materialist paradigm –that the mind has its origin in the brain– is unable to explain the rise of civilization on our planet. It is simply unable to explain the empirical evidence that simultaneously – over a few hundred years – several cultures of our planet independently rose to civilizations. In their own views the ancients received a gift package of civilization from the gods and if we change our perspective in this direction we can gain access to a much deeper understanding of what actually occurred. For this we however need to realize that the global mind has evolved since then, so that we do not simply project our own current mind with its biases onto the past. Already Fig 8 gives a hint that our mind is very different from that of the ancients. In chapters two, three and six we will explore the continued evolution of the mind in much greater detail.

The idea that history is based on the evolution of the mind may however seem very radical. It implies recognizing internal shifts with divine or metaphysical origins as the prime factors behind the course of history and seeing that this follows a preset plan. In this view, humanity has been inspired by the spiritual domain, for instance by geometric imprints, for all of its existence, and this also, as we will see more of in chapter four, long before it became civilized. A new detailed theory based on generally accepted facts will then here be proposed that there is an actual interface between the physical and metaphysical realms from which we can understand much about our lives and the purpose of our existence. This theory goes directly counter to the old materialist paradigm that dominates the educational system, academia and the media, where our minds are believed to be generated by isolated brains. This view tends to keep us isolated in our egos and prevents us from seeing the much larger evolving context of which we are part and may contribute to.

In addition, the materialist paradigm does not hold up intellectually and has prevented mainstream historians from recognizing that the dawn of civilization is something actually requiring an explanation. Yet, also they have had to recognize as enigmatic that the first civilizations emerged as suddenly as they did and that some of these early civilizations displayed a remarkable precision and creativity, sometimes surpassing our own, in many of their activities. It has also had to be recognized that for many of the novelties that these civilizations created there is very little evidence of any preceding trial and error. The construction of pyramids, for instance, and the logistics this required, seems to have appeared almost out of nowhere.

Such a sudden appearance of diversified civilizations, based on many new mental capabilities, is however exactly what you would expect if a compartmentalized mind at a given point in time appeared as a precise mental hologram, in this case originating in an eight-partitioned Earth grid. Otherwise, you would have expected a slow and gradual appearance of novelties at random and unrelated points in time, which is simply not the case. Instead, a veritable quantum leap took place in several different cultures downloading similar packages at the beginning of the Mayan Long Count. This implies that they, and also we, are part of something greater than many might think.

This metaphysical origin of civilization does not mean that the physical environment was unimportant, especially since fertile river cultures mostly seem to have been pre-requisites for civilization to take hold. But the existence of a river valley that may have been there for tens of thousands of years by itself does not explain why people independently around certain rivers, especially the Nile, Eufrat, Tigris and Indus, suddenly at a certain point in time manifested very similar phenomena, which we now associate with civilization.

Hence, there is compelling evidence that Egyptians, Aztecs, Jews and Mayans shared the view that the creation of civilization was brought about by four pairs of aspects of the divine (demi-gods or alchemical energies) compartmentalized by a Creator God. Order was then created from the world that had existed previously, whose consciousness was experienced as floating. Based on the convergence of such ideas from quite disparate cultures and the supporting empirical evidence, the simplest explanation is then that this is exactly what happened. The global mind field, and the human mind ever since, are divine creations. Since even today our minds share their origins in the same eight-partitioning we have much to learn about ourselves from this new perspective.

Some within academic science may however be inclined to say theories that point to a metaphysical basis for the human mind do not belong within science. In our own day and age of aggressive atheism the resistance may be even greater if such a theory concludes there is a divine origin to the human mind. But when there is extensive empirical evidence that favors the view that mental shifts actually drive history, and alternative theories for the origin of the mind are very hard to find, such an attitude is tantamount to saying that science cannot deal with the truth, which seems inconsistent with its reason for being. From a scientific point of view, all theories should be evaluated based on the same criteria with requirements of empirical evidence and not based on whether they are consistent with temporarily dominating biases or not.

The evidence of a downloading of a new global mind also affects the most popular "alternative" theories, which is that extraterrestrials or people from an earlier "lost civilization" taught our ancestors how to create a civilization. What all of these ideas have in common with the mainstream is that they fail to explain why people at the time of the beginning of the Mayan Long Count underwent an *inner* change, and especially a compartmentalization of their minds that was necessary for the creation of a civilization. Such an inner change is also necessary to explain the evolution that would later follow, visible for instance in mathematics and systems of writing that we will return to later.

If we are to gain a deeper understanding of our past I feel we cannot forever dismiss the original messages of the ancients, which were clearly metaphysical in nature and involved different deities. How much sense does it make for us, five thousand years later, to say that we know better than those that were actually there as civilization dawned? In my view at least, if we are to expand our knowledge of our origins we need to incorporate the views of the ancients and then embrace the theory based on empirical evidence that has the highest explanatory power. I believe that the theory presented here as to why civilization arose meets these criteria and that the reason the pyramids were built was the inspiration that a new mind gave. Sometimes the mind can move mountains.

CHAPTER 2:
THE MAYAN CALENDAR SYSTEM— THE BLUEPRINT FOR THE CONTINUED EVOLUTION OF THE GLOBAL MIND FIELD

"The earth and myself are of one mind." Chief Joseph

PHYSICAL VS. METAPHYSICAL CALENDARS

For those that accept the basic perspective of the previous chapter the view of the ancients and of themselves may now have changed considerably. No longer does the Old Kingdom of Egypt appear as something incomprehensibly alien that we cannot make sense of and which we cannot naturally place within the context of human history. No longer do the ancient Egyptians appear as if they belonged to another race. Instead, they had the same brains as we do. The reason they could do some things we could not do (at least not with the tools they used) is that the global mind at the time was different and that they were in an unusually pure resonance with this. We can get a sense of this evolution from the "Dingir holograms" in Fig 8. To gain a deeper understanding of this phenomenon we however need to go deeper into the Mayan calendar, which we will do in the next two chapters and again in volume two of this series.

Following the initiating metaphysical event of the Mayan Long Count and the building of the first pyramids and cities described in the previous chapter, civilization would spread to many different cultures and diversified its expressions. People got adapted to the new mind, and at least in the Near East no longer felt compelled to erect equally spectacular buildings as initially. Yet, as we can see from Figs 2, 7 and 8 ever since the initial dawning of the mind all of human history falls within the time frame of the same wave. In this chapter we will then look at the continued evolution of civilization toward our present time, and go a little deeper into the question of how we have evolved to what we are now. We will now explore if also the continued evolution of civilization can be explained by a repeated downloading of an eight-partitioned hologram. The metaphysical realm from which the latter emanated seems to have been fully visible to and experienced by the ancients, but be largely invisible to ourselves.

Accordingly, we will have to use some of the symbolism of the ancients also to explain the continued evolution of humanity. This seems possible as, ever since the beginning of the Long Count, people all over the world have built pyramids and temples in terraces, which presumably reflect a sequence of heavens, or if we like holograms or spiritual imprints that humanity would download on its climb upwards. Early in the wave in Egypt and Mesopotamia, people sometimes built pyramids and ziggurats in seven levels. Later, in Asia and among the Maya, we also see pagodas, temples and pyramids with five, nine, or thirteen levels. These buildings all seem to be telling us that the heavens had a certain number of levels and pointed to a sequential order with which the climb to the highest level would need to be made. Yet, with the exception of the Maya, the cultures that built these rarely provided any explanations as to how and when this climb to the different levels was going to take place. For this reason, the following two chapters will be devoted to understanding the Mayan calendar system, which is a critical tool for anyone tracking the evolution of the mind and the boundaries of consciousness.

It is, however, possible that the Mayan calendar has now gained a bad reputation after all that was shown on YouTube or in TV documentaries or written about it in books concerning "December 21, 2012", much of which lacked any serious scholarship to back it up. Nonetheless, among the different interpretations proposed, there is a clear division. The dividing line falls between those, including myself, proposing that the Mayan calendar concerns the evolution of the mind and human beings creating according to the principle of "As inside—So Outside," and those proposing that this calendar primarily describes physical and especially astronomical events. In this hype, the "physicalists" suggested that the above date would màrk the end of the world, a galactic alignment, solar flares, a collision with Planet X, or something else of this order. Still, it is not surprising that these things did not come to pass or had any tangible effects. Not only were none of those notions described in any ancient Mayan texts, but the correct metaphysical shift point was also arguably October 28, 2011.

I suggest that the reader, at least for the time being, leaves the discussion generated by this hype behind and explores with me where a nonphysical understanding of the Mayan calendar may take him or her. Even so, there is one common misunderstanding I think is necessary to clarify before we move on; the misunderstanding that the Mayan calendar would have the distinction of being cyclical in contrast to other calendars. If anything, it is the other way around. The Gregorian calendar, for instance defines the year with a precision down to less than a second and can therefore be said to be a perfect cyclical calendar. Likewise, European and Vedic astrology are purely cyclical systems based on the Earth's precessional cycle.

Although the Mayan calendar also has many cyclical aspects, for instance in the waves we are beginning to discuss here, this is not what makes it unique. Instead, what makes the Mayan calendar special is that it, unlike any other calendar system of our planet, describes directed processes going from seed to mature fruit in thirteen steps. This tells us that history is not just repeated, as you would expect if it was based on endlessly repeated astronomical cycles. The precessional cycle is thus not part of the evolutionary waves of the Maya, and despite many claims to the contrary, a 26,000 year time period is found nowhere among their inscriptions. While this cycle may have its place in other contexts, being a physical cycle it has no relevance for our study of the non-physical mind.

Here the purpose is to understand and chart the global mind and the rise of civilization, and for this only a metaphysical calendar such as the Long Count is meaningful. The Mayan calendar may help us understand the origin of our civilization because it has certain unique and meaningful characteristics, but to grasp these we need to listen to what the ancient Maya themselves were saying about its origin. Then, based on the empirical evidence demonstrating that there exists a connection between the evolution of consciousness and the Mayan calendar, we may gain a full picture of the course of human history.

THE ORIGINAL FUNCTION OF THE ANCIENT MAYAN CALENDAR SYSTEM

Even though rising to a civilization only 3,000 years later themselves, the Maya in their inscriptions returned many times to the initial creation event at the beginning of the Long Count. Their kings would reenact this and so demonstrate that the Tree of Life had provided the origin of their own civilization. For them, the creation by the gods was at the heart of everything they represented in their art and architecture. Even if the effects of the Long Count wave had become much more complex at this later point in time, in the first millennium CE the Maya still experienced themselves as related to its initiating event. It was thus the Mayan people that described the different "heavens" most exactly, not only by building their terraced pyramids, but also through the development of an advanced metaphysical calendar system.

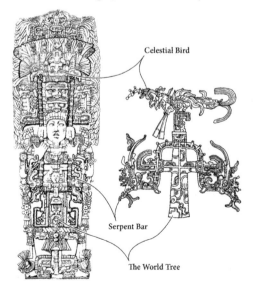

Celestial Bird

Serpent Bar

The World Tree

Figure 9. King 18-Rabbit of Copan performing a serpent bar ceremony while dressed up as the World Tree with a bird at a top. Through such a ceremony, at a particular shift point he connected himself to the initial World Tree erection event at the beginning of the Long Count.

Among the Maya, whose Classical culture lasted 200–900 CE, and Postclassical culture 900–1200 CE, pyramid building was in fact always intimately connected to their calendars. Therefore, the Maya hold a special place among all the peoples embracing the ancient civilization paradigm. They developed calendars that related their lives to the original eight-partitioning as well as to all subsequent consciousness shifts. This was especially important for their kings (Fig. 9), who belonged to royal dynasties that sought to trace their lineages back to the initial event of the Long Count. It was through this connection that the kings gained their authority, meaning that keeping this calendar became somewhat of a lifeline for them. (It is then hardly an accident that the institution of monarchy disappeared among the Maya essentially at the same time as the use of the Long Count calendar.) For this reason, the Maya always dated their pyramids in terms of the Long Count, as these were built for the purpose of celebrating shifts between time periods in a calendar going back to its initial event. The kings erected steles relating their own birth and accession to the throne to such shift points in order to highlight they were at the center of the order that had been created by the Tree of Life. To them, performing ceremonies at the shift points of the Long Count was thus a way of connecting themselves to the divine origin of civilization. With all the focus on our time and 2012, it may not have been sufficiently recognized that the ancient Maya looked at their calendar as sacred and the initiating event of the Long Count as a work of the gods. For anyone seeking to understand the state of consciousness of the ancient peoples on our planet, such a point of departure will however be necessary.

The activation of the Long Count was a metaphysical occurrence to the Maya. We know this also because, despite their proficiency in astronomy, they described the time periods of the Long Count and its wave movement in units of time that were different from those of the solar year. It is for this reason that even if the Maya knew the regular solar year to be 365+ days, their Long Count calendar was based on metaphysical time units such as tuns (360 days), katuns (20 tuns), and baktuns (400 tuns). Consequently, the shifts in the Mayan calendar were based on a nonmaterial reality, which, as we have seen, had the power to alter the human mind. Not surprisingly then, their prophecies were also related to non-astronomical time units like tuns, katuns, and baktuns, as we may still read about in the *Books of Chilam Balam* (Jaguar Prophet).

From the perspective of the Mayan calendar all events are part of an interconnected evolutionary wave of history (Fig. 2), and nothing happens that is not part of this framework. For this reason, we may be more connected to the pyramid builders than we might think, since this evolutionary wave leads from them to us. Thus, the order that was established at the beginning of the Long Count underlies all of its continued evolution and our current civilization. This is true even if, as the reader of my previous books will know, other waves have later been added to it. This means that the Mayan calendar is also useful if we are interested in mental shifts in our own time. In this perspective the original rise of civilization directly influences how we look at life in our own time.

SOLVING THE MAYAN CALENDAR

During the past two centuries the ancient Mayan calendar has been elucidated and explored by Mayanists, historians specializing in the history of the Maya, and it is through their work we know its basic structure. In general, these academic historians have however not recognized that the Mayan calendar has any relevance for understanding historical evolution at large and what this means to our own lives. The person, who first recognized this was José Argüelles. Through his book *The Mayan Factor* in 1987 and the Harmonic Convergence event he promoted in the same year, he spread the knowledge that this ancient calendar system existed and that it might also have relevance for our own time. Nonetheless, despite several seminal ideas, he did not solve the calendar in the sense of providing systematic evidence for how it relates to human evolution.

My own work, whose basic principles have also been adopted by some other authors such as Barbara Hand Clow, has focused on the evolution of consciousness. To verify this notion I have in my previous books presented a systematic biological and historical analysis of the basis of the Mayan calendar.

It is this basis, which we will now use for a detailed study of the evolution of the mind.

The Long Count calendar went out of use about a thousand years ago, so no one knows with certainty what it meant to the ancient Maya. Yet, we do have at our disposal the aforementioned inscription from Palenque describing the beginning of the Long Count and another inscription from Tortuguero that describes the end of its first thirteen baktuns that we have just been through. Together with the information from the *Books of Chilam Balam* as to how the Maya viewed the prophetic meaning of different calendar periods such as katuns, tuns, and kin, etc., we then still have a fairly good idea of how they understood their calendar. However, this outline by itself does not prove anything. It is only as its validity can be verified by actual historical processes in different parts of the world that we know this calendar to be meaningful for studying the evolution of the mind. If there was no such historical evidence from areas other than the Mayan, we would still be completely in the dark regarding the meaning of this ancient calendar system.

Thus, even if we know its basic outline, knowledge about the Long Count is not something that we can just pick up to use as a guidebook to the cosmic plan and the future. Instead, we have to understand the Long Count from how it matches our extensive modern base of knowledge about world history. From this we may discover its patterns and then give it meaning. The essence of such studies from my earlier books will be repeated here together with some new angles on history, which are of special relevance for understanding the rise of the ancient civilizations and the evolution of the human mind.

THE CONTINUING RISE AND FALL OF CIVILIZATIONS

Figure 10 briefly summarizes the continued development of civilizations during the Long Count. A criterion for inclusion in this chart is that a culture has a system of writing. Nonetheless, this overview has several limitations, including a strong European/Mediterranean slant that I will explain shortly. It is also far from complete. To these limitations should be added the uncertainties associated with datings of early times, in this case collected from Wikipedia. For reasons explained in the next chapter, the purpose here is not to prove that the times of rise and fall of every civilization always fit perfectly with the baktun shifts of the Long Count. Rather, the point is for the reader to see how many dramatic turning points in the history of civilization conform approximately, and sometimes even exactly to these shifts.

Step in Wave	Civilizations
Baktun 1, DAY 1 3115-2721 BCE	Old Sumerian (3000-2340), Early dynastic period, Egypt (3100-2666), Indus Valley (3300-1300)
Baktun 2, NIGHT 1 2721-2326 BCE	Old Kingdom in Egypt (2666-2181), Crete (2700-1500)
Baktun 3, DAY 2 2326-1932 BCE	Akkadian Empire (2334-2193), Neo-Sumerian (2119-1940)
Baktun 4, NIGHT 2 1932-1538 BCE	Old Babylonian period (1932-1500) Middle Kingdom Egypt (2055-1650)
Baktun 5, DAY 3 1538-1144 BCE	Hittite Empire (1600-1200), Middle Babylonian Empire (1532-1000) Mychene (1600-1100), New Kingdom Egypt (1550-1077) Shang dynasty China (1556-1046), Olmecs (1500-)
Baktun 6, NIGHT 3 1144-749 BCE	
Baktun 7, DAY 4 749-355 BCE	Neo-Assyrian (744-605) Persian Empire (550-330 BCE) Greek city-states (776-330 BCE)
Baktun 8, NIGHT 4 355 BCE-40 CE	
Baktun 9, DAY 5 40-434 CE	Roman Empire (14-434 CE) Mayan Kingdoms (50-830 CE)
Baktun 10, NIGHT 5 434-829 CE	
Baktun 11, DAY 6 829-1223 CE	European proto-nations (843) German-Roman Empire (962)
Baktun 12, NIGHT 6 1223-1617 CE	
Baktun 13, DAY 7 1617-2011 CE	European nations (1648)

Figure 10. The rise and fall of some civilizations as compared to baktun shifts in the Long Count. For sources see: Wikipedia and [1].

Even though there are many points in this table that could be dealt with in greater detail, I do not think this should prevent us from seeing the overall picture: the rise and fall of civilizations conform very well to shifts between DAYS and NIGHTS in the Long Count. The evolution of humanity through its various civilizations may here be looked upon as an integral whole, going from seed to mature fruit throughout the seven DAYS of this calendar. You cannot understand the rise and fall of any particular civilization in isolation from the others, because mentally speaking they are all part of one and the same process. Overall, but not without exceptions or complicating factors, history can be seen here to have evolved through a wave movement where the baktuns that are DAYS are time periods for the rise of civilizations.

Hence, in the DAYS of the Long Count, completely new civilizations have often emerged or existing civilizations undergone renewals. As stated, an example of the latter is the New Kingdom that arose in Egypt at the beginning of the third DAY of this wave, together with several civilizations in other parts of the world. The New Kingdom in Egypt meant a renaissance expressed through the temples in Luxor, Karnak, and Amarna and by pharaohs such as Thutmose III, Hatsheput, Akhenaton, and Ramses II. This exemplifies that once a civilization, such as that of the Early Dynastic period in the first DAY, has arisen, it will not stay the same forever but will have its upturns and downturns. A wave is a wave and the historical process it generates is not linear, even if it has a forward direction.

It is because all civilizations are the products of the same global wave that syncronicities are created all over the world when it comes to their rise and fall. At the end of this same third DAY, which is also the beginning of the third NIGHT, there was a dramatic decline of civilizations seemingly everywhere. In the Eastern Mediterranean this decline was ascribed to attacks by so-called Sea Peoples. However, these would hardly have any relevance for the simultaneous demise of the Shang Dynasty in China or the end of the Olmec and Indus Valley civilizations roughly at the same time. Nonetheless, following this third NIGHT, considered as the dark ages of Old Greece, the golden age of this culture began in the fourth DAY. Through its renewal at this time—and the timing is indeed important here—it provided a foundation for the thinking of the Western world in its continued evolution.

The rise of the Neo-Assyrian Empire to the world's leading power under Tiglath-Pileser III,[2] a role overtaken by Persia around 550 BCE, also marks this time. Persia then came to include as much as 44 percent of the world's population,[3] and so if there was ever a time when one empire ruled the world, this might have been it. Even so, the golden era of the Greeks and the Persian Empire was set to end as Alexander the Great's rapidly created empire disintegrated some time into the next NIGHT. As a result, in this so-called Hellenistic era the Mediterranean world was left without a dominating empire. As with many other eras that were NIGHTS this one has been thought of as a time of cultural decline. However, with the beginning of the fifth DAY, the Roman Empire would rise to dominate the region until its fall at the beginning of the fifth NIGHT, a time which marks the beginning of the Dark Ages in European history.

Clearly then, there is ample historical evidence that the times of rise and fall of significant leading-edge civilizations coincide closely with Mayan calendar shifts. Yet, naturally, we cannot always date the rise and fall of civilizations exactly. "Rome was not built in a day," and it did not fall in one day either. Historians debate if the Western Roman Empire fell when Alarik sacked Rome in 410 CE, when Attilla became the ruler of the Huns in 434 CE, or when the last legally recognized Emperor Julius Nepos died in 480 CE.[4] When we are considering a drawn out process such as the fall of a civilization as large as the Roman, no indisputable date for this is obvious. Nonetheless, it is clear that the fall of this empire took place around the time of the beginning of the fifth NIGHT in 434 CE, and the rise of Attilla to become the leader of the Huns just happens to coincide exactly with this date. Still, it would not be correct to say that the Western Roman Empire collapsed precisely on a certain day or year. Again, waves move like waves, and this is why history is not simply linear. This may also be a consideration for anyone who thought the particular day the Mayan calendar was supposed to end in 2012 would be dramatic. Even though the Mayan calendar does define metaphysical shift points very precisely, the timing of the visible manifestations of these is subject to many complicating factors.

Following the Dark Ages of the fifth NIGHT, 434–829 CE, Europe awoke to a new civilization with a new organization at the beginning of the 9th century CE. Thus, when looking at the history of civilizations, it is also in its place to study the evolution of their systems of governance. This includes the very concept of nationhood, which becomes very relevant as the sixth and seventh DAYS begin. Monarchy and nationhood, as we saw in chapter one, were phenomena that emerged in Egypt with Menes and in Sumer, "land of the civilized kings," as a result of the initial eight-partitioning. The creation of the nation as a system of rule was then a reflection of a particular heaven that brought boundaries and a center (Fig 5a). Not surprisingly, steps in the continued development of nationhood take place at the beginning of the DAYS in the Long Count, which each brought a new eight-partitioning. The activation of the sixth DAY of the Long Count in 829 CE was, for instance, soon followed by the establishment of the two main "proto" nations of Europe,[5] France and Germany, which were separated in the Treaty of Verdun in 843 CE. Most other European proto-nations[6] would also take shape during the continued development of this baktun.

However, it was only with the seventh DAY that the nation state in a modern sense was born. The event usually considered to mark the emergence of this form of governance is the world's first international conference, the Westphalian Peace Treaty, which concluded the Thirty Years' War of 1618–1648. Only at this time did the European nations finally give up the idea of reviving the Roman Empire standing above the rest. It was at this treaty that European nations for the first time recognized each other as equals, at least in principle. It was also a dissociation from the religious role an emperor had, which as we saw before goes all the way back to the pharaohs and their central role in the eight-partitioning. A somewhat simplistic way of describing this shift is that in northwestern Europe at the beginning of the seventh DAY, the kings started to belong to their nations rather than the other way around.

This DAY would also bring Europe to global dominance. At its height, the British Empire would include about 25 percent of the population of the world, to which we should add people living in the French, Dutch, Spanish, and Portuguese empires. (The more recent rise of the United States, and rise to renewed prominence of nations such as China, Japan, and India results from waves other than the Long Count that will be discussed in volume three.)

THE UNITY OF WORLD HISTORY

It is obviously not the purpose here to cover all aspects of human history in detail, and so the focus will be on events especially relevant for understanding the nature of the global mind and its wavelike evolution. A model based on such concepts would indeed explain why several different cultures, as far apart as Peru, Mongolia, Greece and Egypt, simultaneously began building pyramids at the beginning of the Long Count. We may from such a perspective, for example, also notice that the rise and fall of the Shang Dynasty in China was essentially synchronized with the New Kingdom in Egypt or other so-called palace cultures of the third DAY in Figure 10.

It may, however, sometimes be difficult to know exactly what happened in the respective civilizations in those early times, or determine the parallels in the course of events. Closer to our own time this is easier. We may, for instance notice that the beginning of the seventh DAY saw a significant shift in the system of governance not only in Europe, but also on the other side of the world in Japan and China. In Japan, the Tokugawa Shogunate finally removed all military challenges to its rule at the siege of Osaka in 1615,[7] and in China the Qing Dynasty was founded in 1616,[8] ruling from 1644. In mainstream historical research these parallels on the opposite side of the world to the Thirty Years' War are looked upon as mere coincidences. However, an alternative way of interpreting such synchronicities in different parts of the world is that regardless of where we live, we are all in resonance with a global mind affecting the entire planet.

What I am suggesting is that it is the same underlying processes that are at play in all the different parts of the world, although we have not previously been able to see the parallels. The establishment of the Shogunate in Japan, for instance, meant the separation of spiritual power, which stayed with the Emperor in Kyoto, from the worldly power that was seized by the Shogun in Edo (Tokyo). This separation of power was a parallel to what happened in Europe at the same time, where through the Thirty Years' War the emperor of the Holy

Roman-German Empire lost his power to serve as intermediary between the pope and the various nation states. The result was that the Vatican lost much of its direct political power and the nation states could all independently decide on their religions. While the scenarios were not identical in Europe and Japan, the result, the separation of worldly and spiritual power, certainly was. Yet, Japan at the time obviously had no direct influence on the course of events in Europe, and the European ability to influence Japan was minimal. Accordingly, this separation of spiritual and worldly power seems to have been a product of a common global mind that people all over the planet were in resonance with.

There are many other such parallel developments, and we have only looked at a few here that are traditionally considered as having separate origins. Yet, especially if you look at them from the perspective of compartmentalizing shift points in the Mayan calendar, it seems quite compelling that they are somehow synchronized. How could this possibly be? The difficulty we have when trying to answer this is that we lack a mechanism with which to explain such a resonance and the ensuing global synchronicities. This, however, is a problem that as we proceed I will suggest a complete solution to. As a preparation for this we should now study the resonance between the global and the human mind more closely.

AS ABOVE—SO BELOW

If the global mind was created by the metaphysical Tree of Life at the eight-partitioning, we may wonder if the partitioning lines emanating from the North Pole correspond to certain precise longitudes and to what extent the various civilizations of history were related to those. If these global partitioning lines can be precisely defined, then the principle of "As above—So below"—representing the relationship between the global and the human minds—would also gain a very precise meaning. In Figure 11a, I have placed the north pole of the polar axis (Tree of Life) in the center of a four-partitioned world with eight different trees, which project outwards from the polar axis, as we may see in the underlying chart from the *Codex Fejérváry-Mayer*. The eight partition lines are then actually longitudinal lines going from north to south rather than what we commonly know as the four directions. Once this eight-partitioning was downloaded 5,125 years ago, all over the world people started to live their lives within the framework of longitudinal straight lines and the directions perpendicular to those, and began honoring the spiritual powers of the four directions. Hence, what we normally think of as the four directions resulted from an eight-partitioning emanating from the North Pole. Such a model is consistent with the earlier mentioned Palenquean creation story where the center of the eight-partitioned world is a "house in the North." We have good reasons to be grateful to the ancient Maya for being so precise about how this original creation event took place.

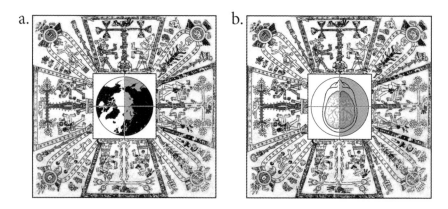

Figure 11. (a) The North Pole of the Earth at the center of the eight-partitioning surrounded by duality trees and corresponding pairs of deities (twins?) in the Aztec Codex Fejérváry-Mayer. *Along the four main longitudes polarized energies are created. (b) The same with a human head at the center, which is now a map of the compartmentalized mind.*

With a model of resonance between the eight-partitioned global mind (Fig. 11a) and the human mind (Fig. 11b), I believe it is possible to come to grips not only with the origins of the wave movement of civilization (Fig. 10), but also with how the evolution of the human mind relates to the planetary mind. The Earth and its inhabitants are in reality what the global mind works upon even if, from our limited perspectives, we do not always recognize this. Here, we are already beginning to build a case that our own minds (Fig. 11b) have become compartmentalized through their resonance with the eight-partitioned global mind. In this way, the compartments of the left and right brain halves, and the frontal and parietal lobes were created by the perpendicular partitioning of the new mind. Viewed in this way (see Fig. 12), an invisible sphere creating the individual human mind is in resonance with a global sphere, which is dissected by planes that partition the world from the North Pole. This different perspective of the human being as someone who "downloads" his or her mind is then something that finds its origin in ancient cosmograms. The global mind is much like a metaphysical cloud (using a term from the cyber world) that everyone may connect to, or be in resonance with.

The building of the pyramids and the dawn of civilization, for instance, seem to have resulted from the downloading of the original eight-partitioning of the Earth (Fig. 11a). On the human level, this perpendicular partitioning was then reflected in the compartmentalization of the brain brought by the mind, which separated it into frontal and parietal lobes, as well as the left and right hemispheres (Fig. 11b). How this resonance looks face on is shown in Figure 12, with the particular polarity that is created by the Long Count. (In Figure 11 this yin-yang polarity is then symbolized by one of the pairs of twins.) The human mind, which separated the brain in the left and right compartments, is thus in resonance with the global mind in a very precise way. It was this compartmentalization of the mind that created civilization with its well-developed division of labor and complex language. Only as humans gained the potential to alter his or her brain activity between different compartments would the potential for true versatility emerge.

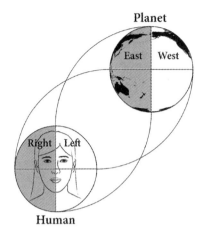

Figure 12. Resonance between the planet and a human being as seen from the front (Pacific Ocean) side of the planet with the polarity characteristic of the DAYS of the Long Count (Sixth Wave).

THE HIERARCHICAL ORGANIZATION OF THE UNIVERSE

To gain a good overview of all of creation, there is one more aspect of the Tree of Life that we need to be aware of. This is that there are Trees of Life at the center of several systems other than the human or global. These are all in resonance with one another according to the principle of "As above—So below" (Fig. 13). On each of these levels, a metaphysical tree provides a three-dimensional coordinate system emanating from a center, around which the life system is organized. Therefore, the different levels in Figure 13 define a nested hierarchy, where each macro system provides the framework within which the micro systems exist. The most encompassing level at the top is provided by the cosmic Tree of Life, whose remarkable physical parallel was discovered by scientists as recently as 2004.[10] *The Purposeful Universe* discusses how the lower levels, beginning with the galactic and solar and all the way down to the cellular and atomic Trees of Life, relate to this cosmic cross. At all of these levels, shifts will occur in synchrony, ensuring that the universe evolves in a coordinated way.

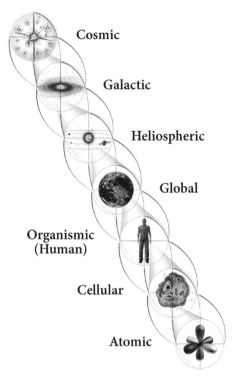

Figure 13. A nested hierarchy of the different levels of the Tree of Life, and their partitioning centers, creating different organizations of the mind in resonance with one another.

In accordance with the previous, the eight-partitioning at the beginning of the Long Count was introduced simultaneously in all the different systems of the nested hierarchy, although it ultimately finds its origin at the cosmic level. Exactly what levels in this hierarchy the ancients described in their myths we may never know, although I believe the Mayan "Raised-up-Sky" refers to the cosmic or galactic level. Yet, the worship among Mesopotamians and Egyptians of the sun god, Shamash or Amun-Ra, respectively, and the reference in Mesoamerican traditions to a "New Sun" at the beginning of the Long Count point to the heliosphere with the sun at its center as another system that was eight-partitioned. In my way of looking at it, it was however not the sun as a ball of fire giving warmth that was worshipped at the time, but the sun as an anchor point for the eight-partitioned heliosphere. You may look upon this as a solar intelligence, but then again this intelligence was only a reflection of a galactic and cosmic intelligence on the higher levels of the hierarchy in Figure 13. The point then is to recognize that the metaphysical eight-partitioning exists simultaneously at several different levels of the cosmos, even if this may be hard to prove directly.

Here I will instead limit the discussion to the two levels where we can prove things and allow us to track and verify the shifting states of the mind. These are the global (or planetary) and the human (or organismic) levels of the Tree of Life, which were also shown in Figures 11a and b. While there are facts that point also to the existence of solar, galactic, and cosmic levels of the mind, in the final analysis what is important to know is how the mental shifts play out in human life and not the details of a complicated transmission process between different levels of the hierarchy.

THE ALTERNATING POLARITIES OF THE GLOBAL MIND

Even if we now have a model for how the human mind is related to the global mind, we still have to answer not only what longitudes the eight-partitioning in Figure 11a correspond to, but also why civilizations will continue to evolve in a wavelike manner, tending to rise and fall. Why, for instance, did the Roman Empire rise and fall? Or why did the Classical Mayan kingdoms collapse? If we are looking for the deeper answers to such questions, we have to understand what causes the shifts between DAYS and NIGHTS. The production of a wave movement requires a wave generator, and so we need to find out what in this case the wave generator may be. Given what we have already seen, it is then natural to propose that the wave generator for the oscillations of civilization in fact is the Tree of Life itself. From this, the eight-house-partitioning would also through resonance create a wave movement for the compartmentalized human mind.

In Figure 10 the DAYS are generally the steps forward for civilization, while the intermediate NIGHTS are more like periods of rest, historically speaking that often result in the fall of civilizations. The Mayan inscription also describes that the Long Count was initiated by a period of eight-partitioning, or in other words a period dominated by a compartmentalized mind. It is on this basis I have proposed the model in Figures 14a and b for the generation of the wave movement of DAYS and NIGHTS in the Long Count. What this model means is that the erection of the eight-partitioning was not a one-time event taking place only in the first baktun of the Long Count, but an event repeated at the beginning of every odd-numbered baktun that has followed since. The global mind field is therefore different in the DAYS compared to in the NIGHTS.

In this model it is indeed the Tree of Life (the polar axis) that serves as a wave generator as it activates the eight-partitioning and creates separations (between the energies of the different twin deities in the Ogdoad or Figure 11) during the DAYS—when a compartmentalized mind can be downloaded—but deactivates these during the NIGHTS. It is then the alternations between the two different fields in Figures 14a and b, which produce the wave movement of rise and fall in history. Shifts between these fields are behind the overall change and all evolution of the global mind. Therefore, it is this wave movement that gives people everywhere an experience of being part of a historic flow that is going somewhere. Moreover, it is this wave movement, which gives humans much of their experience of a connection to spiritual forces and a divine creation in the form of inspiration. Even those that deny a divine connection will often experience themselves as part of such a flow. Without these alternations the human mind would not evolve and civilization would stagnate. No one would be inspired to bring about change.

Curiously, the yin-yang polarity of the global mind shown in Figure 14a was already evident in the Sumerian cuneiform for An (Fig. 5a), which shows that ever since the beginning of the Long Count people have looked upon the heavens as polarized. As we can see from Figure 8, the experience of this duality—referred to in the Bible as the Tree of Knowledge of Good and Evil—also increased over time, at least in ancient times. More generally, many cultures in different parts of the world associated all the four directions with different qualities, and not only with this yin-yang duality. As we see exemplified in

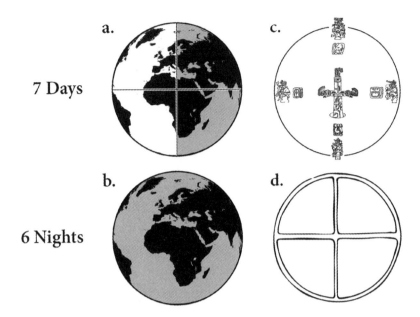

Figures 14a and b. The fields of the global mind in the DAYS and NIGHTS of the Long Count, respectively, as seen from the backside of the planet. In the DAYS (14a) the Tree of Life is activated and creates compartmentalizing lines along the midline and equator. In the NIGHTS (14b), on the other hand, a unified deactivated field is created. (14c) Mayan Tree of Life in the center of the four directions, surrounded by symbols of their different spiritual qualities. (14d) Nordic sun wheel symbolizing a four-partitioning of the sun.

Figure 14c, the Maya saw the four directions as organized by the Tree of Life and associated them with different glyphs, colors, and deities reflecting their different qualities. It is those four directions that often form the basis of ceremonies, such as the Native American Sun Dance, with a symbol for the Tree of Life at its center. Such a partitioning of the world into different fields with different qualities is indeed what you would expect if the boundaries in Figure 14a were creating a compartmentalized global mind.

We may exemplify these different qualities with how the yin-yang polarity dominating the global mind in the DAYS of the Long Count (Fig. 14a) favored the Western Hemisphere, and hence also the left half of the brain in resonance with it (Fig. 12). In particular, after the Long Count came to fruition at the beginning of its seventh DAY in 1617, for about 400 years, a baktun, this polarity has generated a marked geopolitical dominance of Western powers. Thus, it was at this shift that the buildup of the British colonial empire began with the establishment of its first trading post in India in 1615 and the Pilgrims arriving in Massachusetts in 1620. In the 20th century the United States, located as it is even further west, would come to take over much of this world-dominating role because of the very same polarity. Concurrently with this political dominance of the West expressions of the left brain such as science, Protestantism, and capitalism also rose. How it will go with the West in the future is another matter that will be the topic of a later volume of this trilogy.

THE CENTRAL GRID LINE OF THE EIGHT-PARTITIONED GLOBE

If the wave movement of civilizations in Figure 10 is associated with shifts between the two different fields of the global mind in Figures 14a and b, then we should also expect that the shifts between a compartmentalized and a non-compartmentalized global mind would coincide with these. Days would be compartmentalized and NIGHTS decompartmentalized and so generate two fundamentally different fields for humans to live and play in. Logically, the effects of the shifts between such different fields of the global mind would then be most evident close to the midline separating the Western and Eastern hemispheres, since it is there that the primary yin-yang polarity is created. This, in turn, would lead us to search for the specific longitude in Figure 14a that corresponds to the midline of the eight-partitioning, in order to be able to study the wave movement this gives rise to.

Figure 15. The outward projection from the Tree of Life creating the separation of the Western and the Eastern hemispheres along the 12th longitude East (marked by Rome).

Such a wave movement of contraction-expansion, resulting from the alternating fields in Figures 14a and b, indeed becomes evident when we study the directions of major military campaigns in Europe in relation to the line shown in Figure 15. (This line is then a blow-up of the line shown in Figure 14a). Such movements can be followed from the beginning of the fourth DAY of the Long Count and onwards as shown in Figures 16 a-g. (Not surprisingly then, the fourth DAY, when the effects of this line first became apparent, is also the time when people through the Greco-Persian Wars became aware of a rift between an Occidental and an Oriental civilization.) These shifts between DAYS and NIGHTS create a wave movement in human history related to, and in fact generated by, this midline created by the Tree of Life.

What is shown in Figure 16, it should be noted, is not just a singular observation but a consistent pattern over time. When the global mind is compartmentalized (as DAYS begin), movements away from the midline are induced, separating people who move away from it in different directions. When, on the other hand, it is decompartmentalized (as NIGHTS begin), the midline boundary collapses, resulting in a movement toward the center abolishing the previous polarity. Therefore, these maps reflect shifts between the two fields shown in Figures 14a and b. (To study this wave, incidentally, is about as close as we may ever come to scanning the global brain for activity.)

The effects of this wave generator, for instance, when the seventh DAY began, were felt as far away as the North American prairie, where new tribes then moved in from the East, or eastern Siberia where the Russians reached the Pacific Ocean. Yet, the effects, as always with a wave generator, are the most evident close to where it is located, which is along the 12th longitude East. The reason that such an adherence to the baktun shifts (within a twenty-year period) is so clearly visible (Fig. 16) is that we are looking at a phenomenon, the relationship between East and West, which directly relates to the compartmentalization of the global mind. In chapter five we will return to look at other longitudes of the eight-partitioning and explain the physical correlates of this planetary midline. For now, it is important to notice the generation of a pattern around the line, which clearly is in accordance with the baktun shifts of the Long Count.

From these tangible effects, we can see that the Egyptian, Sumerian and Mayan ideas of an eight-partitioning of the earth through a metaphysical heaven is a meaningful basis for understanding the course of human history, with its ups and downs. Remarkably, then, history follows a clear pattern of evolution, and yet our schools do not teach us about it! The pattern in Figure 16 in fact includes very significant events in European history such as the rise (c) and fall (d) of the Roman Empire and the beginning (d) and end (e) of the Dark Ages. To further highlight the importance of these events, the empire created by the Mongol Storm (f) was the largest of all history, and the Thirty Years' War (g) was one of its most devastating conflicts. The latter, in fact, caused the death of a larger proportion of the population in Europe proper than any other war, including World Wars I and II.[11]

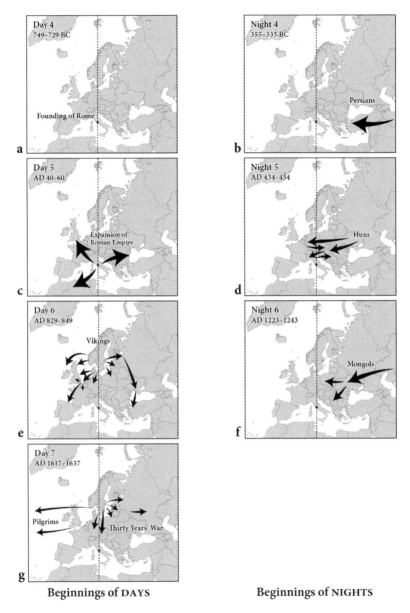

Beginnings of DAYS   **Beginnings of NIGHTS**

Figures 16 a-g. Alternating significant (military or violent) movements from and toward the planetary midline in the initiating twenty years of DAYS and NIGHTS of the Long Count, respectively. Detailed descriptions of these movements are presented in Solving the Greatest Mystery of our Time *and* The Mayan Calendar and the Transformation of Consciousness.

The effects of the wave movement of the Long Count, generated by the partitioning line of the 12th longitude East, hence cannot in any sense be qualified as minor. Taken together we may understand how this wave movement gave Europe a central role, which led to the export especially of science, capitalism and Protestantism to the rest of the world during the course of DAY 7. Judging from this, history is governed by entirely different forces than we have been led to believe and perhaps too much emphasis was placed on the kings and battles when these were only secondary effects of a much larger scenario. The true meaning of history seems to have been hidden.

The "grid line" separating, or if you like, compartmentalizing the Eastern and Western hemispheres of the planet then, in fact, has a real existence and plays a primary driving role in history. This planetary midline (Fig. 15) goes from the North Pole down close to Copenhagen, Berlin, Rome, Tripoli, and Cape Town to the South Pole. In Gabon, in Central Africa, it meets the equatorial plane, which plays a similar, but less marked, role for compartmentalizing the world. The latter seems to have driven civilization north in the Northern Hemisphere and south in the Southern. For this reason, the leading edge of civilization during the course of the Long Count has DAY by DAY moved away from the equator, taking it from Egypt to Northwestern Europe with parallels in other parts of the world.

Together with the equator the 12th longitude East has served as a wave generator not only for migrations and military campaigns, but also, through resonance, for the further evolution of the civilized compartmentalized mind. Because of our resonance with the yin-yang polarity between East and West (Fig. 14a), a polarity between different compartments of the human mind has then also been created. Traditionally, people in the West have been more analytical compared to the East, where they are more holistic. (To see this, it is enough to compare the different types of medicine that have come out of the two hemispheres.) The people closest to the midline (that is in Europe in the Northern Hemisphere) have been most marked by the global polarity generated by the Tree of Life and so also driven out to spread its effects elsewhere.

THE RISE OF EUROPE AND THE POWER
OF THE FOUR DIRECTIONS

In this midline we have found the explanation to Europe's special role in later times for exporting the compartmentalized mind that created civilization. This has typically happened under the symbol of the cross, which originally (Fig. 14d) was a symbol of the partitioning of the four directions.

The modern world, however, is not organized in relation to this actual midline, but by the system of longitudes that has the Greenwich meridian at its center, a system that also plays a central role in our timekeeping. Naturally, this tends to confuse people into thinking this meridian or longitude separates the East and the West. The Greenwich meridian, in contrast to the twelfth longitude East is however unimportant for separating the Eastern and Western hemispheres. It was chosen for the mere reason that it was the most convenient reference point for measuring longitude for the British fleets that would sail out to colonize the world. Hence, the Greenwich meridian is mostly a reflection of the Western dominance that characterized the field of the Long Count (Fig. 14a), especially towards its end.

From Figures 16a through g, it is already clear that the global mind and its defining partitioning lines have a strong effect on people in resonance with it. Yet, we then need to ask where the energy comes from for these military campaigns that the Tree of Life seems to have generated. It is clear it is not electromagnetism, since the midline is pointing towards the center of the eight-partitioning located in the direction of true north. We should also note here that the Egyptian pyramids are aligned with true north and not with magnetic north. This means two noteworthy things: Firstly, the directions in which these pyramids are pointing are consistent with the power of the eight-partitioning longitudes presented here. Secondly, there is no reason to associate electromagnetic pole shifts with the Mayan calendar. No pole shift has been connected with this calendar in the past, and there is no reason to expect that this will be the case in the future either.

If these shifts in fact were the products of an unknown source of energy, things would become complicated, as the movements would then apparently violate the law of conservation of energy; energy in an isolated system remains constant over time. For now at least, I tend to think that the directional boundaries emanating from the Tree of Life do not really add energy, but merely direct and guide the human beings to use their already existing energy in specific ways. Regardless, from the maps in Figure 16 we may see that the energies unleashed, or directed, by these shifts in the Long Count must have been very strong given the force of the movements in different directions.

These movements present a new twist on the building of the Egyptian pyramids, as it was the very same compartmentalizing power of the global mind that four millennia later, for instance, gave rise to the outpourings of the Vikings (Fig. 16e) or other events in these maps. The compartmentalizing power of the eight-partitioning has thus been expressed in different ways in the different baktuns shifts. Yet, there is a commonality in the immense power focused at these different shifts points, for instance, by bringing people such as the Mongols all across Eurasia. Given such expressions of power, we should maybe not be surprised that much earlier the Egyptians with a similar shift on their backs, also had the will and capacity to build the Great Pyramid in a relatively short period of time. At first sight it may seem quite remarkable to us that so seemingly different events, widely separated in time, in fact may have been fueled by the same power. Yet what we are retrieving here is a worldview where everything is connected through the global mind and its four directions. Such comparisons then attest to the power of this global mind and the four directions that are part of it.

The compartmentalization of the human mind was thus not a one-time event. Instead it is a result of a wave movement that stepwise has become expressed more widely in the history of humanity. We should therefore look upon the building of the pyramids and the emergence of the Egyptian and Sumerian civilizations, which began the whole process, only as reflections of the very first step in this process of the compartmentalization of the global mind. The civilizations we saw in the DAYS in Figure 10 are simply continuations of the same wave movement of the Long Count. In this respect, each DAY also means a more marked separation, especially between the Eastern and Western hemispheres, because of the increasing compartmentalization of the global mind.

MATHEMATICAL PROOF

The model of the global mind presented here provides for a completely different way of looking at history compared to the conventional, in which religions, kings, battles, and inventions are just viewed as popping up accidentally without any meaningful context. All events here are instead seen as parts of an evolutionary process of the global mind. In this model a wide variety of phenomena, which otherwise would have been regarded as separate, become recognizable as the results of one and the same process with an origin at the metaphysical level.

Here, as a first example of how the special capabilities of the human mind have evolved, we will look at the development of mathematics throughout the Long Count, which is summarized in Figure 17. Typically, the oldest numerals in Babylonia (3100 BCE)[12] and Egypt (3000 BCE)[13] are known from the very beginning of the Long Count. We can also see in this figure that this specific creativity of the human mind, mathematical thinking, continues to evolve in parallel with the wave movement of civilization in general (Fig. 10). This, of course, is not surprising if, as I have argued here, the evolution of civilization itself is a product of the global mind. Since mathematics is a typical expression of the geometric structure of the human mind, it would be expected that it too would develop with the DAYS of the Long Count (Fig. 14a). Put plainly, the science of mathematics has only progressed because the global mind has evolved.

As we saw in Figure 14a, it is in the DAYS of the Long Count when the global mind is more compartmentalized that the planetary field is polarized. For this reason, certain mental abilities, created through resonance with the Western Hemisphere and mediated by the left half of the brain, have been especially favored in those time periods. In previous books, I have touched upon some of these special aspects of the development of civilization, including writing, money, science, governance, and religions. Later, in chapter six, equipped with a clearer understanding of the mind, we will again study several such phenomena.

Step in Wave	Evolution of Mathematics
DAY 1 3115-2721 BCE	Numerals (Sumer, 3100 BCE and Egypt, 3000 BCE) Multiplications Tables (Egypt and Sumer)
NIGHT 1	
DAY 2 2326-1932 BCE	First and Second Degree Equations (Babylonia, 2000 BCE)
NIGHT 2	
DAY 3 1538-1144 BCE	
NIGHT 3	
DAY 4 749-355 BCE	Greek Mathematics and Geometry Thales (d 546 BCE), Pythagoras (d 495 BCE)
NIGHT 4	
DAY 5 40-434 CE	Alexandrian School of Mathematics Diophantos (d 284 CE)
NIGHT 5	
DAY 6 829-1223 CE	Arabic Algebra (830) Fibonacci (1202)
NIGHT 6	
DAY 7 1617-2011 CE	Logarithms (1617) Infinitesimal Calculus (Fermat), Analytical Geometry (Descartes 1636), Probability Theory (Pascal 1654) Calculus (Leibniz 1676, Newton 1687)

Figure 17. The evolution of mathematics during the DAYS of the Long Count.[14]

To understand this, we should remind ourselves that it was the initiating event of the Long Count, the eight-partitioning, which introduced the straight lines in the human mind. This immediately explains why the branch of mathematics now called geometry took its beginning at this point. How could there be geometry or sacred geometry before people had minds organized by straight lines? Also arithmetic, going back to the very process of counting, most likely found its origin in the dualities created by the mind about 5,000 years ago. Thus, as I discussed in *The Purposeful Universe*, the first step for humans to invent counting was to recognize the concept of "two-ness" in the mirror images of pairs that are part of how we have been created, biologically speaking, two arms, two breasts, etc. Two-ness is thus much more clearly a part of ourselves and of nature than three-ness and four-ness and the number two may be more archaic than the numbers three and four and above, which presumably did not exist before the eight-partitioning of the mind. Hebrew, for instance, has a special form of plural for identical pairs and in some languages, counting is still today based exclusively on the numbers one and two, so that one, two, three, four, and so on are counted as one, two, two-one, two-two, and so forth. That the numbers one and two are more archaic than the others is clearly visible also from the different Indo-European languages, which have similar words for one and two, but dissimilar words for three and four etc. This indicates that numbers higher than two only began to be used after the "Tower of Babel" event (Fig 7) and that numbers and languages are products of the very same compartmentalization of the mind.

This supports the idea that the basic duality introduced by the eight-partitioned mind is at the root not only of geometry, but also of counting and numbers. Indeed, it is only from the beginning of the Long Count we know of symbols for numerals. Creating numerals and counting then presumably meant the first steps toward the development of mathematics. As the mental ability to isolate concepts and elaborate them abstractly was developed by the compartmentalized mind, so were methods for computing, such as addition. From addition—the most basic form of computation—subtraction, multiplication, and division were derived, and from this, mathematics moved on to much more abstract ideas brought by the following DAYS.

However, because human beings do not behave according to mechanical laws under the influence of the Long Count wave, there will for any specific phenomenon be some apparent anomalies when tracking its evolution. This is also true for the evolution of mathematics in Figure 17 and the gap in the third DAY of its evolution is noticeable. Scholars have explained this with the advancement of the earlier Babylonian scribes in DAY 2 that, unlike in later cultures, went through a thorough training in mathematics. (They were so good, you might say, that humanity could skip the class of the third DAY.)

Despite this, and other possible anomalies, the important thing to see here is the big picture, which is that the evolution of mathematics matches extremely well with the DAY-by-DAY development of the global mind. This is especially evident if you focus on the beginning, midpoint, and end of the Long Count, DAYS 1, 4 and 7, which are the DAYS when the most significant changes usually manifest. In this series, the first DAY brought the first numerals and the rudimentary means of calculation used in both Egypt and Sumer.

Thales of Miletos, often known as "the first Westerner" or "the first mathematician" then very notably appeared in the fourth DAY. The reason historians have placed so much emphasis on Thales' role is that he is the first person known to have proved his theorems. Accordingly, after the significant mental shift at the midpoint of the whole Long Count in 551 BCE, it was no longer good enough to argue you had been inspired to your discovery by the gods. Instead, logical proof was needed and people like Thales, Pythagoras, and later Euclid delivered such proof. This change in thinking reflected an enormous shift taking place at this midpoint, not only in mathematics, but as we will see in the next volume, more broadly in how human beings saw their relationship to the gods.

Finally, the beginning of the seventh DAY, coinciding with the scientific revolution in Europe, meant an explosion of breakthroughs in advanced mathematics. Thus, as the human mind at this time became fully compartmentalized, mathematicians in central and Western Europe produced vastly more advanced mathematical theories than ever before. Descartes, for instance, developed the branch of mathematics called analytical geometry, which in turn established the coordinate system. This branch of mathematics is noteworthy as it is a direct expression of the perpendicular lines of the compartmentalized mind that again were being activated. At the same time, mathematicians developed methods for rapid computation, such as logarithms and calculation machines, while Pascal developed probability theory and Fermat paved the way for the calculus that was later fully developed by Leibniz and Newton.

The scientific revolution at this time meant that physics for the first time was studied by means of mathematics (Kepler 1619, Galilei 1632, and Descartes 1638). A new analytical mentality based on the light on the left hemisphere of the mind then dawned (Fig. 12) not surprisingly close to the compartmentalizing planetary midline. Also this happened according to the principle of "As above—So below" at the same time as the Western Hemisphere began to dominate on a global scale (Fig. 14a). As stated, the latter was reflected, for instance, through the beginning of the buildup of the British Empire. Other activities in Western Europe at this shift, such as the world's first stock exchange in Amsterdam in 1618, further highlight the role of mathematics in the mental shift to the seventh DAY.

The stepwise development of higher and higher levels of mathematics with every DAY of the Long Count is thus one of the clearest ways of tracking the evolution of the global mind. It can be seen to proceed from DAY 1 to DAY 7 from the very first numerals to calculus, or in the words of the Maya, as a process from seed to mature fruit. Presumably, it was then such mental shifts that the ancient Maya, who were also proficient in mathematics, experienced and symbolized by various deities in order to understand how the mind and the spiritual reality changed between different time periods. The value of studying this here is that it makes it clear that the mind, as it is expressed through human individuals, follows a *directed* evolution throughout the seven DAYS (or thirteen baktuns). The solution to the Mayan calendar is then to truly see this as a description of the evolution of the global mind, with all the consequences for the human beings in resonance with it.

The various aspects of this global mind, however, manifest differently in different parts of the world, partly due to the compartmentalization as shown in Figure 11. By mapping the evolution of these aspects through the facts of history, we can see how the global mind has evolved in accordance with a time plan. As part of this evolution, the global mind develops a more marked compartmentalization of human thinking with every DAY of the Long Count. The world has then with every such step become more and more civilized, and people at the same time become more separated from nature. In chapter six we will come back to study other specific products of the mind that are all parts of the "package" bringing civilization.

Already from this chapter it may be clear the mind is not something that originates in the brain. Instead, the mind of the human individual is also fundamentally related to the earth and follows a metaphysical time plan for its evolution. But then, "who" or "what," is at the origin of this process of mental evolution in seven DAYS and six NIGHTS? Where did the mental imprint of the eight-partitioning come from? The Maya attributed it to the First Father, the Egyptians to the sun god Ra and the Babylonians to the sun god Shamash. In general then, the ancients saw the abilities they gained to create civilization as a gift from the divine. Presumably, any modern concept of God, which all have their cultural taints, might be equally applicable.

I do not think any mortal can describe the source of the eight-partitioning objectively. However, what I think we can say with some certainty is that this process cannot be explained by any material factor or being. While I may personally prefer words such as the Presence or the Divine Spirit-Mind for the source of the spiritual imprints I am not going to argue with someone who simply leaves this question open by saying that the imprints of the mind are from the metaphysical realm. This is a realm we cannot understand by using our minds, since it exists beyond the mind.

Yet, it is natural if we ask the questions to what extent the divine also controls our minds and if we have a free will etc. The continued focus will here however be on the empirical evidence. I believe this is most helpful for us all to draw our own conclusions about what exists before or beyond the mind. But I believe there is something there and I will refer to the global mind and related concepts as divine. This is also because the ancient peoples of the Earth would have referred to the origin of the wave movement of seven DAYS and six NIGHTS as "the gods" – or "God" and here I will follow their lead.

The peoples of Mesoamerica developed a particular mythology to describe the divine origin of this wave movement. As we have now looked at empirical evidence for how the Mayan calendar describes the shifting reality of human history we will in the next chapter explore how this was symbolically expressed and experienced by the people that created this calendar.

CHAPTER 3:

THE PLUMED SERPENT—
THE CREATOR OF THE CALENDAR

THE MESOAMERICAN CONTEXT

The relationship between the Maya and the Aztecs has several parallels to that which existed in antiquity between the Greeks and the Romans. As the Greeks and the Romans belonged to the same Mediterranean cultural context, the Maya and the Aztecs belonged to the same Mesoamerican context (Fig. 18a) and so had significant aspects of their worldviews in common. The region of Mesoamerica (meaning Middle America) spanned roughly from the current-day border between Mexico and the United States down to western Honduras and El Salvador and included several different cultures therein. Like the Greeks, the Classical Maya were organized in city-states (Fig. 18b), each with its own special traits and ruled by its own dynasty of kings. The Aztecs, on the other hand, much like the Romans built a large empire of tribute-paying tribes. As with the Greeks, the Maya were bent on intellectual endeavors and developed an advanced calendrical system and a system of writing, none of which was equally developed among the Aztecs. In addition, and mirroring the Greeks and Romans, the two Mesoamerican civilizations shared a number of deities between themselves. Even if there are significant differences between their pantheons, there are also obvious similarities, and in some ways we may learn about the Maya from the Aztecs.

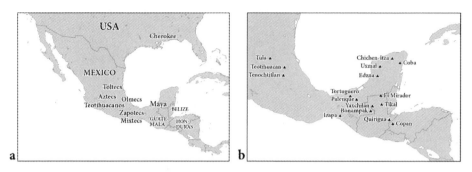

Figure 18. Maps of (a) the Mesoamerican region and some of its peoples in relation to modern nations. (b) The Mayan region and Central Mexico with some of its ancient cities.

These parallels are important as from a modern research perspective there is a big difference between approaching the Classical Maya and the Aztecs. The Aztec culture was very much alive when it had its fateful encounter with European civilization. In contrast, the Classical Maya, who in the time period 200–800 CE used the most advanced calendar system in the world, by the time the Spanish arrived had abandoned their ancient sites. At the time of the shift between the tenth and eleventh baktuns of the Long Count in 829 CE, most of the Classical Mayan culture had in fact already collapsed,[1] and inscriptions based on the Long Count were no longer written (the last, from 909 CE, is found in Tonina). At this shift point the center of Mayan civilization moved north from what is now Guatemala to the Yucatan peninsula, where a spectacular center for it would arise in the city of Chichen-Itza. In this region the so-called Postclassical Mayan civilization emerged, with a different emphasis from the Classical, which would also be reflected in the calendar system. Chichen-Itza was later itself abandoned around 1220 CE.[2] In the centuries that followed, the Aztecs created their empire in central Mexico, which lasted until the fall to the Spanish of their capital Tenochtitlan on August 13, 1521 (Ce Coatl, One Serpent in the Aztec calendar).

While the Maya wrote the most enlightened inscriptions regarding their calendar system about 900 years before the arrival of the Europeans, the Aztec worldview and calendar was described in some detail by contemporary Spanish chroniclers. According to one of them, Sahagun,[3] the Aztecs thought when the Spanish Conquistador Hernan Cortes landed in Veracruz in 1519 that he was the so-called Plumed (or Feathered) Serpent deity, known in their language as Quetzalcoatl; the deity all visitors to Mexico hear about, and yet find mysterious and hard to understand.

WHO WAS THE PLUMED SERPENT, REALLY?

The reason Cortes was able to conquer the mighty Aztec empire was, according to Sahagun's account, partly that their Emperor Moctezuma II had mistakenly taken him to be an incarnation of the god Quetzalcoatl and so allowed him entry into his capital. The reason he did so may have been that at the time in Mexico there existed a prophecy that the god Quetzalcoatl would one day return. He had been prophesized to do so from the Atlantic East Coast in a special calendar year, One Reed. Cortes met both of these expectations and because at his landing site in Vera Cruz he had raised a Christian cross—reminiscent of that of Quetzalcoatl (Fig. 19)—the Aztecs took him to be the god returned. In this way, some believe the prophecy of a return of Quetzalcoatl contributed to the fall of the Aztec Empire.

Who, then, was this deity of the Plumed Serpent that in the view of the ancient Mesoamericans had given them their calendar and civilization? If we are going to study the rise of civilization based on the timeline of the Mayan calendar, we need to have some idea about how this Plumed Serpent and its relationship to civilization was viewed. We will then initially explore this based on the myths that the Toltecs and Aztecs left behind.

The actual origin of the Aztec prophecy of a return of Quetzalcoatl is to be found in the Toltec city of Tula. In the tenth century, a priest king by the name of Ce Acatl Topiltzin, who had been born on the day One Reed appeared in this city.[4] This man became part of the priesthood of Quetzalcoatl and had added the name of this deity to his own. Topiltzin Quetzalcoatl taught the Toltec people new arts and crafts and built a new temple so that their culture flourished. He taught them to offer serpents and butterflies rather than sacrificing humans and became highly valued by his people. His popularity, however, did not go down well with another priesthood, which instead was loyal to the deity Tezcatlipoca, the dark mirror of the god Quetzalcoatl. The Tezcatlipoca priesthood opposed the teachings of Topiltzin, and because it was able to gain the upper hand in the power struggle, he was forced to leave Tula.

Figure 19. Quetzalcoatl carrying shield with eight-partitioning cross in Codex Magliabechiano.

According to one version of the legend, Topiltzin Quetzalcoatl escaped to the Yucatan to play a part in the Toltec-Maya center in Chichen-Itza then emerging (Fig. 18b). Another version says that in the year One Reed he left Mexico from its Atlantic coast on a raft made from serpents, promising to return in a year that also had the spiritual quality of One Reed. It was typical of

Mesoamerican prophecies that they were based on such day signs in the sacred 260-day so-called sacred calendar. As Cortes later landed on the same coast in the year One Reed (1519), Moctezuma did not quite know how to respond. His hesitancy allowed Cortes, with his 530 Spanish soldiers, sixteen horses (never before seen by the natives), and allied Mexican tribes,[5] to defeat an emperor who had the power to raise an army of one hundred thousand warriors. However, we should consider that the Aztecs saw themselves as living in a time of darkness, and due to their large-scale human sacrifices might have had good reason to be apprehensive of the return of Quetzalcoatl, the god of the dawn.

In this account the Plumed Serpent was thought of as a human being, Topiltzin, in whom the spirit of Quetzalcoatl had incarnated. Still, the Plumed Serpent was clearly primarily regarded as a god as evidenced by the impressive temples that had been dedicated to it for a long time in Mesoamerica. From the Spanish chroniclers we know that among the Aztecs Quetzalcoatl was seen not only as the protector god of the merchants and the patron of the arts and crafts, but also was mentioned as the bringer of their calendar and civilization. Not surprisingly, then, Quetzalcoatl was also the patron god of the Aztec priesthood of knowledge.[6] Hence, he was primarily a god, and as such many Aztec codices depict him with his defining attributes (Fig. 19). In his guise as the wind god, Ehecatl, he was also associated with a calendrical energy as the creator of winds of the spirit.

Another legend tells us that Tezcatlipoca at one point tricked Quetzalcoatl into an incestuous relationship with his sister, Quetzalpetlatl, while he was intoxicated with the alcoholic cactus drink pulque. Out of remorse (Quetzalcoatl was also the god of boundaries), he threw himself into the fire and his heart was transmuted into Venus the Morning Star. Venus as the Evening Star instead came to be seen as a manifestation of his twin Xolotl. From these stories it seems that to the Aztecs Quetzalcoatl could exist in many different guises that he could be transmuted between. To the Aztecs, then, the Plumed Serpent was not only a god and a man, but also a planet, a calendrical energy, and maybe even a metaphysical principle as well. Indeed he appeared to them as a multifaceted deity, whose essence it may not be immediately clear to us how to grasp.

Also to the Maya, the Plumed Serpent, who in the Yucatan went by the name of Kukulcan, was one of the principal deities said to have existed since the beginning of time. He is in fact mentioned at a very early point in the *Popol Vuh*, the so-called Bible of the Maya, which describes another version of their creation story:[7]

"So there were three of them, as Heart of Sky, who came to the Sovereign Plumed Serpent, when the dawn of life was conceived: 'How shall it be sown, how should it dawn? Who is to be the provider, the nurturer?'"

Even if the Aztec sources tell us fascinating things from the prophetic lore of Mexico, this quote gives another impression of the Plumed Serpent. The *Popol Vuh* presents him as the supreme deity, who, after contemplating together how things should be on Earth and what living species they were going to create, Heart of Sky came to ask how creation was going to be initiated.

A picture of the Plumed Serpent as an entity on a supreme level thus emerges from the *Popol Vuh*. Among the Maya the Plumed Serpent was ultimately seen as a metaphysical entity existing before everything else. This tells us that we may have to take some of the mythology of the Aztecs with a grain of salt if we are to probe deeply into the underlying truth of the calendar system of the Maya. To find this, the best place to go is to Chichen-Itza, a city that the Postclassical Maya, possibly with a Toltec influence, built in honor of this very entity.

THE SYMBOLISM OF THE PYRAMID AT CHICHEN-ITZA

If we recognize how intimately the building of pyramids, in fact all over the world, was connected to the initial creation event described for the Mayan Long Count (chapter one), we also have reasons to expect that the Mayan pyramids have something to say about their calendar system. Nowhere is this clearer than from the Pyramid of the Plumed Serpent (Fig. 20)—the most famous of all Mayan pyramids—located in Chichen-Itza on the Yucatan Peninsula.

Remarkably, unlike all other major Mayan pyramids, when viewed from above like the Great Pyramid at Giza, this pyramid is also eight-partitioned. This, however, is only one of the things these two showcase pyramids of the

Old World and the New World have in common. Like the Great Pyramid in antiquity, Chichen-Itza was in a recent international Internet vote chosen as one of the Seven Wonders of the World.[8] Seven, the number of the wonders of the world also happens to be an especially relevant number, because at this pyramid this number is manifested in a most spectacular way. Those who built the Pyramid of Kukulcan highlighted this number through a spectacular light show, and this light show will help us to definitively determine who or what the Plumed Serpent really is.

Figure 20. The descent of Kukulcan on the eight-partitioned pyramid in Chichen-Itza at spring equinox.

This light show presents itself at every equinox at one of the four staircases that create the eight-partitioning of the pyramid. On such a day, performances and dances lead up to the time in the late afternoon when the shadows from its terraces align in a very special way for about half an hour. At this time, *seven* triangles of light appear as scales on the back of the Plumed Serpent, which lead into its head and seem to descend to the ground (Fig. 20). In our own time, about one hundred thousand people gather at Chichen-Itza at the spring and autumn equinoxes to view this descent of Kukulcan. By far the majority of these visitors are local Mexicans—often with Mayan roots—celebrating the new season. Some ten thousand will also come from the four corners of the world to witness the spectacular descent of the Plumed Serpent to the Earth. However, this thousand-year-old light show can only be clearly seen during a few days around the equinoxes (unless, of course, it is cloudy, which happened to me once).

The moment the shadows project onto the staircase and give rise to seven triangles of light strikes you with awe. Ordinarily when we see things from ancient times they are physical objects, but this is different. This is one of the few cases where pyramid builders have created a light show we can still witness today. The reason that this impression goes into your marrow is that as it happens—and this can hardly be communicated in words—you understand the challenge the builders must have faced to produce this effect for only two specific days a year. (It is not as if you can move a pyramid of this size a "little bit" if it does not produce the desired effect. Moreover, you would have to wait for the equinoxes every year to evaluate the result.)

This light show provides another curious commonality with the Great Pyramid at Giza. Today the eight-sidedness of the latter, presumably its most important facet, can be seen from the air, but it also becomes visible from the ground at the equinoxes because of shadows produced on these very days.[9] If the message at Giza at the equinoxes is so important, there are reasons to believe the light show at Chichen-Itza on the same days has an equally important message.

Typically, tour guides at Chichen-Itza will tell you that this pyramid is a solar calendar. Each of its four staircases also has ninety-one steps, which if you add the top level sums up as 4 x 91 + 1 = 365, the number of full days in a year—the duration of the so-called Haab calendar of the Maya. On a superficial level it is then true that this is a solar calendar, but arguably this is fairly trivial knowledge. Given time, anyone can find out that the number of days in a year is slightly more than 365 days and, with enough of a workforce build a pyramid accordingly. However, not everyone can produce the light show, which requires constructing a building with very great precision. Not surprisingly, then, it is through the light show that the significant metaphysical message of the pyramid is conveyed. This message unfortunately remains hidden to casual visitors, as most tour guides are not aware of it. In reality, the message of the pyramid is very profound, because it tells us who the Plumed Serpent really is and why it was so revered.

In the light of this, we may again want to ponder the mysterious nature of this deity, the primary deity of the whole city of Chichen-Itza. Why would someone see a Plumed Serpent as a supreme creator god and as an object of worship, and why regard it as the bringer of civilization and the calendar? Without a deeper explanation, it may seem incomprehensible, or even bizarre, for a culture to associate such a role with a serpent. To complicate things further, the Aztec and Mayan writings I referred to earlier really have nothing to say to clarify the matter. Instead of going to their legends, we will then have to ask ourselves what the pyramid is really saying and why they built it the way they did.

What is easy to see about this pyramid is that the house used for ceremonies on its top was the center of the eight-partitioned world mountain, where the sky connects to the Earth.[10] It is also evident that it was from this center that the Plumed Serpent emanated. Thus, at the equinox light shows, the wave movement of seven triangles of light and six of darkness emanates from this center. If we further recognize that the movement of a serpent may be the clearest manifestation in the physical world of a sine-wave movement, then we may begin to understand why they chose a Plumed Serpent as a symbol for the waves of creation. What the Maya worshipped was therefore not the serpent as a reptile, but the metaphysical waveform that develops the creation that we are all part of. Put plainly, the Plumed Serpent was the name for the wave movement of seven DAYS and six NIGHTS.

Accordingly, despite what the lore seems to imply, the Plumed Serpent is not an individual god, planet, reptile, or human, but an invisible power in the creation process. It is for this reason that the Heart of Sky in the *Popol Vuh* goes to the Plumed Serpent to ask how life is to be seeded. Part of the message of the pyramid is, thus, that from the center of the world mountain emanates a wave movement of seven pulses of light and six of darkness, adding up to thirteen. If we identify these triangles of light and darkness with the thirteen baktuns of the Long Count (see Figs. 2 and 10), then, and only then, will things start to make sense. That the Serpent is "feathered" simply refers to the fact that these are not land-based waves like those of the movement of a snake, but creation waves "flying in the air," emanating from the Heart of Sky in the heavens.

In chapter one we saw that it was indeed the beginning of this very seven plus six-wave movement of the Long Count calendar that had initiated civilization and the building of pyramids. In this light, it is no wonder the Plumed Serpent was worshipped as a seeder of life, the bringer of civilization, the calendar, books, commerce, arts, crafts, and knowledge. The role of the Plumed Serpent in the *Popol Vuh* makes sense if we are willing to go deeper than the astronomical interpretations and see the underlying metaphysical reality that it symbolizes. What was presented in the previous chapter to explain the shifting nature of the DAYS and the NIGHTS of the Long Count is then consistent with the mythological view the Maya had of the Plumed Serpent.

Unlike some pyramids in the Old World, the pyramid of Chichen-Itza was, however, not built in seven levels, which seemingly would have been a simpler way to convey the message that the Plumed Serpent consists of seven DAYS of creation. Like the central pyramids in many other Mayan sites, such as Tikal and Palenque, it was built in nine levels, a number that in fact adds significantly to its message. To further emphasize his relation to the number nine, Kukulcan was symbolized by the calendrical energy of Bolon Ik, Nine Wind.[11] This tells us that there are nine winds, and indeed the nine wave movements of seven DAYS and six NIGHTS generated by this entity must have been experienced much like spiritual winds. As we will see, *nine waves, each made up from seven peaks of light and six valleys of darkness, is a condensed description of the Mayan calendar system*. Not surprisingly, then, this message is communicated by the Pyramid of Kukulcan in Chichen-Itza, which was one of the last ones built by the Maya and in the modern world has become their showcase pyramid.

THE NINE WINDS

If there are nine waves in the Mayan calendar system, a crucial question becomes how to identify these and how to know if they are real. By real, I mean that through empirical evidence they can be shown to have an effect on the real evolution of life. That the *Popol Vuh* describes the Plumed Serpent as the seeder of life does not by itself prove this to be the case, since there are many ancient myths that may simply have been created for entertainment. However, we have already encountered one such wave, the Long Count, which in the previous chapter we found to be real as it was behind the emergence and evolution of human civilization in a tangible way. Remarkably, this is exactly how the Toltecs and Aztecs saw Quetzalcoatl—as the god of dawn and the bringer of civilization. Since in Figures 10 and 17 we saw that each of the DAYS indeed means a new dawn in the development of civilization, we can conclude that seen in the right way, this description of the Plumed Serpent is really to the point. In Figure 19, we can also see that Quetzalcoatl was the bringer of an eight-partitioning cross and indeed, from what we know about the history of the Long Count, the eight-partitioning played the decisive role for the development of this wave.

Of these nine waves, only the Long Count of thirteen baktuns seems to have been ruled by an entity called Six-Sky-Lord.[12] From this, we may surmise that the sixth level of the nine-storied pyramid symbolizes the Long Count, and for this reason I will use the name Sixth Wave interchangeably with the Long Count. This Sixth Wave is by far the most commonly represented among the steles of the Classical Maya. The reason for this predominance is presumably that this wave most directly influenced the life of the ancient Maya. References to the other eight waves are much less common. Yet, especially in Coba,[13] but also in Yaxchilan, there are steles that include several different wave movements. The time periods of the nine waves of the Plumed Serpent have been listed in Figure 21.

Wave	Time Unit	Duration (Metaphysical time)	Duration (Physical time)	Activation of Wave
9th	uaxaclahunkin	18 kin	18 days	March 9, 2011
8th	tun	$20^0 = 1$ tun	360 days	January 5, 1999
7th	katun	$20^1 = 20$ tun	19.7 years	1755 CE
6th	baktun	$20^2 = 400$ tun	394 years	3115 BCE
5th	pictun	$20^3 = 8,000$ tun	7,900 years	103,000 YA
4th	kalabtun	$20^4 = 160,000$ tun	158,000 years	2.05 MYA
3rd	kinchiltun	$20^5 = 3,200,000$ tun	3.15 MY	41 MYA
2nd	alautun	$20^6 = 64,000,000$ tun	63.1 MY	820 MYA
1st	hablatun	$20^7 = 1,280,000,000$ tun	1.26 BY	16.4 BYA

Figure 21. Summary of the time units of the nine waves of the Plumed Serpent, and the metaphysical and physical durations of these time periods. The right column marks the dates of activation of the respective waves.
(YA = years ago, MYA = millions of years ago, BYA = millions of years ago)

In Figure 21 the second column shows the Mayan names for the units of time (whether they are DAYS or NIGHTS) with which each one of the nine waves of the Plumed Serpent are developed. In columns three and four the table also provides their respective durations in both metaphysical time units and as translated to astronomical time units of solar years and days. Each of the time periods becomes twenty times shorter, and hence the frequency of the wave twenty times higher, as we climb to new and higher waves from the bottom of the table (which reflects a nine-storied pyramid). Because of the durations of the waves of thirteen such time units, these are becoming shorter as we climb the pyramid. They are, as we may see in the fifth column of Figure 21, then also activated in a certain sequential order. Hence, the First Wave, which was activated at the Big Bang (about 16.4 billion years ago), was the only activated wave until 820 million years ago, when the Second Wave was also activated. The higher waves, Third, Fourth, etc., with their stepwise increased frequencies, then progressively come into play. This is what is behind the acceleration of time that has become a common experience, especially in recent decades.

When a new wave is activated it thus adds to those already activated and does not replace the ones with lower frequencies. Instead, the different waves are activated on top of the others until on March 9, 2011, the Ninth Wave, with the highest frequency, was finally activated. At this point all the waves of creation were for the first time oscillating together. On October 28, 2011, these nine waves had all come to their thirteenth step (seventh DAY), which was a significant synchronizing event and a tipping point in the creation of the universe. At that point, the wave movement in thirteen steps of the Plumed Serpent had run its course in all nine waves, thus completing the buildup phase of the evolution of the universe. That this is not the full story, as the waves have actually continued after October 28, 2011, the reader may read about in Appendix I, but for the purpose of this particular volume, which deals only with the past, this is not necessary to assimilate.

MATRICES OF CREATION

The nine different waves develop different kinds of phenomena that are summarized briefly in Figure 22, although in this volume we will only focus on the Fifth and Sixth Wave. What is shown in this table are only rough descriptions to give the reader a sense of what all the nine different waves are about rather than precise definitions. There are many other aspects to what these different waves create.

Yet, if the Plumed Serpent, as the *Popol Vuh* implies, has seeded all life, then we would expect each of its nine waves to begin with a seeding event, which in thirteen steps will lead to a mature fruit. These seeds would then be developed through wavelike processes of seven DAYS and six NIGHTS in principle according to the pattern that we saw for the Sixth Wave in chapter two. To clearly see the common pattern, beginning with the seeding event in the different waves we then need to compare the events in them as in Figure 23.

Wave (or Underworld)	Basic Time Period	Phenomena Evolved
9th (Universal)	uaxaclahunkin	"Multi-D," unity consciousness
8th (Galactic)	tun	"3-D," smart technologies, female energies, Asian economies
7th (Planetary)	katun	"3-D," materialism, Americanism, industrialism, democracy
6th (National)	baktun	Mind, "3-D," civilizations, constructions, nations, writing, science, religions
5th (Regional)	pictun	Soul, tribal cultures, diversified tools, art, spirituality
4th (Human)	kalabtun	Homo, brain development, fire, tool-making
3rd (Anthropoid)	kinchiltun	Erect postures, bipedalism, tool-using
2nd (Mammalian)	alautun	Lateralized multicellular animals, plants to support higher life
1st (Cellular)	hablatun	Cells, galaxies, stars, planets

Figure 22. Different phenomena developed by the nine waves. Here the previously used names for different Underworlds corresponding to these waves are put in parenthesis. The term Underworld used previously refers only to the thirteen first time periods. (D = dimension)

The matrix in Figure 23 has been constructed for all but the two highest waves (because of their high frequency, changes in them are harder to track exactly). In this, the steps in the different waves have been normalized so that even if the waves are developed by time units of different duration, such as hablatuns, alautuns, etc., the phenomena of the different waves are compared based on the numbers from one to thirteen that the respective time periods have in the wave (Fig. 23). We can then, for instance, see the phenomena these respective waves seed at their very beginnings: First Wave (the Big Bang), Second (first animals), Third (first monkeys), Fourth (first humans), Fifth (first cultures), Sixth (first civilizations) and Seventh (first democracies). All of these are in our modern educational system treated by different disciplines, and yet they can all be recognized as seeding events, especially if we are aware of their relationship to the Plumed Serpent. The actual seed in the Long Count was as we saw in Chapter 1 (and Fig 19) the eight-partitioning, while in the other waves they are somewhat modified, which we will touch upon in the next chapter (Fig 26).

(Step in Wave) Ruling Quality	1st Wave 13 hablatun	2nd Wave 13 alautun	3rd Wave 13 kinchiltun	4th Wave 13 kalabtun	5th Wave 13 pictun	6th Wave 13 baktun	7th Wave 13 katun
DAY 1 Sowing	16.4-15.1 (BYA) Big Bang	820-757 (MYA) First multicellulars	41-38 (MYA) First monkeys	2.05-1.90 (MYA) Homo habilis	102,500-94,600 BP Ochre production, burials	3105-2721 BCE First nations	1755-1775 CE Idea of democracy
NIGHT 1	15.1-13.9	757-694	38-35	1.90-1.74	94,600-86,700	2721-2326	1775-1794
DAY 2 Germination	13.9-12.6	694-631 Early multicellulars	35-32 Aegyptopithecus	1.74-1.58 Homo ergaster	86,700-78,900 Flower burials	2326-1932 Akkadian empire	1794-1814 Napoleonic wars
NIGHT 2	12.6-11.4	631-568	32-28	1.58-1.42	78,800-71,000	1932-1538	1814-1834
DAY 3 Sprouting	11.4-10.1	568-505 Ediacaran, trilobites	28-25	1.42-1.26 Homo erectus	71,000-63,100 Botswana serpent	1538-1144 New Kingdom	1834-1854 Democracy in France
NIGHT 3	10.1-8.8	505-442	25-22	1.26-1.11	63,100-55,200	1144-749	1854-1873
DAY 4 Proliferation	8.8-7.6	442-379 Fishes	22-19	1.11-0.95 Homo erectus	55,200-47,300 Drachenloch altar	749-355 Persia, Greece	1873-1893 Labor movement
NIGHT 4	7.6-6.4	379-316	19-16	0.95-0.79	47,300-39,400	355-40 CE	1893-1913
DAY 5 Budding	6.4-5.1	316-252 Reptiles	16-13 Kenyapithecus wickeri	0.79-0.63 Homo antecessor	39,400-31,500 Cave paintings	40 CE-434 Roman Empire	1913-1932 End to autocratic empires
NIGHT 5 Destruction	5.1-3.9 Meteors bombard	252-189 Perm-Triassic extinction	13-9.6	0.63-0.47	31,500-23,700 Extinction of Neanderthals	434-829 Dark Ages	1932-1952 Fascism and WW II
DAY 6 Flowering	3.9-2.6 Prokaryotic cells	189-126 Proto-mammals	9.6-6.4 Australopithecus afar	0.47-0.32 Archaic Homo sapiens	23,700-15,800	829-1223 European proto-nations	1952-1972 Decolonization
NIGHT 6	2.6-1.3 End of anaerobes	126-63	6.4-3.2	0.32-0.16	15,800-7,900	1223-1617 European nations	1972-1992
DAY 7 Fruition	1.3-0.0 Eukaryotic cells	63-0.0 Higher mammals	3.2-0.0 Australopithecus africanus	0.16-0.0 Homo sapiens	7,900 – 0 Rock art of human figures	1617-2011 European nations	1992-2011 Fall of Soviet Union

Figure 23. Matrix of phenomena during the corresponding thirteen first steps in the seven lowest waves of creation. BYA= billion years ago, MYA= million years ago, BP = before present. Note that each wave has a time scale of its own.

The details in the diagram in Figure 23 have been discussed in all three previous books of mine, and to lay out all the evidence here for each of the continued steps in column 1 would detract from the main focus of the present book. The diagram is presented to give a quick overview of a rich and complex subject and the reader who desires a more detailed discussion is referred to my previous books. How biological life was seeded in the four lowest waves was, for instance, extensively discussed in *The Purposeful Universe* and a brief summary of this theory has been added in appendix II. Comparisons of the Sixth, Seventh, and higher waves were on the other hand presented in my earlier two books. *The Mayan Calendar and the Transformation of Consciousness*, for instance, included several examples of how the Seventh Wave developed industry from the sowing in the mid-1700s to the fruition in our own time.

The point to realize here is that by comparing one by one the thirteen steps in all of these waves, it becomes evident that qualitatively speaking they develop in parallel. This is true irrespective of the different frequencies of the nine waves in Figure 21 and regardless of their different roles in the evolutionary process shown in Figure 22. The evolution of the animals from the first multicellular organisms to the higher mammals in the Second Wave for instance parallel the evolution of democracy in the Seventh Wave from the Albany congress in 1754 to the worldwide spread of this system of governance at the collapse of the Soviet Union in late 1991. What this tells us is that each of the thirteen time periods in these waves represents a unique evolutionary step and that *this step has a similar quality in all the waves*. Hence, in terms of the basic progression of the movement of the Plumed Serpent, there is really no difference between biological and mental evolution, which both follow the same pattern of seven DAYS and six NIGHTS.

In all the waves, evolution thus results from a relatively smooth *wave* movement in thirteen steps. DAYS and NIGHTS collaborate to produce what appears as an intentional result in a directed process going from seed in the first DAY to mature fruit in the seventh DAY. In the present volume this waveform of the Plumed Serpent will mainly become visible through the evolutionary process of the Sixth Wave of thirteen baktuns that we discussed in the first two chapters. This then started with a seeding (in this case of the first nations and civilization), beginning a process which was completed with the proto and highest forms (of nations), respectively (Fig. 10).

THE ONE AND ONLY SOVEREIGN PLUMED SERPENT

The fact that this pattern is the same in so many different wave processes is, however, at closer thought, truly remarkable. It could only be so if evolution does not hinge on accidental or physical factors, but follows a preset metaphysical plan. This common pattern in the different waves is the chief reason that people in Mesoamerica came to worship the Plumed Serpent. Think about it! Why would a pattern like this—verifiable with modern scientific datings—be repeated in quite different processes of evolution? In theory, it would have been possible that the universe was created by wave movements, which each followed a pattern of its own. Biological evolution could, for instance, have proceeded by slow gradual changes as in the Darwinist model, or through jumps randomly dispersed in time, but none of those alternatives are consistent with the empirical evidence. Moreover, the frequencies of the different waves could conceivably have been unrelated to each other, rather than consistently differing by a factor of twenty. Instead, the evolutionary processes have developed in parallel according to the same pattern of seven DAYS and six NIGHTS in the different waves. This consistent wave pattern of evolution in thirteen steps means that each one of its steps has a distinct and unique quality (Fig. 24). It was the experience of these qualities that became the basis of the prophetic art of the ancient Mesoamerican civilizations.

The peoples using this calendar and practicing its prophetic art would use deities, birds, and other symbols to describe these qualities of the thirteen steps. (Our most extensive source for these is from the Aztecs, where the task of deciding on such symbols probably fell upon the priesthood of Quetzalcoatl.) When we look at the characters of these thirteen deities in Figure 24 we may indeed notice that they alternate so the DAYS (odd-numbered steps) are usually dominated by deities that we would see as nurturing and life-generating, whereas

Number Quality		Ruling Aztec Deity	Associated Bird	Growth Stage	Stage
1	DAY 1	Xiuhtecuhtli, god of Fire and Time	Blue Hummingbird	Sowing	Initiation
2	NIGHT 1	Tlaltecuhtli, god of the Earth	Green Hummingbird		
3	DAY 2	Chalchiuhtlicue, goddess of Water	Falcon	Germination	Activation
4	NIGHT 2	Tonatiuh, god of the Sun and the Warriors	Quail		Reaction
5	DAY 3	Tlacolteotl, goddess of Love and Childbirth	Hawk	Sprouting	Anchoring
6	NIGHT 3	Mictlantecuhtli, god of Death	Owl		
7	DAY 4	Cinteotl, god of Maize and Sustenance	Butterfly	Proliferation	Midpoint
8	NIGHT 4	Tlaloc, god of Rain and War	Eagle		
9	DAY 5	Quetzalcoatl, god of Light	Turkey	Budding	Breakthrough
10	NIGHT 5	Tezcatlipoca, god of Darkness	Horned Owl		Destruction
11	DAY 6	Yohualticitl, goddess of Birth	Scarlet Macaw	Flowering	Proto-Completion
12	NIGHT 6	Tlahuizcalpantecuhtli, god before Dawn	Quetzal		
13	DAY 7	Ometeotl/Omecinatl, Highest Creator God	Parrot	Fruition	Completion

Figure 24. Deities and symbols of the thirteen steps of the wave movement of the Plumed Serpent based on Aztec descriptions.

deities that are war-like or destructive rule the NIGHTS (even-numbered steps). To compare the qualities of these deities to what actually happened historically in the corresponding evolutionary steps is always fascinating, and this presumably was part of the basis for the prophetic art of the Mesoamerican priests.

From the upturns and downturns in the civilizations of Mesoamerica this wave pattern of creation had presumably become evident to their peoples through events related to the Long Count. Around 434 CE, the beginning year of the tenth baktun, new powerful dynasties had, for instance, been established in Copan and Palenque,[14] the cities marking the most eastern and the most western points of the Mayan region, respectively. Even more dramatically, as the eleventh baktun began in 829 CE, all of the old dynasties of the Classical Maya collapsed.[15] By the time the twelfth baktun began in 1223 CE, Chichen-Itza was also abandoned, and at the beginning of the thirteenth baktun (seventh DAY), the

Itza-Maya sent an emissary to the Spanish in Merida offering collaboration.[16] To the Maya, it was the wave of the Plumed Serpent that brought all of these shifts in power about, and even if these were not always in their favor, they recognized the wave as real. Understanding the Plumed Serpent fully would be the same thing as knowing in what direction the political winds would blow. Many would have liked to stay on top of such political changes and use this knowledge to their advantage. For this reason, they developed a prophetic art around their calendar, as we may learn about from the *Books of Chilam Balam.*

That the Plumed Serpent is always one and the same wave is also very consequential. This unified expression of creation must have been what prompted the ancient Mesoamericans to look upon this wave as its central deity. At its heart, it means that factors that ultimately are metaphysical are needed to explain the creation and evolution of our universe, and we can call one aspect of those the "Plumed Serpent." The forward direction of these evolutionary waves is also the explanation to a long-standing problem in modern physics, namely why there is a so-called arrow of time. Once we see the unity in the way that our universe is being created, we need not wonder why the peoples of Mesoamerica developed a religion with the Plumed Serpent as its central figure.

Seen in the model presented here, life is therefore not something that happened to pop up on our planet as a mistake or a whim of nature. It instead seems that the very reason for the existence of the universe is to generate life, and it does so through a wave movement called the Plumed Serpent by the ancient peoples of Mexico. Unlike in the Darwinist view, biological evolution is then here not seen as a result of accidents, which could lead it in any direction. The waves of creation instead bring life in a certain preset direction, and if we are to believe the *Popol Vuh*, it was the purpose of the gods, for instance, to create human beings.

THE MYSTERY OF QUETZALCOATL EXPLAINED

After having seen the metaphysical nature of the Plumed Serpent as a wave movement of creation, we may now return to the old lore about this entity, which was recounted in the beginning of this chapter. This lore will make more sense from the metaphysical understanding that has now been presented. To see this, our point of departure will be that the Plumed Serpent is the light aspect of a set wave in thirteen steps as shown at the pyramid in Chichen-Itza.

Already its wave form may in fact help to clarify why Quetzalcoatl was associated with Venus, since this is a planet that may be seen as exhibiting a kind of wave movement between light and darkness. After its emergence as a morning star, Venus rises higher and higher in the sky until it reaches its apex. Then it starts day by day to decline until it disappears as the morning star and reappears as the evening star. In this sense, the planet Venus really undergoes a wave movement from light (morning star) to darkness (evening star) and back. From this, we may understand that Venus was seen as a symbol of the wave movement of the Plumed Serpent, which likewise alternates between DAYS and NIGHTS.

When it comes to the most well-known human incarnation of Quetzalcoatl,

Figure 25. Lady 6-tun from Yaxchilan communicating with a serpent spirit.

Ce Acatl Topiltzin, we should first notice that he is believed to have reigned between 923 and 947 CE.[17] This was indeed within a period of light, a DAY, in the Long Count (see Fig. 10), and so a time when civilization would be expected to flourish. In the worldview of the ancients, it was natural to see human individuals, such as Topiltzin, as merging with entities in the spirit world, such as the Plumed Serpent, and for this reason this man was given the name of Quetzalcoatl. All the good deeds of this priest-king would then be looked upon as manifestations of the light of this spiritual wave movement and consequently as manifestations of Quetzalcoatl.

We may also note that the central pyramid in honor of Quetzalcoatl in Chichen-Itza was built in a DAY time period, which reflected the light of this deity. The entire era of the Aztecs, 1248–1521 CE,[18] on the other hand, fell within a period of darkness, namely baktun 12, which is NIGHT 6 of the Sixth Wave. The Aztecs were apparently aware of this darkness, which was what led them to expect a return of the light of the Plumed Serpent. More recently, some scholars have questioned[19] whether Moctezuma actually saw Cortes, who happened to arrive in this dark period, as a god. I think it is quite possible that he did not. Still, the paradox is that this does not preclude the possibility the Aztec priesthood was discussing whether Cortes was a manifestation of Quetzalcoatl or not. What the Aztecs may have discussed among themselves was when the light of the Plumed Serpent wave was going to return. The Spanish would not have understood such a discussion, since it refers to the higher metaphysical truth about the Plumed Serpent, who was not a "god" in the same sense that they thought of one. Regardless, the Aztecs were not in a good position to answer when the light would return, since they did not follow the Long Count. Moreover, they had changed the calendrical energy of Quetzalcoatl from Nine Wind to One Reed, which most likely added further confusion. Unfortunately, the calendars of Mesoamerica were not completely pure, and were sometimes modified for religious or political reasons.

At this point in time, the Maya are believed to have essentially abandoned the Long Count. We do not know exactly when they did so, because so few (only four) of their codices have survived, but we may look upon the disappearance of this metaphysical calendar as part of the decline of the cosmology of the ancients. Certainly by the time of the conquest, the so-called "katun wheels" and the "52-year calendar rounds" had mostly replaced the Long Count calendar. As a result, they might not have been certain about the time of the return of the Plumed Serpent either, even if attempts to determine this are apparent in the *Books of Chilam Balam*. Furthermore, at the beginning of the sixth NIGHT Chichen-Itza had collapsed as a culture, despite its reverence of Kukulcan, and so maybe their faith in this entity was lost by then. The Plumed Serpent was not an easy wave to ride even for those who knew about it and honored it. It was a beloved deity, which, however, was also known to sometimes molt its skin and change its guise as new waves were activated.

The Spanish conquistadors who were riding another wave, the pre-Seventh Wave (which is outside the scope of this book to discuss), cunningly seized the opportunity, and in the beginning of the 16th century the entire ancient Mesoamerican civilization collapsed at their hands. With the fall of the Aztec Empire, the last vestige of the pyramid-building ancient mind disappeared from the Earth. For the indigenous civilizations of the Americas, this was a disaster both culturally and in terms of population. According to some estimates, the native population of Mexico declined from twenty-five million to one million in the following hundred years.[20] This was not the first time, and not the last time, either, that the actual manifestation of the creation energies described by the Mesoamerican calendar system failed to conform to expectations.

After these three chapters describing the dawn and evolution of the human mind we will in the next chapter look at what humans were like before the mind had been activated.

CHAPTER 4:
CAGING IN THE CAVE MAN

TRANSITIONING FROM ANIMAL TO MAN

The nine different waves mentioned in the previous chapter (Fig. 22) each develops a particular set of phenomena and is each a worthy topic of study. Among these, the four lowest waves, discussed in detail in *The Purposeful Universe*, create the physical and biological evolution of the universe. In contrast, the four highest waves, discussed in *Solving the Greatest Mystery of Our Time* and *The Mayan Calendar and the Transformation of Consciousness*, create the evolution of the human mind and civilization. Between these two groups of waves there is the Fifth Wave (that in previous books I have called the Regional Underworld), and this is the wave we will focus on in this chapter.

The Fifth Wave, which was initiated 102,700 years ago, provided the background to the rise of civilization discussed in chapters one and two, and so if we are to understand the transformation humans underwent with the dawning of the mind we should study this wave. This Fifth Wave has, in other words, provided the bridge between the biologically speaking fully developed human being, which came out of the Fourth Wave (summarized in appendix II), and the civilized human being that came into existence with the Sixth Wave. To describe this transformation requires an attempt to grasp what consciousness was like before the beginning of the Long Count, and what humans were like before they had developed a resonance with the global mind. This is the daunting task of our own compartmentalized minds to understand the non-compartmentalized minds of our prehistoric forefathers and foremothers.

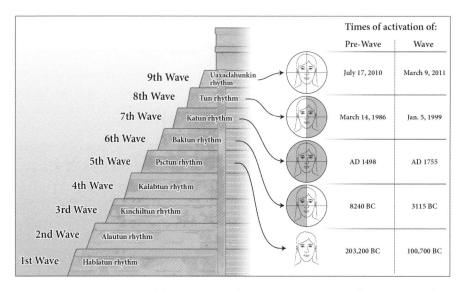

Figure 26. Nine-storied Mayan pyramid with the nine waves of evolution and their respective rhythms. To the right of this are the shifting polarities of the human mind at the higher waves of the pyramid as well as the times of activation of these waves and their pre-waves.

Homo sapiens, the product of the seventh DAY (beginning 158,000 years ago) of the Fourth Wave was fully endowed with a mind only 5,125 years ago. This happened because of the eight-partitioning of the global mind, which had been preceded by a preliminary form of this 10,250 years ago (Fig. 2). This leaves a time period of about 150,000 years since the emergence of *Homo sapiens* that we need to examine in order to understand what happened in between and what humans were like before the dawn of civilization. Questions we may then want to ask are: "What was the imprint at the beginning of the Fifth Wave?", "How did hominids evolve into humans?", "Did humans of the Fifth Wave have a soul?" and "Did early humans have a mind and, if they did, what was this like?"

Given what we learned about the seeding of a new geometric structure of the mind, the eight-partitioning at the beginning of the Long Count, we must assume that before this point in time humans lacked a fully developed mind.

Yet, some kind of bridge must have existed between the near animal of the Fourth Wave and the civilized human being of the Sixth Wave (5,125 years ago). This bridge between animal and man is quite difficult to scrutinize, as hard facts concerning these ancestors are scant, and datings uncertain between these two points in time. We will have to approach their reality based on the only material available, namely pieces of art and, in particular, the cave paintings.

The Fifth Wave, like all the Nine Winds of the Plumed Serpent, was a wave movement of seven DAYS and six NIGHTS. In this case, each of the DAYS and NIGHTS lasted for the duration of a pictun (about 7,900 years long, Fig. 21). This means that this particular wave, which developed the bridge from animal to man, has a frequency twenty times higher than the Fourth Wave. On the other hand, it had a frequency twenty times lower than the Sixth Wave that developed human civilization (Figures 10 and 17). This low frequency meant that by modern standards the lifestyles of human beings changed very slowly throughout the Fifth Wave.

Especially from its first half, archaeological findings in the Fifth Wave are very sparse. In addition, those actually found are difficult to date, as carbon-14 dating loses its accuracy 50,000 years into the past, and other less reliable means of dating then need to be utilized. Nonetheless, what some refer to as the world's first art studio in South Africa, a place where colors were mixed in shells,[1] is dated with such methods to about 100,000 years ago. This tells us that human beings at the beginning of the Fifth Wave started to create external representations of an emerging inner life, probably in the form of painted bodies or cliffs. A new form of self-awareness must thus have emerged at this time. Although this very early form of art is lost to us, the very fact that it existed points to a big step taken at this time distancing the human beings from the animals. The oldest known piece of art was discovered in Botswana and is estimated to be about 70,000 years old.[2] Given what we saw in the previous chapter, it is not very surprising that this is a serpent.

The fact that the oldest undisputed burial of humans dates back 100,000 years,[3] to the very beginning of the Fifth Wave, is also consistent with the notion that this wave meant that humans came to perceive themselves as being endowed with an inner life, a soul or a spirit.[4] Later, from maybe 80,000-100,000 years ago, we have the remains of the so-called flower burials among Neanderthals in the Shanidar cave in present-day Iraq.[5] This indicates a belief in an afterlife had emerged in the Fifth Wave, which in turn would mean that people had begun to experience themselves as souls, whose existence could transcend the physical existence. This soul would not be the mind, which emerged only with the Sixth Wave, and thus humans in these two waves had distinctly different characters. Through this awareness of soul they were also profoundly different from the animal-like hominids of the Fourth Wave that had preceded them. As a result, we have a few indications that similarly to how the mind was downloaded from a spiritual realm at the beginning of the Sixth Wave, the soul had been downloaded already at the beginning of the Fifth.

Barbara Hand Clow has analyzed this Fifth Wave in her book *Awakening the Planetary Mind* in terms of its seven DAYS. She concludes it was during this wave that humans became spiritual and emotional beings. Based on early remains from burial sites, she suggests that at the time humans had gained a sense of their souls. She also relates the remarkable finding from the so-called Drachenloch Altar built by Neanderthals in current-day Switzerland—very tentatively estimated to 75,000 years old. This contains thirteen bear skulls, seven of which point toward the cave entrance, while six are found in niches cut into the back of the cave. Even if we will never know for certain, it is thus quite possible people in the Fifth Wave were already aware of the metaphysical rhythm of the waves of creation presented in the previous chapters. Such responsiveness to the metaphysical realm alone gives us reason to call the humans that lived then spiritual beings. Caring and compassion also seems to have emerged between human beings in the Fifth Wave as evidently incapacitated persons were helped to continue their lives.

Presumably, the emergence in the Fifth Wave of spirituality and empathy with other members of the human race may be explained from the particular pattern of shifting polarities shown in Figure 26. This pattern of shifts between the yin-yang polarities that dominate the mind in different waves is a key facet of the Mayan calendar. As a consequence, the veils separating us from the light and world of spirituality will be different in different eras. This has been discussed in my previous books and will be discussed again in the next volume of this trilogy. For now, what I think deserves to be noted is that the Fifth Wave lacks such a veil, or filter, and that so people at the time might have been more empathic. Moreover, the frontal lobe of the brain, thought to be the area in the brain where all ideas of God are created,[6] had by then been fully developed. Taken together, this would mean human beings in the Fifth Wave experienced a unity with others, as well as with nature and spirit. This would be in contrast to either the Fourth or the Sixth Wave when they were endowed with filters. As we saw earlier, in the Sixth Wave the human mind became polarized, and it was this polarity (also known as the Tree of Knowledge of Good and Evil) that led human beings to create civilizations, and with them patriarchal religions.

THE FIFTH WAVE OF EVOLUTION

We may note in Figure 26 that the Fifth Wave is the midpoint of the climb to the top of the nine-storied pyramid. This level is then really a turning point in the evolution from animal to man, or from physical body to mind. The reason is that the Fifth Wave was the wave that created the soul of the human being and made him or her into something more than just biological and physical matter. If the Drachenloch Altar may serve as a guide, then the experience of seven DAYS and six NIGHTS of this Fifth Wave also brought a spiritual dimension to human life. Through this wave, the humans became spiritual beings, and within a materially speaking very primitive culture they began to express themselves artistically. Presumably, this wave also made them sensitive to a whole range of subtle "energies," some of which I believe we may now have lost. Yet, the Fifth Wave fell short of giving the humans a civilized mind, and in the following I will provide some substantiation of this claim.

Very few manmade physical artifacts older than 50,000 years have been found, and before this time stone tools were very crude and unsophisticated.

However, artifacts more recent than 50,000 years made not only of stone, but also of bone, have been found to be more sophisticated. Thus, we may separate these more recent tools into different categories, such as projectile points, engraving tools, knife blades, and drilling and piercing tools based on their different functions.[7] This marked specialization in tool-making then happened at what we know to be the midpoint of the whole Fifth Wave (102,700 / 2 = 51,350 years ago). The midpoint of a wave always means a very profound shift, and in this case the diversification of tools indicates that a very rudimentary partitioning of the mind then for the first time began to manifest.

However, it is only from about 40,000 years ago that we find statuettes, cave paintings, and objects used by people to adorn themselves.[7] The world's oldest statuette, *Venus of Hohle Fels* (Fig. 27a), recently discovered in Germany (2008),[8] is from this time. So are cave paintings in Arnhem's Land in Australia[9] and the European caves of Chauvet, Peche Merle, and Altamira. The slightly more recent *Lion Lady* (Fig. 27b) tells us that someone we may recognize as human lived on Earth then, and that she presumably wanted to have the soul of a lion, or merge with one. (At the time, large numbers of this animal still inhabited Europe.) It thus seems 40,000 years ago an aesthetic revolution was taking place simultaneously and independently in Europe and Australia, a synchronicity, which attests to the global nature of human consciousness already at this very early point.

While it may be an enigma to mainstream archaeology that there was a sudden burst of art 40,000 years ago, it is not so from the perspective of the Mayan calendar that describes waves simultaneously influencing the whole Earth. Instead, the timing of this enhanced aesthetic activity is from this perspective exactly what you would expect. I pointed this out already in *Solving the Greatest Mystery of Our Time*[10] when stating that the aesthetic revolution took place at the beginning of the fifth DAY of the Fifth Wave. To understand why the earliest known cave art was created about 40,000 years ago, we need only recall that in all the nine waves the pattern of seven DAYS and six NIGHTS is the same. The qualities of those are summarized in Fig 24 and some corresponding

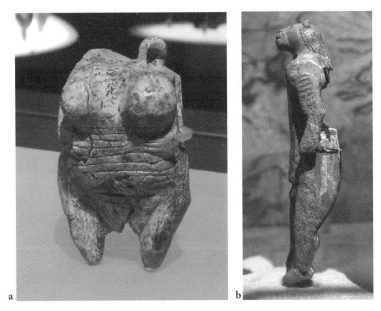

Figure 27. (a) Venus from Hohle Fels is a figurine made from mammoth tusk found in a cave in southwestern Germany and dated to 35,000-40,000 years old. (b) the Lion Lady, previously called Lion Man of the Hohlenstein Stadel is a 40,000 year old 30 cm high stauette carved from Mammoth tusk found in a cave in Southwestern Germany.

phenomena in the 5th Wave are shown in Fig 23. The ninth step in any wave, here called its fifth DAY, then always means a breakthrough in the expression or experience of light. Because this particular time period carries a breakthrough to light, the ninth step in the wave of thirteen was associated with Quetzalcoatl, the very deity of light. In Figure 28, we can see examples of phenomena that have manifested at the beginning of the fifth DAY in the various waves.

In the particular case of the Fifth Wave, the fifth DAY (40,000–32,000 BP) then brought the aesthetic revolution of statuettes and cave paintings. Human beings, at this time, began to express their inner light through art. While the oldest caves with art were most often dated to around 30,000 years, very recently (2012) a new dating technique has pushed up their age to what I had earlier expected based on the Mayan calendar. The famous site in Altamira is, for

Wave	1st	2nd	3rd	4th	5th	6th	7th
DAY 5 Quetzalcoatl	Solar system	Reptiles, Transition to land		Fire	Cave paintings	Christianity	Democracy
NIGHT 5 Tezcatlipoca	Meteor bombardment	Perm-Triassic extinction		Wurm ice age	Neanderthal disappear	Dark Ages	Nazism, WW II

Figure 28. Some phenomena of breakthrough and destruction, Quetzalcoatl and Tezcatlipoca, in the fifth DAY and fifth NIGHT, respectively, of different waves. From the Third Wave almost nothing is known about this shift.

instance, now dated to 40,000 years old,[11] and even slightly older cave paintings, presumably made by Neanderthals,[12] have been discovered in Spain. From this time cave paintings and carved objects become much more common, and even a flute has been found from this era.[13]

In each wave the fifth DAY is followed by the fifth NIGHT, symbolically dominated by Quetzalcoatl's dark mirror, Tezcatlipoca. Generally this brings some kind of destruction, or even extinction (see Fig. 28), following the preceding breakthrough. In the case of the Fifth Wave, this fifth NIGHT (32,000–24,000 BP) seems to coincide with the well-known extinction of the Neanderthals, who had been living side by side with *Homo sapiens* for a considerable time. Although it is not known how and why the Neanderthals disappeared, recently it has been shown that we still carry genes from Neanderthals today,[14] indicating that the two main groups of *Homo* that existed in the Fifth Wave interbred. This means *Homo sapiens* may not have killed the Neanderthals. If humans then lived in a time and era of unity (Fig. 26), there is no reason to take for granted they were as belligerent toward each other as they have been in some later times.

THE DISCOVERY OF CAVE PAINTING

The most spectacular forms of human self-expression known from the Fifth Wave are no doubt the cave paintings. Such cave painting from what prehistorians call the Paleolithic (50,000–10,000 BP) are found in a relatively limited area in southern France and Spain, even though a few sites are known from elsewhere as well (350 caves are now known in Europe).[15]

The modern world first became aware of these cave paintings through a discovery in Altamira in Spain around 1870. A gifted amateur archaeologist by the name of Marcelino Sautuola had taken his eight-year-old daughter Maria to a cave on his property, where she noticed paintings on the ceiling (Fig. 29). As Sautuola made the connection between these paintings and the prehistoric objects he found on the floor of the cave, he realized that these paintings must be very old. The scientific establishment at the time, however, was not willing to accept them as authentic, which spawned a protracted controversy that went on for some thirty years.[16] Few believed the paintings were as old as they actually were, and only when carbon-14 dating was introduced in the 1950s was the remarkably high age of the European cave art definitively ascertained.

Figure 29. From the great hall of polichromes in Altamira, Spain. Drawing by Marcelino Sautuola.

As several other similar sites were later discovered, it has become clear that the motifs, techniques, and styles of the cave paintings have remained quite constant over the millennia. Doubtless it was because of the low frequency of the Fifth Wave, compared to the higher waves that the style of the cave art changed so slowly. Therefore, at this early point in the history of art, "isms" (such as Cubism, Dadaism, etc.) did not rapidly replace each other. Instead, essentially the same style prevailed in the caves for thousands, if not tens of thousands of years, even if some minor trends are apparent. For the reader who wants to familiarize himself with the cave paintings, I recommend a remarkably fine Internet presentation of the famous site of Lascaux.[18]

The cave paintings made in the second half of the Fifth Wave naturally present a challenge to our ability to understand the people that created them. Over the past hundred years, researchers have thus proposed several theories to explain how, and for what purpose, the cave art was made. Our special interest here is what it may tell us about the soul or the mind, or absence thereof, in the people who created it. To explore this we may start by considering what we know about their lives at this time. From paleontology, for instance, we know that in Europe at the time humans were living in a world dominated by huge herds of animals. Some of these represented formidable threats, such as hyenas, bears, and lions, against whom often the only advantage humans had was their command of fire (see Fig. 28). In those days, the idea of finding a safe haven must have seemed farfetched, and human life probably meant a constant fight for survival against some very powerful animals. Other animals, such as horses and reindeer were instead prey for the humans. Still, it seems clear the paintings were not just preparations for hunting, as the caves also depict several animals not hunted. Regardless, animals were the most common motifs of these cave paintings. In Lascaux, for instance, more than half of the subjects depicted are horses. The caves also portray many other species, such as bison, auroch, and owl.

WHO WERE THE "I'S" THAT PAINTED IN THE CAVES?

It is not surprising that the purpose and meaning of the cave paintings have been topics of intense discussions. After all, no modern person would enter a cave hundreds of meters long and face its various dangers for the mere sake of creating a piece of art. Thus, from a modern standpoint it does warrant an explanation why this art was done to begin with. Based on the work of prehistorians Jean Clottes and David Lewis-Williams, connecting the Paleolithic cave paintings to shamanism (to be discussed in Volume 2), I believe the cave paintings were undertaken as part of some form of vision quest. In my view, humans in the Fifth Wave were living in a world of spirits, and the shamanic state was then the state of consciousness. That this would be a default state is an important point where my assessment may differ from that of others. As a consequence of this shamanic state, they may not have needed the same guidance regarding their purpose in life as a modern person engaging in a vision quest. Instead, I speculate it was only in the secluded environment of the cave that these artists could fully experience their inner light and inner visions, which would be enough of a reason for creating this art. This would then lead them to also experience that they had souls. Because the animals represented the greatest powers in the world at the time, the artists presumably also sought to reflect and integrate the souls of these animals. I then do not think the cave paintings were made "in order to" achieve something else. The purpose was obviously not to sell them and most likely not even to share them. Instead, it was in my view an affirmation of their spiritual selves that only with the 5th Wave would be realized.

Maybe in a human species barely emerging from the animal kingdom, the experience or even creation of one's soul came to be its own reward as the Fifth Wave broke through in its fifth DAY. Such a purpose could also answer why these people, who had no veil separating them from nature, chose to make

Figure 30. The Sorcerer from the cave of Trois Freres in France.

their paintings in caves. People who spend a long time in the dark will begin to see visions as expressions of an inner life similar to a shamanic state of contact with the spirit world. Maybe outside, humans were constantly preoccupied with the activities necessary for survival in a reality, which was experienced as merely physical. This could mean either hunting or being hunted with no place, either mental or physical, for self-reflection or experiencing one's own soul. Perhaps it was simply to experience their souls that they took the great pains to enter long tunnels in cold and moist caves.

This would mean that the fifth DAY of this Fifth Wave, starting 40,000 years ago, truly meant a breakthrough to experiencing the human soul, and cave art would have been a means of this. In this respect, only while they were secluded in the darkness of a cave would they become aware of the reality of the soul in a way that was both empowering and self-affirming. They would then have been able to experience things inside of themselves that would not have been possible in the daily life of fight or flight. Such self-consciousness could indeed have been a highly prized experience for them—the discovery through their art that they had a thinly shielded inner self and a soul that allowed them to experience "I am."

The shamanic merging of their souls with the spirits of animals may then have reinforced this self-affirmation. This would have led them to create the beings in their art that have become known as therianthropes: hybrids of humans and animals. Such beings may still appear in shamanic journeys today where a shaman merges with the soul of a power animal/totem or encounters a therianthrope in the spirit world. While there are not many representations of human beings in the early cave paintings, there are indeed therianthropes, such as the Lion Lady (Fig. 27b), or the Sorcerer from the cave at Trois Frères (Fig. 30). The Sorcerer, painted fifteen feet above the ground in a location where no modern artist could see himself working, is a combination of several different animals with a torso seemingly provided by a human being. I believe such a shamanic state created by the fifth DAY of the Fifth Wave was the default state of consciousness for all humans in the era of the cave paintings. In addition to the therianthropes, there are also in the cave paintings animals, or beings that we are not sure even existed, such as, for instance, the "unicorn" at Lascaux.

PRE-EIGHT-PARTITIONING ART

My basic premise for studying any form of art is that people create it as a reflection of how they experience reality, and I see no reason not to also apply this to the cave painters. The fact that realistic paintings of humans are completely absent in the caves and only a few, almost cartoon-like, figures are known may thus tell us something about how the artists experienced themselves and others around them.

This absence of representations of humans in the caves would not be surprising if it were not for the fact that many animals are beautifully painted with a high degree of realism. The most natural conclusion to draw from this absence of human portraits is that at this time the artists had not developed a very strong self-consciousness, not to mention ego. This would indicate that the uniquely human self-consciousness had then only barely emerged. It may even be that at this early time the animals surrounding them made a stronger impression on the artists than their fellow humans and so were favored as motifs. At the time, long before the human soul had downloaded the boundaries of the mind separating it from nature, maybe the powerful animals provided a stronger, more attractive motif to identify with.

Is there then any way of substantiating such far-reaching conclusions about the early humans painting in the caves and their contemporaries? Well, in addition to what is present, we may also take note of what is absent in the cave paintings. Examples of things missing are fishes, trees and plants in general. There are also very few birds. More importantly, in the caves we never see any landscapes with rivers, lakes, or mountains that would provide a context for the animals portrayed. The oldest landscape painting known in the world is in fact much more recent (about 8,200 years old from Catal Hüyük in present-day Turkey).[19] The absence of landscapes in the caves is consistent with the view that the cave paintings were made by humans lacking the mental boundaries that would be necessary to provide the context for a landscape or a scene. Such contexts for the art would not begin to be expressed until what archaeologists refer to as the Neolithic era or, in other words, after the activation of the pre-Long Count 10,250 years ago.

Hence, among the paintings are very few *scenes* organized in a meaningful way. Mostly, each animal gives the impression of having been created separately, despite different animals sharing the same space on the walls. The cave paintings often present the animals as if they are floating in space (see Fig. 29 or the so-called "Falling Cow" at Lascaux).[18] What this tells us is that the artists had not yet experienced reality as organized and structured in accordance with perpendicular vertical and horizontal lines, in contrast to later after the downloading of the geometric boundaries of the mind. To me at least, and I have visited a few of these caves, it does not seem either as if the images had a mythological content. This would suggest that the cave painters lived in a spirit world prior to "the expulsion from the Garden of Eden" (that is to say the downloading of the eight-partitioning) and that only after this "event" would myths created by compartmentalized minds come into existence. Unlike, for instance, the later Egyptians they had not yet experienced the beginning of a creation and so maybe had nothing to reference to develop a mythology.

Quite a few geometric signs are, however, present in the caves in the form of dots, circles, and short lines (see Fig. 31). Even in the earliest caves with art we can sometimes observe cruciforms, some of which are also perpendicular. As you would expect from the theory presented here, there is also a trend towards increased use of perpendicular signs.[20] Presumably then a very rudimentary mind

Figure 31. Nonfigurative Paleolithic signs in the cave of Niaux, France (13,000 BP).

already existed, maybe even from the midpoint of the Fifth Wave, preceding what would later develop with the dramatic partitionings in the pre-Long Count and the Long Count. Although the artists are nowhere near the long, precisely straight lines of the Egyptian pyramids, Figure 31 does show some very early steps towards those. However, what is crucial to notice is *the complete absence in the cave paintings of sun wheels or eight-partitioning symbols.*[21] This is worthy of note not only because this is what provided the Mayan definition of the initiation of the Long Count, but also because sun wheels and eight-partitionings are common motifs in cliff paintings less than five thousand years old. An example of sun wheels and eight-partitionings from the Long Count is shown in Figure 32, demonstrating a markedly increased degree of structure compared to in the caves before its activation (Fig. 31).

There is therefore no reason to believe that the early cave painters had yet experienced an eight-partitioning of the Earth. The often floating character of the cave art, as well as its shamanic traits, provides evidence that the Paleolithic painters did not possess compartmentalized minds. These findings should be related to the discussion of the eight-partitioning in chapter one and support that this was indeed an enormous novelty. It dramatically altered not only the outlook of human beings on life, but also their ability to create the linearly structured architecture typical of civilization. As the mind was downloaded the human ideal of art would also radically change, which is something we will return to in chapter six.

Up until the beginning of the pre-Long Count it thus seems human beings had only extremely rudimentary minds. However, 10,250 years ago, with the activation of the pre-civilized global mind brought by the preparatory Sixth Wave (Fig. 2), humans started to develop a new creativity. A new reality or, put more exactly, a new frame for experiencing reality then emerged based on this preliminary eight-partitioning. The direct evidence that they gained minds with frames comes from the fact that it was around this time that people started to build rectangular houses for the first time. The cave men were then with the new boundaries, if you like, caged in by a new frame of the mind, and

Figure 32. Cliff painting made by Chumash Indians in Santa Barbara, California, from about 1000 CE (within the Long Count).

this frame included a veil that partially separated them from the natural world (see Fig. 26). The pre-Long Count brought humanity what we may call a pre-civilized mind, which initiated the Neolithic era. After the inception of this, no cave paintings are known from Europe. Presumably, as the early compartmentalized mind emerged (10,250 BP) its boundaries generated a stronger experience of an inner self in the human beings. This alone provides an explanation as to why such cave painting came to an end, since self-affirmation could then be gained in other ways. With the mental shift that took place, humans became more intent on control of nature than on merging with the spirits of the animals.

WHY DID THE LARGE MAMMALS GO EXTINCT?

Throughout the Paleolithic era large herds of mammals, sometimes giant varieties of those existing now, roamed the plains of the world. However, around the time of the beginning of the pre-Sixth Wave, 10,250 years ago, especially in Europe and the Americas, several species of large mammals, such as the woolly mammoth died out. The extinction of fifteen genera of mammals in North America can, for instance, be reliably attributed to a brief interval between 11,500 to 10,000 radiocarbon years BP.[22] More than half of the number of species of mammals became extinct shortly following the arrival on this continent of the Clovis people. Similar extinctions took place all over the world, and while there are other possible explanations to these, the most likely and probably most widely accepted is that at this time humans implemented new hunting practices.[22] An argument favoring the hunting hypothesis is that where humans did not reach, for example to Wrangel's[23] or St Paul's islands, the woolly mammoth survived for a much longer time.

My interpretation of these extinctions is that the downloading of the pre-civilized mind about 10,250 years ago had significant consequences for how humans hunted. We know from Göbekli Tepe and other sites from this era that people at that time became able to project rectilinear boundaries. Endowed with such minds with boundaries, they probably started to employ vastly more effective hunting techniques than before. In this view, the establishment of inner boundaries was crucial for the development of practical hunting techniques, such as the creation of traps, or groups of hunters collaborating to catch animals by encircling them. The new mental cage then helped the humans to cage in the animals in the external world, all according to the principle of "As inside— So outside," and with this they gained superiority. To use methods of snaring or trapping may seem obviously advantageous to us, who already have minds with boundaries. Yet, without such a mind the outcome of a hunt would most likely be determined by who was the fastest and/or had the sharpest teeth and claws. Under such conditions primitive humans would often come out on the losing end. The emergence of a mind with boundaries may have shifted this game entirely, and the extinction of the great mammals coincides very well in time with what we would expect from the beginning of the pre-Long Count of the Mayan calendar (Figures 2 and 26). A factor that I will not expand on in this volume is that humans also seem to have become more aggressive with the downloading of the mind and that this might have improved the hunt.

In terms of sustaining the long-term survival of the hunters, these new hunting techniques may even have turned out to be too effective. Large numbers of mammals rapidly went extinct, and this may be an early, or even first, example of civilization's notorious inability to stay in balance with nature. The compartmentalized mind tends to always outsmart the non-compartmentalized mind, sometimes even to its own detriment. According to most estimates, the extinction of large mammals happened in an instant, in about 400 years of geological time. In addition, these extinctions may have been the deathblow to many hunter-gatherer cultures, forcing some of them to turn to agriculture for their survival.

THE CREATION OF THE AGRICULTURAL REVOLUTION BY THE PRE-SIXTH WAVE MIND

It is also interesting to note that the domestication of plants and animals for food production commenced at about the same time as these wild animals went extinct. Thus, we see the first domestications of plants taking place independently, for instance, in Southwest Asia (olives, wheat, peas, 10,500 BP), China (rice, millet, 9,500 BP), and New Guinea (sugar cane, banana, 9,000 BP),[24] and in four other areas.[25] This occurred simultaneously with or shortly after the activation of the mind of the pre-Sixth Wave. What is noteworthy about these early agricultural societies in different parts of the world is that they were not in contact with one another and the particular crops they domesticated were not even the same. For these reasons, we can completely rule out agriculture as something they learned from one another. Yet, regardless of the location on Earth, people at this particular time simultaneously started to practice agriculture. It seems the only prerequisite was that there existed edible plants suitable for domestication.

This simultaneous and independent emergence of agriculture is fully consistent with the notion that it then became possible to download a new global mind, the one that inaugurated the pre-Long Count from the metaphysical realm. The knowledge about this early compartmentalized mind, which as we will see in chapter six had incorporated linear dimensions of both space and time, may in fact help us understand how agriculture began. To begin with, this early mind brought a rudimentary experience of sequential time and cause-effect relationships, which is something that is necessary for sowing, harvesting, and storing. Equally important may have been the idea to create fields with boundaries for growing crops and to set these apart from the rest of nature according to the principle of "As inside—So outside." It seems unlikely that without a mind with inner boundaries any intensive agriculture would ever have emerged on this planet.

The domestication of animals, which was also introduced at the beginning of this pre-Sixth Wave, presumably had a similar origin. The first animals (other than the dog) to be domesticated were sheep and goats in Southwest Asia (10,500 BP) and pigs and silkworms in China (9,500 BP).[26] In the case of animal domestication the role of mental boundaries seems to be even more critical than for plants, since an important factor will then be to fence in the animals. Even coming up with the idea of fencing animals (or herding them with the help of dogs) in the first place must have required a great mental shift. Again we have a case where the modern mind with its boundaries may not easily recognize how large a step this might have been for a non-compartmentalized mind. It may seem obvious to us now that if we are going to keep animals we need to fence them in, or at least prevent them from wandering away. For a human being who ten thousand years ago was just emerging from a default shamanic state and had been at the mercy of dangerous beasts, it may have seemed very unnatural to consider the fencing in of an aspect of nature—animals—to keep this separate.

What I propose here is that the fencing in of animals would also have required a mind with rudimentary boundaries on the part of the humans. Only as the human beings themselves became caged in by this new mind would they be willing and able to cage in animals and fields of crops according to "As inside—So outside." Agriculture and the associated settled lifestyle thus, in my view, emanated from a specific shift in consciousness, the one from shamanic to mental that took place 10,250 years ago as the pre-Sixth Wave began.

In this way, the human beings through two shifts, 10,250 and 5,125 years ago, both well-documented in ancient Mayan inscriptions (Fig. 47), went from cave man to civilized man—most markedly in the Fertile Crescent. As Jared Diamond highlighted in *Guns, Germs, and Steel*, it was not a racial superiority that placed the dawn of civilization in this area. Instead, it was partly that grains and animals suitable for domestication already existed there. These animals and plants had in fact existed there for some time, but no agriculture would emerge before it became possible to download an early mind with boundaries 10,250 years ago. The intensified food production in this particular region would, as the Sixth Wave began in 3115 BCE, facilitate the emergence of civilizations in the real sense of city life. A surplus of food provided by agriculture in fact was a prerequisite for the courts, priesthoods, armies, and craftsmanship that would then emerge.

In this transition to agriculture it was not the primary concern of human beings to protect the animals and nature. On the contrary, it would be more accurate to say that the compartmentalized mind has conquered, and often destroyed, everything in its way. In the Fifth Wave the human population grew from about half a million people 100,000 years ago to six million people 12,000 years ago.[27] At the time of Jesus Christ it had further grown to around 300 million. Its average yearly rate of growth, in other words, increased five-hundred-fold after the downloading of the early civilized mind, presumably because of the combined effects of the extinction of the wild animals and establishment of agriculture. Exactly the same trends are continuing into our own time to the notable detriment of nature.

THE ERECTION OF MEGALITHIC MONUMENTS

Another interesting phenomenon that came with the initiation of the pre-Sixth Wave period is the erection of megalithic monuments of a size the world had never seen before. Some of these megalithic monuments were built according to techniques that our modern minds are not always able to understand. It is for instance well-documented how huge stones were quarried and transported

220 kilometers from Wales to form part of Stonehenge,[28] and there are other examples that may be even more difficult to comprehend. Illiterate cultures then began to create what we now see as mysterious sites, such as Göbekli Tepe, Carahunge (Armenia), Ħaġar Qim (Malta), Carnac, Ales Stenar, Stonehenge, and Avebury, although only a few of these are more than 7,000 years old.

Unlike the Egyptian pyramids, pre-Long Count monuments are not yet characterized by exact geometric forms with straight lines. Yet, they often attest to an intention, not fully realized, to create sharp geometric forms and I suggest that they were all built to align with the incoming geometric imprints. Still, the impetus for the earliest of these megalithic monuments may later have been forgotten and their original purpose lost over time. Göbekli Tepe, for instance,[29] is known to have been backfilled relatively soon after the pre-Long Count had begun. My interpretation of this is that some time after the early mind had been downloaded people would rather put their creativity into practical pursuits, such as agriculture. Hence, rather than feeling compelled to erect monuments in honor of the source of the new mind, they were busy making use of it, and as they did they forgot about its origin and may not quite have understood why their ancestors had built such temples.

For similar reasons, the original purpose of the Egyptian pyramids and Stonehenge, at the beginning of the Long Count could later not be understood by people, who saw the compartmentalized mind as an integral part of themselves, rather than as an external divine imprint. Coming generations could only speculate about the meaning that the monuments originally had. The experience of those living at the beginning of the pre-Long Count or the Long Count had been fundamentally different from that of those that came after (Fig 8), who tried to make sense of the megalithic monuments from the perspective of their already assimilated minds.

As some Neolithic monuments mark alignments at solstices and equinoxes, some modern scholars have interpreted this to mean that people then were focused on astronomy. While it is entirely possible that with the new mind they used astronomical alignments in order to determine shift points in the solar year, I would like to suggest that the interest of people at the time was not in the astronomical alignments as such, but primarily in the metaphysical power of the four directions and of the sun. Hence, the pyramids at the beginning of the Long Count attest to people feeling the immense power of the eight-partitioned global mind related to the four directions. I believe it was these powers that people actually experienced and wanted to relate to spiritually at the time when many such monuments were built. As we could see in chapter 2 there is no need to speculate about the power of the four directions. These powers are very real.

In my view then, it is not likely that without the divine inspiration from the eight-partitioning people would ever have embarked on megalithic

Figure 33. T-shaped column from the world's oldest temple in Göbekli Tepe. My own interpretation of these steles is that they symbolize the Tree of Life (compare to the Mayan image at the center of Fig. 3a). These T-shaped pillars are from a layer dated to 8600-9100 BCE.[30]

building projects. Consequently, I propose the seeming interest in astronomy was a secondary phenomenon based primarily on their interest in identifying the origin of the powers of the four directions. If the eight-partitioning of the Earth was a microcosmic reflection of the eight-partitioning of the heliosphere (Fig. 13), we can also see why they would be interested in certain solar alignments. The sun, for instance, only rises exactly in the east and sets exactly in the west on the equinoxes, and those days may have become special for the very reason that they are connected to the four directions

(Fig 16). This may have been the primary reason for following the movements of the sun and erecting megalithic monuments that marked equinoxes and solstices.

Among the many aspects of knowledge the Pyramid of Chichen-Itza conveys, the descent of the Plumed Serpent at the equinoxes may then have been to honor the power of the east and the west and the power line connecting these directions. Since the four directions on Earth are related to the sun in a direct way, as well as to the eight-partitioning of the heliosphere, these may have been the very basis for the worship of the sun that became common in early civilizations. Indeed, symbols of partitionings (Figs. 14c and d) have come to be called sun wheels, and the famous eight-partitioned Aztec Calendar Stone has the sun god Tonatiuh at its center. I can see no reason that the sun would be symbolized in such ways unless it was itself recognized as the center of an eight-partitioned heliosphere.

That sun worship would have its origin in the eight-partitioning and the four directions is also hinted at in Egyptian mythology, where in one myth the sun god Ra was born out of the Ogdoad (eight-partitioning). This is just another way of saying that the sun only became the god Ra through becoming eight-partitioned and the center of the heliospheric mind (Fig 13). The sun by itself may not have been worshipped. Rather, it was the eight-partitioned sun that was worshipped since this provided an interface with the divine realm and as we have seen the Mesopotamian sun god Shamash was related to the eight-partitioning (Fig 6). In this, we would then have a rationale for why Neolithic people were interested in determining the cardinal directions and also why early civilizations came to worship the sun. It seems indeed, as is claimed by the Maya and the Aztecs that a "new sun", an eight-partitioned sun, was born 5,125 years ago.

THE UNKNOWN POWERS OF THE ANCIENTS

My own speculation regarding how the megalithic sites were built, technically speaking, is that in this pre-civilized era humans had some powers and abilities that we with our compartmentalized minds no longer share. Although humans in Neolithic times had downloaded an early version of the compartmentalized mind, they were still partially unfettered cave men. If human beings 10,000 years ago were still partly immersed in the spirit world of the Fifth Wave, then their state of consciousness would have been very different from what it is now. Even if we are not likely to ever be able to fully reproduce or experience what this state of consciousness would be like, we may still speculate about it. To begin with, people may in this transitional era, like the cave painters, have had small egos and been willing to put enormous efforts into creating something they experienced as a strong spiritual calling. If this inspiration was combined with the urge of the early compartmentalized mind to create structure in the external world, the results could have been the huge megalithic monuments that now seem so mysterious to us.

The shift activating the pre-Long Count may then possibly have given a new focus to the powers that people already had or even unleashed new powers and knowledge that later have been lost to us. An example of such knowledge that modern people have lost is to know what plants or animals in nature to eat or domesticate. Hence, the evolution of the mind does not only mean that we have gained new powers. It may also mean that we have lost powers and certain knowledge that the compartmentalized mind shuts out, and this may have included some powers related to how to handle huge stones. What I feel we can say with some certainty about these ancestors is that they were in a considerably more intimate spiritual relationship with nature than we generally are now. If they had a spiritual contact with the plants, which taught them which ones to domesticate, maybe their spirituality also taught them how to move and shape large stone structures to create spectacular monuments.

This is of course speculation. Yet, it is not more speculative than ideas that extraterrestrials, or members of a lost high-tech civilization, told our ancestors what to do. There are alternative explanations to many of the things some say only extraterrestrials can do and in a recent impressive documentary Chris White has debunked many of the arguments put forth in support of the so-called ancient astronaut theory.[31] On my own part, I feel the power of the mind, and the shifts between mental states the Mayan calendar describes, are aspects of reality that has been missing in the discussions about the origin of the megalithic structures that preceded civilization. Human beings at this early time, by necessity, had a different relationship both to spirit and to the mind than we do now and so may have had quite different powers.

All over the world there exist legends saying that Neolithic monuments were "built by the gods," and maybe it was because they had such a different relationship to the global mind that the humans living at this early time would later come to be remembered as "gods" or "giants." People in the Fifth Wave without mental boundaries or veils could well have been immensely more dedicated to the callings from the divine than humans at any later point in time. This unveiled spirituality might have come to its height with the seventh DAY of the Fifth Wave 8,000 years ago. Perhaps many mysteries of the past would be solved if we consider that the mind changes according to a preset pattern and that people in earlier eras were living in other states of consciousness than we are now.

The time when the humans were "gods," in the sense of being mentally unfettered, may well be what the ancient Egyptians referred to as the Zep Tepi, the First Time.[32] In this context we may also consider whether the famous Sphinx at Giza, the world's largest monumental sculpture, should be regarded as such a pre-Long Count monument belonging to the same category as Göbekli Tepe. Could the Sphinx be from Zep Tepi? There is no immediate answer in the form of contemporary texts alluding to when, or why, the Sphinx was built. However, a debate has raged between on the one hand Egyptologists claiming this sculpture must have the same age as the pyramids and on the other hand those, especially John Anthony West and geologist Robert Schoch,[33] claiming the Sphinx maybe as old as 10,000 years. The reason the latter two suggest this higher age is that its erosion pattern indicates it was built when the Sahara was fertile because of rainfall.

I find the arguments for the higher age of the Sphinx quite convincing. Maybe the Sphinx, which faces east, was built around the beginning of the pre-Long Count as a very early expression of the power of the four directions that humans were only then beginning to experience. After all, the sphinx is a very archaic therianthrope known to us already from the Lion Lady (a sphinx in reverse, Fig. 27b), and from Nevali Cori.[34] If the Sphinx was built at Giza as an expression of the power of the East, it is not so farfetched to believe the pharaohs, who later built the pyramids, decided to place them at the site of the Sphinx. Their placement there would then be a way of reconnecting to the four directions and honoring their ancestors from the Zep Tepi. In this understanding, the Egyptian pyramids would simply further express the strength of the directional powers already noted by their ancestors. If there were not such a connection of the Sphinx to the Zep Tepi, why would they have built the pyramids in what was already a forbidding desert?

It seems to me, however, that both sides in this Sphinx riddle have wrongly assumed that this monument must be the product of a civilization. For instance, a main argument of noted Egyptologist Mark Lehner against an old age of the Sphinx was that there is no evidence of a civilization having existed in Egypt at such an early time.[35] Yet, it seems clear that Göbekli Tepe was not built by a civilization, and in my view there is no need to assume that the Sphinx was built by a civilization either. If human history is primarily a product of a divine plan for the evolution of the human mind, then the shift in consciousness at the beginning of the pre-Long Count could have had many direct effects. Therefore, our own minds will not be able to interpret these correctly without taking earlier states of consciousness into consideration. Our hunter-gatherer ancestors may simply have felt a calling to build a monument such as the Sphinx to honor the Sun, the East and the King of the animal kingdom. If we accept the principle of mind over matter, human prehistory may be very different from what we have previously thought because it developed according to a quite different logic. People at the time may just have acted without what we call thinking.

COMING FULL CIRCLE

In the first chapter, I essentially placed emphasis only on the straight and perpendicular lines of the eight-partitioning. In order to gain a complete view of the sacred geometry creating this new mind we must, however, also consider the circle as part of this new mental template. There are, however, examples of objects in nature that are circular, and so it is not obvious that everything humans made that is circular or spherical has a metaphysical origin. The sun and the moon are, for instance, circles visible to everyone. Yet, I believe it was only at the time of the eight-partitioning that the circular form became the boundary of the human mind. Even if the circle had always been visible to humans in the form of the sun and the moon, it was only with the Long Count and its preceding wave that humans became aware of this as a distinct form and started to represent it in monuments and art.

The oldest near-circular forms are already present in Göbekli Tepe from the beginning of the pre-Long Count (the carbon-14-dating points to an age of 9600-8800 BCE for the circles and 8800-8000 BCE for the pillars,[30] which is somewhat earlier than 8240 BCE, when the pre-Long Count began). However, it is only at the beginning of the Long Count proper that almost perfectly circular structures, such as Newgrange (3200 BCE), Stonehenge (3100 BCE) (Fig. 34a), and Avebury (3100 BCE) are built. This means that these monuments on the British Isles, and maybe others elsewhere too, were built as reflections of the circular form that then came down from the heavens enclosing the eight-partitioning.

To further strengthen the argument that circular forms could be downloaded at this time, we may note that the contemporary Sumerian symbol for heaven, the Dingir, and the Star of Inanna are also circular. It may also be argued that the Egyptians incorporated the number pi (π) when building the Great Pyramid, possibly in recognition of the power of the circle as a mental structure. Thus, the ratio of the perimeter to the height of this pyramid is 22/7, which in ancient times was a commonly used approximation of this number.

The circle and pi may then have been looked upon as having a divine origin and for this reason included in the design of the Great Pyramid.

Yet, we do not have to be this sophisticated to see the connection between the rise of civilization and the circular enclosure of the mind. The ancient Egyptian and Chinese symbols for city and village (Figs. 34b and c), respectively, point directly to the relevance of the circular enclosure for the emergence of civilization. The Egyptian hieroglyph for "city" actually provides the most direct evidence possible that this culture associated civilization with a circular eight-partitioning. We can look at these symbols of city life as another direct statement from the ancients as to what caused the rise of civilization. As I see it, we no longer have reason to wonder about the rise of civilization's connection to the eight-partitioning, at least not if we accept what the ancients themselves are communicating.

As part of this sacred geometry the wheel should also be taken into consideration, as it is often said to be one of the most important of human inventions. The oldest wheel uncovered is from Slovenia and estimated to be 5,250 years old.[36] This provides another example of how human beings create in accordance with the principle of "As inside—So outside." Therefore, only as there is a metaphysical imprint of a circle will humans start to make wheels. Thus, even if circular forms existed in nature for eons before this invention, it was only as it became part of the inner reality of the human beings that they began to manifest it in the external reality.

The circular enclosure may even have been the most important aspect of the mental shift. This circular boundary may have made the human beings fully self-aware and led to the birth of the human individual. Since circular forms, unlike straight lines, exist in nature, I have however chosen to present these arguments at this later point in the book, only after presenting evidence that the Mayan calendar is indeed a description of the evolution of the sacred geometry of the mind.

The tremendous importance the circular form and enclosure may have had for social interactions also deserves consideration. All gatherings, ceremonies,

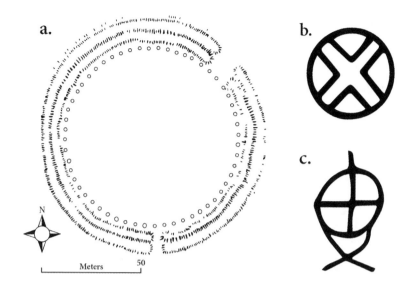

Figure 34. (a) Aerial view of the circle of Stonehenge I from 3100 BCE, before the stones were added. Note especially the near-perfection of the inner circle of wooden poles. (b) Egyptian hieroglyph to denote city.[37] (c) Ancient Chinese ideogram to denote village or town.[38]

and dances in tribal societies may, for instance, relate to circular enclosures in the minds of people. Maybe even the very existence of a larger community, or a tribe with an identity of its own, is a product of this circular mental form. When answering if this could be the case, our natural tendency may again be to simply project our current mind backwards, believing these practices have been going on for hundreds of thousands of years. Yet, we have no way of knowing for how long circular social gatherings have taken place or how long distinct tribal identities may have existed. I would like to suggest that they might not be much older than the enclosure of the human mind, which would place their maximum age at about 10,000 years. The circular form in the human mind would then have been what caused the experience of being part of a community in the first place.

Stonehenge, among others, may then have been created, whether consciously or unconsciously, as a physical expression of the circular mental enclosure downloaded at the beginning of the Long Count. Certainly its age would indicate this to be the case. Pointing to this is also that the number of poles in Fig 34a is 56 = 7 x 8, the product of the number of DAYS in the Long Count and the eight directions.

I thus do not think that we should regard the interest in the circular form by the ancients as a mere fascination with a geometric concept as such. The importance of the metaphysical circular imprint goes much deeper as it provides the boundaries of the mind, which I have already outlined as spherical in the models in Figures 11 and 12. Hence, the circle or actually, as we will see in the next chapter, the sphere of which the circle is a cross section, provides boundaries fully creating an experience of a separate self in the human beings. If it was this spherical boundary that was behind the new hunting techniques, agriculture, pottery, and the emergence of human social life, maybe we should not be surprised if the ancients erected megalithic monuments in its honor.

While the Fifth Wave may have incorporated a soul in members of *Homo sapiens*, the downloading of a spherical enclosure as the Sixth Wave began doubtless meant a further significant step in the transformation of consciousness into the material universe: the birth of human self-consciousness. This self-awareness, as just mentioned, seems to have been missing in the cave painters. Similar to the straight line, the circle may, however, seem too trivial for modern people to recognize as the origin of the human mind. It may especially be so, since by now we just take it for granted that the geometry of the mind is a part of ourselves and we have trouble discerning it. Where such a circle would come from may also appear just as mysterious as the origin of the eight-partitioning that it provides an enclosure for.

THE PLUMED SERPENT FLIES EAST

The winged disk symbols known from many parts of the Near East, such as Mesopotamia, Persia, Anatolia, and Egypt (Fig. 35), also deserve to be discussed in the context of the geometry of the mind. In these areas, and some other parts of the world as well, winged disks appear on reliefs and the top of gateways and temples going back to the beginning of the Long Count. Overall, these disks were associated with the Tree of Life, which they can be seen hovering over on many seals from Mesopotamia. In Egypt, they are known from about 2600 BCE (when the Great Pyramid was built).[39] It is widely believed that the wings indicate that these disks have an origin in the heavens and were perceived as having a divine origin. They were also intrinsically connected with providing protection of kingship and were thus in Egypt often associated with Horus,[40] which the pharaoh was a reincarnation of. The winged disks were there typically also shown with a pair of serpents, the royal cobras. Many suggestions have been made as to what these disks represent. They are often said to be associated with the sun, sometimes also to symbolize a perfected soul.

Figure 35. (a) Winged disk with eight-partitioning from Nimrod in Assyria. (b) Egyptian symbol of winged disk with serpents.

What I suggest is that the winged disks symbolize the influx of the geometric structure of the circle and the boundaries of the human mind this would create. Such disks emanating from the Tree of Life represent the circular enclosures, metaphysical geometric imprints, which together with the eight-partitioning created the civilized mind. That something was winged meant that it was a divinity emanating from the heavens or the god of heaven. Also, the serpents themselves may well have symbolized the wave movement, which brought this sacred geometry to the humans (Fig. 35b). Here we then have a direct parallel between the Near East winged sun disk with cobras and the Mesoamerican Plumed Serpent. Much like the Assyrian relief of a winged disk in Figure 35a, also Quetzalcoatl brought an eight-partitioned cross (Fig. 19), which in turn is identical with the Egyptian symbol for city.

This provides for an astounding convergence of symbolism that allows us to see how different ancient cultures in many parts of the world recognized a Feathered Serpent as bringing a mind-altering eight-partitioning imprint creating monarchy and civilization. Each ancient culture in Mesoamerica or the Near East had a special cultural way of representing these imprints, but we may now realize that the core meaning of these symbols is the same. Thus, like today where there is a modern mind with many commonalities all over the planet, there also existed something we could call a common ancient mind.

If the winged disk was a symbol of the circular enclosure of the mind, it explains why this played such a critical role not only for civilization, but also more directly for its associated kingship. (The symbolism became important at all royal buildings and monuments. Some winged disks have kings in them.) The winged disks were indeed aspects of the heavens that the ancients downloaded and then they would create enclosed social structures, which during the Long Count proper had the monarch at its center. From this we can understand that in Egyptian mythology the winged disk was associated with Horus, who by defeating his enemies helped consolidate its civilization.[41] To see the winged disk as a symbol of the perfected soul also makes sense if we recognize that what gave the human beings self-awareness of this soul was the downloading of this very enclosure. The various interpretations of these symbols may thus not be mutually exclusive. (Incidentally, the so-called "orbs", spheres of light currently visible on digital photographs, especially at spiritual events, are most likely modern expressions of the circular imprints that in ancient times were symbolized as winged disks.)

WHEN CIVILIZATION DOES NOT TAKE HOLD

Based on these studies of the circular imprint I suggest that Göbekli Tepe reflects the first step, the first rudimentary expression of the circular and eight-partitioned geometry of the pre-Sixth Wave. Later, around 3100 BCE, this would be expressed more sharply in Stonehenge or the Egyptian pyramids. It was thus the beginning of the pre-Long Count that created the roundish structures at Göbekli Tepe. However, it was only in the next step, when the Long Count began, that Newgrange and Stonehenge with almost perfectly round forms were created. Likewise, we could see the relatively straight pillars of Göbekli Tepe, or the rectangular buildings in Catal Hüyük and Jericho, as preparatory steps for the sharp, extended straight lines of the Egyptian pyramids. From these comparisons, we can recognize that the downloading of the corresponding mental forms, both circles and the straight lines they enclose, really occurred in two steps at the beginnings of the pre-Long Count and of the Long Count, respectively.

In terms of timing, the erection of both Stonehenge[42] and Avebury[43] in fact seem to match the building of the Egyptian pyramids remarkably well. At Stonehenge the oldest east-west alignment (then hypothetically corresponding to that of the Sphinx) has been dated to 8000 BCE. This is shortly after the beginning of the pre-Long Count in 8240 BCE. "Stonehenge 1" (Fig. 34) was then erected around 3100 BCE as a circular enclosure as mentioned made from 56 wooden poles at the beginning of the Long Count (simultaneously with the first mastabas in Egypt). The huge sarsen stones and the so-called station stones,[42] however belong to "Stonehenge 3," and were then simultaneous not only with the Giza pyramids (Fig. 1), but also with the clearest eight-partitioning of the Dingir (see Fig. 8). These stones form a perfect octagon combined with a heptagon[44], and so not only does Stonehenge seem to be perfectly timed with the Great Pyramid, its message, the eight-partitioning of the human mind in an evolution in seven steps, seems to be identical with it. This message we have also seen is carried in the more recently built pyramid in Chichen-Itza.

Avebury shows a parallel timing with its first earthworks being from 3100 BCE and the stone circles from circa 2600 BCE. The last phase of construction at Stonehenge (1600 BCE) coincides essentially with when the last Egyptian pyramid (Ahmose's in 1540 BCE) was built. These dates indicate that the constructions of Stonehenge and Avebury reflect and parallel the same metaphysical reality that was manifested in the construction projects in Egypt and Sumer. Again we have evidence for the existence of a common global mind affecting different areas in synchrony.

Thus, it seems as if people living on the British Isles at this early time were already downloading the new compartmentalized mind. The erection of Stonehenge seems timewise to parallel that of the Egyptian pyramids and so also reflects the new mental hologram that then became available. The current wisdom of archeologists is,[45] similarly to what I suggested regarding the contemporary Egyptian pyramids, that the importance of Stonehenge and other similar megalithic sites was in the act of building them. This again would attest to the intention of connecting heaven to earth, which would have been a prerequisite for manifesting a new civilization.

The fact that unlike in the Near East we see no evidence at this time of a civilization in the British Isles is, however, notable. Maybe the British Isles, because of their northwestern location, were not yet ready for civilization to take hold. While the influence of the eight-partitioning may have been strong enough for people there to build megalithic monuments in its honor, the conditions may otherwise not have been strong enough for civilization, and the monarchy that this was organized around to truly take hold. If nothing else, the population of Britain is estimated to have been less than a twentieth of that of Egypt in 2600 B.C.E. Even by the time the Romans invaded Britain (Fig 16c), they saw no signs of city life anywhere.[46] Similar "insufficiently" powered civilizations may have erected megalithic monuments in other parts of the world as well without developing a centralized monarchy. Certainly, Scandinavia with its exquisite bronze work and the world's largest megalithic ship formation at Ales Stenar, would have had an insufficient population to develop a civilization at this time.

In the case of the British Isles a viable symbol of the eight-partitioning would, as we will see, emerge later, and this would then only partially be land-based.

Based on the previous it seems like the time line of the Mayan calendar, and the evolution of the Dingir (Fig. 8), should be consulted whenever the purpose and role of a megalithic monument is to be investigated. If the Egyptian pyramids and Stonehenge were built to reflect the same metaphysical reality, why then would this not be true for other megalithic sites as well? I suspect that thousands of sites and earthworks exist on our planet reflecting the primordial mound, the four directions and the eight-partitioned sun, but only in a few of these places did civilizations take hold. The reasons civilizations took hold in certain places, but not in others, are probably not simple. Factors involved are the natural environment, population size, the presence of raw materials and domesticable plants and animals, as well as the location of an area in relation to the earth's grid (Fig 14a).

Midpoint summary: In this chapter, I have suggested that in the Fifth Wave the human soul was incorporated in the humans, expressed among other things in the cave paintings. The cave art does not indicate that its creators had compartmentalized minds organized in accordance with horizontal or vertical lines. It also does not express the self-consciousness that would later be generated by the spherical boundaries of the mind. The human beings were caged in by this new mind in two steps. The first happened around the beginning of its pre-wave 10,250 years ago. This, as mentioned earlier, is very clearly noted in the Mayan inscriptions as the beginning of a new creation. At that point, several things happened that changed the human beings and attest to their downloading of an early form of a mind with inner boundaries. The cave paintings with their apparent lack of context and scenes then disappear.

The few archaeological sites from around the time of the beginning of the pre-Sixth Wave, such as Göbekli Tepe and probably the Sphinx, also attest to the downloading of a new mind. Megalithic monuments significantly older than the beginning of the pre-Long Count have never been found. This is consistent with the absence prior to this time of a mind necessary for such creativity. The beginning of the pre-Sixth Wave also coincides closely not only with the extinction of large numbers of mammals, but also with the beginning of agriculture. Both of these phenomena may be explained by the emergence of a compartmentalized mind with boundaries. That these changes took place at the same time is a compelling reason to believe they had the same cause.

This shift point marking the emergence of a mind with circular boundaries led to massive changes in human life, including the introduction of private property and the ensuing lowering of the status of women. The increased safety generated by the extinction of many species of animals and the increased food supply from agriculture also prepared the way for civilization that emerged with the Sixth Wave proper, activated in 3115 BCE. While the circular enclosure was downloaded in many different parts of the world at the beginning of the Long Count, such as in the British Isles, the conditions for the emergence of civilization were not yet ripe everywhere.

From this summary, we can see that the emergence of many different phenomena that otherwise would seem unrelated can be attributed to the emergence of one single factor—the mind. Because the mind obviously evolves, we may conclude that it is not hardwired into our brains. Rather, the mind is something we, for lack of a better word, "download" from the "metaphysical realm." Because of this ability to download the mind there existed a common ancient mind all over the planet. We will now look at how this may be possible.

CHAPTER 5:

THE CONNECTION OF THE GLOBAL MIND TO THE EARTH

CONSCIOUSNESS AND THE MIND

In the first three chapters, we saw some examples of the crucial role the evolution of the mind has had for the rise and development of human civilization. In the previous chapter, as a contrast we saw what people were like before they possessed an eight-partitioned mind with a spherical boundary. What was also outlined is how civilization was prepared for through a series of predetermined mental steps already affecting the early Paleolithic people. This presentation was only a general outline, and further arguments in favor of a geometric transformation of the mind could be developed based on the archaeological record and reliably dated megalithic sites.

Nonetheless, what we have seen so far is sufficient to draw the conclusion that the evolution of a mind independently of the brain is the chief factor behind the rise and evolution of civilization. As controversial as it may seem, this means that the mind cannot be a product of the brain. Such a conclusion implies a need to integrate spiritual aspects in our understanding of reality and shift away not only from the materialist, but also from the Darwinist paradigm. It also provides for a new way of understanding the humanities, especially history and psychology.

Crucial for such a paradigm shift is the idea, proposed in chapters one and two, that the human mind is in resonance with the global mind and evolves as a part of this. In the previous chapter we found further support for such a relationship, for instance, in the synchronized global onset of cave paintings and megalithic monuments, as well as of agriculture and the extinction of the great mammals in different parts of the planet. Yet, the reader may ask, are these synchronized global events only coincidences, or is there really such a thing as a global mind serving to synchronize them? The present chapter is devoted to answering this question and aims to demonstrate that the proposed theory about the rise of civilization literally stands on firm ground.

Before verifying the existence of such a global mind, which we all have a part in, I should briefly discuss consciousness and how we may distinguish this from the mind. In the way I use the term consciousness—as our subjective experience—it is more basic to our existence than the mind. Consciousness here means the spirit, or soul, at the center of our subjective experience, and so it is not the same thing as the mind. Yet, human consciousness may be modified by the mind, for instance, with the downloading of its spherical boundaries, which increases human self-consciousness. For this reason, whenever there is a shift in the state or organization of the mind there is also a shift in the state of consciousness, and so I have sometimes talked about "evolution of consciousness" interchangeably with the "evolution of the mind," even if, strictly speaking, consciousness does not evolve. A significant difference between the two concepts is that the mind, in contrast to consciousness, does not really belong to us, even if we often think it does. Therefore, the mind is something that can be approached objectively and, as we will see, be strictly defined. Consciousness, on the other hand, may be so basic to our existence that it does not fall back on anything else. For this reason, I think it serves little to enter an abstract philosophical discussion about how to define it correctly.

Nonetheless, I do think it is worth contemplating the etymology of the word consciousness. The English word consciousness is derived from Latin, and if picked apart as *con* = with, *sciere* = to know, and *ness* = the state, it seems to mean "the state of knowing with." While the English word does not really spell it out, we may note that the Swedish word *medvetande* or the German *Bewusstsein* for consciousness do indicate a possible answer to what or whom we may "know with." If, as I suggest, we connect Swedish *veta* (to know) to *ved*, wood, or German *wissen* to *Wald*, forest, we gain the Germanic meaning of consciousness as "the state of knowing with wood," or "the state of knowing with the Tree of Life." If we could invent an English word on the same basis, consciousness would be called something like *Bewoodedness* or *Withwoodedness*. This points to what may be at the heart of human consciousness, as we already know that the Tree of Life plays a key role for defining the mind of the human being. The point to realize is that consciousness does not exist in isolation. It emerges from knowing "with" something else, and this will be crucial for understanding the global mind.

THE PINEAL GLAND

Before we look at how the resonance of the human beings with the global mind is established, we need to get an idea of how the mind sphere, with its various metaphysical imprints, specifically interacts with the human brain and body. While the images in Figures 11 and 12 may convey the general idea of this relationship, they do not answer exactly why and how the mind interacts with or is anchored to the brain.

To understand the interface between mind and brain, we need to ask where in the human brain the central anchor point for a sphere in resonance with the global mind would be localized. The connecting point would then correspond to the center of the eight-partitioning on the level of the human being, meaning that it would also be the center of the abovementioned compartmentalization of the human brain. This in turn would give this center a very special role, to coordinate the activities in the different brain compartments created by the mind. In relation to this center, certain activities could also be blocked out by veils (see Fig. 26), depending on the particular wave of evolution that the brain is influenced by. Hence, we can think of this center as the focal point of human consciousness.

We have already started to zoom in on where this central point may be located by pointing out that the human mind partitions the brain in a left and right hemisphere. By itself, this partitioning defines one of the planes of the three-dimensional coordinate system of the human mind sphere (Fig. 36). Moreover, the polarization along the brain's midplane generates what we can think of as a bicameral mind, creating the well-known differences between the two brain halves.[1] However, to fully establish a mind sphere with three axes, it is also necessary to define its central point, its so-called origo, as well as the vertical axis that is part of this coordinate system. As it turns out, there is really just one organ in the brain that can play such a central defining role, and this is the so-called pineal gland. This small, 5 to 8 millimeter long gland in the brain has the shape of a pinecone[2] that is covered by yellow-gold granules. Because this has a tip it points out a direction in the plane that separates the hemispheres, and from this direction a three-dimensional coordinate system may unambiguously be defined.[3] The pineal appears in the development of a fetus at the same time as the differentiation into a specific gender begins, about seven weeks after conception, and also later in life it will play a role in sex differentiation. This seems consistent with the previous observation that the pineal is in a position between the right and the left hemispheres of the brain, traditionally associated with the two genders.

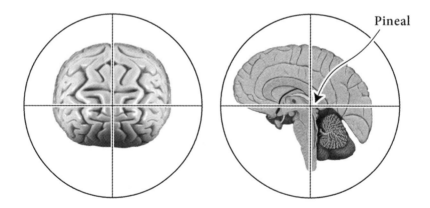

Figure 36. Images of the human brain from the front and in cross-section with the mind sphere and eight-partitioning surrounding the center of the mind at the pineal gland.

To put things simply, human beings experience and create reality from the perspective of what the pineal gland "sees." If they have not downloaded a three-dimensional mind sphere they will create beautiful, spiritually intense paintings of animals lacking a context or framework, like the cave painters did. This is because without an eight-partitioned mind sphere the pineal gland would "see" and experience the unity with these animals without any structuring axes. On the other hand, if humans have downloaded the three-dimensional sphere, as they did at the beginning of the Long Count, they will build pyramids and frame their paintings, as they would then "see" reality through a perpendicular framework. Therefore, at any given point in time the resonance with the global mind conditions what the pineal can see. What is required for such a resonance is that both the human mind and the global mind, has a clearly defined center around which its compartmentalization is organized, and on the human level the pineal plays this role.

THE SEAT OF THE SOUL

With such a central role of the pineal gland as an anchor point of the human mind, we should not be surprised if from ancient times there are a number of myths indicating that this gland plays a significant role for human spirituality. The pineal has, for instance, often been seen as the biological correspondent of the so-called Third Eye, located in the center of our foreheads. The name "Third Eye" may then be quite suitable, since the pinealocyte cells of the pineal gland in many non-mammalian vertebrates have a strong resemblance to the photoreceptor cells of the eye. Thus, the pineal is light sensitive even though it is an enigma how any light would reach this folded retina[4] in the center of a human brain.

The pineal is indeed a unique component of the brain in that it is unpaired. From the perspective of it being the anchor point for the eight-partitioned mind, what may be even more relevant is its location at the geometric center of the brain.[5] If the mind sphere of the Sixth Wave provides a framework for the human beings, it seems this must indeed be anchored in a central position of our brains. This means it is located in a plane separating the two hemispheres of the brain, pointing from there in a direction perpendicular to the *corpus callosum*, the nerve connecting the two hemispheres. In turn, the consequence of this is that the pineal defines a three-dimensional coordinate system with itself at the center (Fig 36).

In the conventional view, the superior mental abilities of the human beings compared to the animals are typically explained by our larger brain/body size. Interestingly, in species other than human, the pineal gland is not located in the center, but almost at the top of the head.[6] What I would like to suggest then is that an equally or even more important factor for our relatively advanced mental faculties is the location of the pineal. This is consistent with the view that the possession of a mind seems to be the prerogative of human beings, at least on our planet, and even if animals have spirits they do not have compartmentalized minds. What this also tells us is that the pineal gland is not a piece of biological matter that for some unknown reason has magical properties. Rather, *the crucial role of the pineal gland as an interface between mind and brain derives from the fact that it is located at the center of the spherical geometry of the mind and as such creates its interface with the brain.*

According to Indian yogis, when someone attains enlightenment after much spiritual practice he or she may see a great inner light with the pineal gland. Hence, there are spiritual practices designed to "open the Third Eye," and maybe we can now begin to understand how, because of its relationship to the mind, the Third Eye is related to human spirituality. The Vedic and Buddhist traditions see the Third Eye as a symbol of enlightenment and refer to it as "the eye of knowledge" sometimes marked by what is called a bindi on the forehead. Sometimes described as the gateway to higher consciousness, the Third Eye in the understanding presented here is the anchor point of the eight-partitioned mind in the human brain and spiritual enlightenment is a result of a decoupling of the mind from the pineal gland.

The idea that the pineal gland plays a role for human consciousness is thus not new. Already in 1636 the French philosopher Descartes suggested that the pineal gland was the point where the soul interfaced with the human body.[7]

Descartes argued that the pineal gland was the only unpaired component of the human brain, and for this reason it would have to be the seat of the soul. The idea of a connecting point between soul and body fitted well with the dualistic philosophy emerging in his time. Descartes, who we may regard as the foremost philosopher of the scientific revolution, formulated its ideal, called rational empiricism. Proposing that there were two separate planes of existence, spirit and matter, he thought it was in the pineal gland that these two met in the form of the soul and the body. While this was a very good hypothesis, providing a role for the pineal as an interface between the mind and the brain (Fig. 36), there was at the time precious little to support it, so the scientific community abandoned the idea. In recent decades an interest in the topic has, however, been rekindled because new evidence seems to support Descartes' view.

The huge pinecone in the Court of the Pine Cone of the Vatican[8] is interesting as a symbol of the pineal on a planetary scale as related to the global mind. The Vatican in Rome has remained the center of the Christian world religion even after the fall of its empire. What is notable about the location of this city is its placement right on the line dividing our planet into an Eastern and a Western hemisphere (Fig. 15). Hence, the Court of the Pine Cone (Fig. 37a) is also located in the plane that separates the two hemispheres of the planet and, as such, it parallels the location of the pineal in the human brain. Moreover, since 1990 this pinecone shares its place in the court with the sculpture *Sphere within Sphere*, pointing to its connection to the inner core of the Earth. This, as we will shortly see provides the brain of the Earth. Curiously, the nearby Saint Peter's Square is eight-partitioned (Fig. 37b) and these two squares are thus placed together in a very special location where they symbolize the interface between the pineal gland with the eight-partitioned mind on a global scale. To top it off, an obelisk (a Benben symbol)[8] has been placed at the center of the eight lines radiating from Saint Peter's Square, and this obelisk is almost contemporary (fifth dynasty, 2500 BCE) with the eight-partitioned Great Pyramid. The Vatican thus very clearly embodies a symbolism of connecting the global mind with the global brain essentially in accordance with the model proposed here.

Figure 37. (a) The Pigna, a 4 meter high pine cone in the Vatican, Rome. (b) Aerial view of the eight-partitioned Saint Peter's Square of the Vatican, Rome.

The understanding that the pineal gland and the Third Eye play important roles in human spirituality thus goes far back in time and, as already exemplified it is expressed in many religions. What is new in the present study is the proposal that the pineal gland plays its role because it anchors the human mind sphere, created by resonance with the global mind. This connection to the global mind allows us to fully understand how the sequence of altered states of consciousness, induced by shifts in the Tree of Life, has changed the human beings, and driven the evolution of civilization forward according to the principle of "As inside— So outside."

THE RESONANCE OF THE HUMAN BRAIN WITH THE EARTH'S ATMOSPHERIC-GEOPHYSICAL SYSTEM

In the previous chapters, we have seen several examples of how the evolution of human history conforms to the pattern created by the waves emanating from the Tree of Life and its eight-partitioning. We now also have a model for precisely how the fundamental perpendicular structure of the individual human mind may be anchored in the brain with the pineal at its center (Fig. 36). However, in order for the human mind to establish a resonance with the global mind, the latter also needs to be anchored in a corresponding center of the Earth, and here we will see how this works. We will, in other words, explore what it is the human being "knows with" in order to stay conscious.

In my book *The Mayan Calendar and the Transformation of Consciousness*, I presented a theory to account for the connection between the human and global minds, a connection at the heart of human consciousness. I will sum up this theory here with some crucial new aspects added. Owing to recent important discoveries in geophysics, there may now be a definitive solution to the problem of how the global mind is related to the Earth.

To understand this solution we need to start with subdividing the interiors of the Earth into different spherical shells: mantle, outer core, etc. These shells are separated from one another by boundary surfaces both in the interior of the Earth and in the atmosphere (see Fig. 38 or the list in Fig. 39). Examples of such boundaries are the Van Allen belts (which are not truly spherical), the surface of the Earth, and the boundary between its inner and outer core.

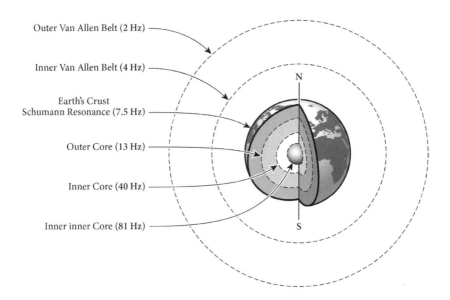

Outer Van Allen Belt (2 Hz)

Inner Van Allen Belt (4 Hz)

Earth's Crust
Schumann Resonance (7.5 Hz)

Outer Core (13 Hz)

Inner Core (40 Hz)

Inner inner Core (81 Hz)

N

S

Figure 38. The Earth's atmospheric-geophysical system with the frequencies associated with significant boundary surfaces between the various shells. Note that the Van Allen Belts are not spherical, and so their frequencies are based on their average extensions.[9]

If we then start by looking at the surface of the Earth, this is known to be enveloped by an electromagnetic standing wave called the Schumann resonance with a base frequency of 7.8 Hz.[9] Despite widespread rumors to the contrary, the frequency of this Schumann resonance is perfectly constant and does not increase over time. The reason the Schumann resonance does not change is that its particular frequency is defined by the speed of light (300,000 kilometers per second) and the circumference of the Earth (40,000 kilometers), which are both constant and so any electromagnetic wave at the surface of the Earth would have a frequency close to 300,000 / 40,000 = 7.5 Hz.[10]

Sphere	Radius from Earth's Center	Frequency
Outer Van Allen Belt	25,000 km	2 Hz
Inner Van Allen Belt	12,000 km	4 Hz
Earth's Crust, Mantle	6,371 km	7.5 Hz
Outer Core	3,500 km	13.5 Hz
Inner Core	1,200 km	40 Hz
Inner inner Core	600 km	81 Hz

Figure 39. Calculated frequencies of guided standing electromagnetic waves at surface boundaries at different distances from the Earth's center.[10]

From a geopsychological point of view, this particular frequency happens to be very interesting as it corresponds to the lower end of the frequencies of the so-called alpha waves of the brain (Fig. 40). These are produced in our brains when we are in a relaxed state. On the other hand, when we concentrate on something or are mentally active, the electrical discharges of our brains produce beta or gamma waves. However, if we close our eyes in such an alert state we activate alpha waves, the first step toward the sleep state where the brain instead exhibits delta and theta waves. The frequency ranges of the different types of brain waves and their corresponding mental states are shown in Figure 40. In practice, measurements of such electroencephalograms (EEGs), including all the different brain waves, are quite complex, as they will also differentiate between the different areas of the brain in which they occur.

Brain Wave Type	Frequency	Distribution in Brain	Mental State
Delta	0-4 Hz	Diffuse, Widespread	Deep sleep
Theta	4-7 Hz	Usually regional	Light sleep
Alpha	7-13 Hz	Regional	Relaxation
Beta	13-40 Hz	Localized	Concentration
Gamma	40- Hz	Very localized	Higher states

Figure 40. Brain wave frequency ranges associated with different mental states.[12]

The question now arises what is the origin of these different types of brain waves and their frequencies. The above observations about the frequencies of the spherical shells of the Earth become interesting when we realize that in the same way as the Schumann resonance is determined by the circumference of the Earth, the other frequencies are determined by the different boundary surfaces in the Earth's atmospheric-geological system as shown in Figures 38 and 39. If we compare the frequencies of these boundary surfaces with the ranges of different types of brain waves in Figure 40, such a comparison suggests that *the frequencies of the different mental states are associated with different circular shells in the Earth's system.* This is a finding with significant consequences for what makes the human beings human.

THE SHELLS OF THE EARTH AND THE NATURE OF MENTAL STATES

We may exemplify the above associations between shells and mental states with how our brains produce delta waves in deep sleep. The frequencies of these brain waves then indicate that in this particular mental state our brains are in resonance with the spherical shell between the two Van Allen belts (Fig. 39). Since in the outer atmosphere there is not much structure to be in resonance with, when our brains vibrate with these frequencies our minds would indeed be likely to be "gone." In this mental state (or actually the absence of such) we would not only lack a structure to connect to, but as a consequence also a subjective experience, which is what is missing in deep sleep. If we then go towards the other end of the scale, i.e. when our minds are engaged in alert concentrated thinking, our brains would be operating in the range of the beta frequencies 13 to 40 Hz. The outer core of the Earth corresponding to these frequencies is produced by liquid magma moving with convection streams generated by heat from the Earth's interior. However, it is increasingly being discovered that both the mantle and the outer core are not uniform in character and so have structures.[13] Thus, when our brains vibrate at the alpha or beta frequencies we are indeed conscious, as the mind then has a structure to relate to (in contrast to at the atmospheric frequencies).

What is most interesting, however, is that when our brains are operating at the lower end of the gamma frequency range, at 40 Hz, they are in resonance with the boundary surface of the inner core of the Earth. This inner core has for some time now been known to be a huge spherical iron crystal presumably containing nickel and other elements.[11] That this is a crystalline structure is consistent with the overall model for the relationship between the mental states and their corresponding brain waves presented here. As a result, when we engage in higher mental activities our brain cells typically oscillate in the gamma frequency range,[14] which means that they are in resonance with the most structured part of the Earth, its inner core. Put another way, at the 40 Hz frequency typical of crystal-clear cognitive functions or memorizing, our brains are in resonance with the boundary surface of the crystalline inner core of the Earth. The close packed hexagonal or cubic crystalline structure in this may then hypothetically provide support for compartmentalized thinking, computation, and even the storage of our memories.[15]

Overall, the progressively more definable localization of activities to specific brain parts with increasing frequencies (column three, Fig. 40) is also consistent with the increasingly orderly structure as we go towards the more central shells of the Earth.[16] Only if the brain is in resonance with a geological structure with clearly defined compartments, such as in a crystal, are its waves likely to be localized to specific brain compartments. It is thus not only that the frequency ranges of the different types of brain waves display a remarkable concordance with those of the geological shells. There is also a remarkable concordance between the nature of these brain waves and what we know about the geophysical structures of the corresponding shells.

This implies that depending on what mental states we are in, our brains are in resonance with different shells in the Earth's atmospheric-geophysical system. Over the twenty-four-hour sleep-wake cycle, known to be controlled physiologically by the pineal, we will then alternate between the different mental states and our brains will change their electromagnetic vibration frequencies correspondingly. The alternations between these states are, in fact, often subordinated to our conscious control. For instance, we can choose when we want to go to sleep and, as we do, the brain will change its frequency. Alternatively, by "concentrating" we can connect to the Earth's outer or inner cores. This indicates that we at least to some extent have a choice as to what states of consciousness we download.

A few new findings reported in the scientific literature have added substantially to this theory since *The Mayan Calendar and the Transformation of Consciousness* was published. The first of these is the discovery by scientists at the University of Illinois in 2008[17] that the Earth also has an inner-inner core, with a radius of merely 600 kilometers. The boundary surface of this corresponds to a standing wave of 81 Hz, which places it in the higher range of the gamma brain waves. Interestingly, there are indications that this frequency range is especially related to the inner subjective experience we call consciousness,[18] which I associated with the pineal gland. The conclusion to draw seems to be that when our minds go into high states of consciousness our brains attain a frequency corresponding to a sphere very close to the center of the Earth, in the inner-inner core. It then makes sense that in our individual brains the pineal, or the mind's eye, corresponds to the center of the Earth.

To my knowledge, this theory that brain waves are connected to different shells of the Earth is the only one proposed that explains why there are distinct brain wave ranges in the first place, and why these wave ranges are limited by the particular frequencies that they are. However, before we continue I need to emphasize I do not believe that the resonance of our brains with an inner shell of the Earth arises just because of an electromagnetic entrainment. If it would merely be a matter of entrainment, we would not have any choice regarding our mental states, and all human beings would presumably share the same state all the time, subordinated to electrical currents in the Earth. Since this is not the case, these standing waves corresponding to the different shells do not entrain our brains. Rather, they are always there as possibilities for us to connect to.

My view is then that *our choice to connect to a particular aspect of the global mind makes our brains oscillate at frequencies that correspond to the geophysical correlates of this aspect of the mind.* Hence, the theory does not assume that electromagnetic waves from the inner core create resonances in our brains. Instead, when we focus on, or chose a particular mental state our brains will start to resonate with the frequencies of the corresponding shell in the Earth's system. The theory, however, does assume the existence of wave-guides for the surface areas of such shells in the interior of the Earth. That such a wave-guide exists at the surface of the Earth for the Schumann resonance is known, but regarding the interior of the Earth we are in the dark.

In this model, thinking is therefore not something that happens in our brains in isolation, but is essentially a product of our soul's interactions with the Earth's system. We will go into more detail regarding this in chapter seven, but to discuss in depth whether this gives us a free will, would lead too far. Yet, it seems that we may choose when we go to sleep, which we do by decoupling our minds as we establish resonance with the outer spheres of the Earth. Yet, we cannot choose never to go to sleep, which as we know is dangerous; perhaps because we will then never decouple the mind from our souls. Thus, there is much to ponder here for the philosophically inclined.

THE HEMISPHERIC POLARITY OF THE EARTH'S INNER CORE

The second notable new scientific finding pertaining to the Earth-brain resonance is even more dramatic in its consequences. This is that the boundary surface between the outer and inner cores of the Earth shows evidence of physical polarities, or in scientific language, anisotropies, between its Eastern and Western hemispheres.[19] Hence, this boundary surface, the one we just discussed as having the same resonance frequency as the lower end of the gamma waves, does not have the same structure on the Western and the Eastern hemispheres. Based on seismic studies of the Earth's inner core, French researchers have explained this difference through a model (Fig. 41) according to which the Eastern Hemisphere of the inner core is molten, while the Western Hemisphere is crystalline. The different types of surface areas of the two hemispheres of the inner core then exist in a dynamic equilibrium. This anisotropy exists because the center of the inner core (C in Fig 41) is not located exactly at the center of the Earth in its entirety (O). This in turn means that a temperature difference, and hence a structural difference, is created between the surfaces of the two hemispheres.

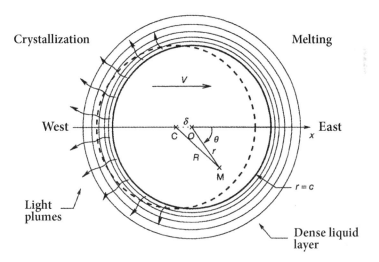

Figure 41. A model of the Earth's inner core showing how the polarity in the structure of the Eastern and Western hemispheres is created by a displacement (∂) of the center of the inner core (C) from the center of the Earth (O) in its entirety.[19]

This model fits remarkably well with the one I proposed earlier, which suggests that sharp analytical thinking anywhere on Earth is supported by the resonance of our brains with the crystalline inner core of the Earth. Traditionally people in the West have been considered as more analytical and compartmentalized in their thinking, which is consistent with the finding that the Western Hemisphere of the inner core is the more crystalline (and hence physically compartmentalized). The relative physical proximity of Westerners to the crystalline Western Hemisphere of the Earth's inner core has then reinforced such analytical thinking in them, while the holistic thinking of Easterners has been reinforced by the smoothness of the Eastern Hemisphere. Possibly adding to this effect is also the slight displacement of the Earth's inner core towards the west (Fig. 41). Regardless, this model strongly supports the model I proposed in my earlier books, namely that the Earth is a global brain with a Western and Eastern hemisphere.

In this model, the geophysicists have also ascertained the existence of a boundary line between the two hemispheres on the surface area of the inner core, a line that they find to be quite sharp. The difference in properties between the surfaces of the two hemispheres of the Earth's inner core is in fact quite profound and more sharply separated along a line than anyone would probably have expected. The hemispheres differ not only regarding temperature but also, as a consequence, regarding physical structure and chemical composition. The two hemispheres of the inner core in fact seem to differ much more consistently than the continental structure on the surface of the Earth and certainly more consistently than our two brain halves. It is difficult then to draw any other conclusion than that the separation in mental functions between the left and the right brain halves of human beings finds its origin in their resonance with the hemispheres of the inner core. Taken together, the model shown in Figures 11 through 13, implying that the human brain is indeed in resonance with the Earth, has thus now found very strong support.

The most remarkable finding in this context was reported in an article published by a research group at Cambridge University in 2011.[20] From seismic measurements, this group determined that at the surface area of the inner core the line separating the two hemispheres is located at 12 ± 2 degrees longitude East. This geophysical result should then be compared to my own hypothesis based on the course of human history (see, for example, Fig. 16) that the line separating the global hemispheres is the 12th longitude East. The longitude separating the Eastern and Western hemispheres of the inner core according to the Cambridge group, then turns out to be as close to an exact verification as is possible of the hypothesis I presented already in my book *Maya-hypotesen* (1994, in Swedish). I reiterated this hypothesis in books I published internationally, for example, "Judging from this study, the arms of this cross, as hypothesized, go through longitude 12° East and the equator".[21]

This concordance of results from different disciplines reinforces my consistent claim that the Earth is truly to be regarded as a global brain, with two different mentalities associated with its two hemispheres. When I first proposed the existence of a planetary midline separating the planetary hemispheres of the east and the west, it was controversial if such a line even existed. The fact that the new geophysical finding has precisely verified this a priori hypothesis deserves to be very seriously considered in any scientific evaluation of this overall theory. The wave pattern in Figure 16 was, in other words, not discerned after knowing of the geophysical fact, but much before this. At the very least we now know that such a midline does exist at the level of the inner core. The exact location of this midline presented in 2011 is fully consistent with the model of the mind, which is the topic of the present book.

Not only the mental sphere of the human being, but also the bicameral aspect of the eight-partitioned mind, has thus now been shown to have firm correspondences at the level of the inner core of the Earth in the form of its spherical shape and a straight line separating its hemispheres, respectively. We can then say with some certainty that what happened at the beginning of the Long Count was that these geometrical structures anchored in the interior of the Earth were activated. Only as this geometry was activated did people in resonance with the inner core start to build monuments that reflected it. Should we be surprised, then, that the Egyptians built the pyramids as reflections of the Benben, the primordial mound of the Earth—that is to say, the inner core of the Earth?

Yet, in terms of a potential paradigm shift the fact that this model has confirmed the reason the Egyptians gave for building the pyramids is only the tip of the iceberg. We should remember that the activation of the human mind takes place according to a preset time plan and is not something we can look upon as a mechanical effect. It is because of this time plan we know the mind has a metaphysical, or, if we like, divine, origin. As I have shown in previous and present books, the time plan for the evolution of the mind and its shifting polarities (Fig. 26) is provided by the Mayan calendar. However, what has been added here is evidence as to how this divine mind is anchored in the Earth. A far-reaching consequence of this is that the human mind depends on the resonance of our brains with the Earth. It then seems the conventional view of the mind as a property of our brains is at odds with reality.

CRYSTALLINE VS. SMOOTH THINKING

We now have an explanation not only for the pattern of movements in relation to the global brain in Figure 16, but also why there are broad differences between the religious and philosophical systems of the East and the West. We may also understand why so many ancient and aboriginal cultures honor the four directions in their ceremonies and often refer to them as individual deities. The reason is that the four directions are related to what we may call powerful metaphysical winds, originating in the inner core of the Earth that truly have an effect on the evolution of the global mind and the history of humanity. From this perspective it merely makes sense to honor them in ceremonies.

An example of the effects of this hemispherical separation is, for instance, that the religious thinking of the ancient Maya and Aztecs in the West was more "crystallized," or in other words more compartmentalized than in the East. Hence, it often involved beliefs in "team work" of different gods linked to a mathematical analysis of metaphysical time. By comparison, Buddhism or Daoism in the East are more integrative philosophical belief systems. The Abrahamic religions emerging closest to the midline are the most markedly dualistic as they express the polarity created at the planetary midline. As I mentioned earlier, Rome, and hence the Catholic Church has derived much of its power from its location on the midline between these two mentalities. The same can be said about the Protestant churches going back to Luther's reformation, which began in Wittenberg on the very same line. Through this model we have also found a direct and simple explanation for the long-standing difference between the East and the West and their respective collectivist and individualist political philosophies, which were so obvious, for instance, during the Cold War.

The point to realize is that we cannot explain the differences between East and West only by the existence of different traditions, which in the conventional view have emerged randomly. Religious, philosophical, and political differences between East and West instead find their origin in deeper thought patterns, directly related to the respective structures of the hemispheres of the Earth's inner core. Thus, Richard Nisbett's *The Geography of Thought* shows a number of examples of how psychological tests have given different results in the Far East and the United States, pointing to the existence of different underlying thought patterns to the respective traditions. For instance, when Chinese and American children were asked to answer whether "a" or "b" goes with "c" in Figure 42, they displayed a significant difference. (The reader may want to make his or her own assessment of what goes with what before continuing to read.)

The American children tended to connect the cow with the chicken rather than with the grass, which was the preference of the Chinese. Because of the more "crystalline" thinking of the American children, they connected the cow to the chicken based on the similarity of the two *objects*. In the "smooth" thinking of the Chinese, on the other hand, the children thought that the *relationship* between the cow and the grass was more important. Several other basic differences in thought patterns between East and West are evidenced through such tests. Generally, when asked to describe an image Westerners will crystallize out the objects in it and their attributes, while Easterners will be more inclined to describe the broader context and the relationships between the objects.

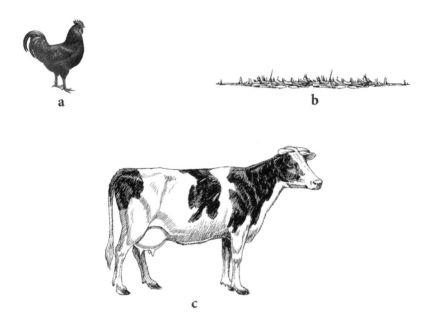

a   b

c

Figure 42. When asked to connect c with a or b, Westerners and Easterners give different answers.

It then seems natural to conclude that the differences in religious and political philosophies between East and West also find their origin in these primary thought patterns related to the two hemispheres of the Earth's inner core. Clearly, Islam, with its base in the East, emphasizes collective forms of religious worship, such as global prayers and pilgrimages. This is in contrast to Christianity, with its base in the West, which emphasizes the need for individually emulating the example of Jesus. Everything else aside, these are religious practices, which are associated with smooth and crystalline thinking, respectively.

THE CENTRAL LONGITUDES OF THE WESTERN AND THE EASTERN HEMISPHERES

Based on this polarity in mentality with very deep roots, it is not surprising that Washington, DC, the current center of Western power, is located at the central longitude (77 degrees West) of the Western Hemisphere, exactly at 90 degrees from Rome. This may be why this location was chosen over Philadelphia for the capital of the United States. It could also be why DC's street pattern is full of alignments with sacred geometry stimulated by this the most basic alignment with the Earth's inner core.[22] Forty-five degrees further west, along another longitude created by the eight-partitioning, are the cities of Vancouver, Seattle, and San Francisco, accounting for a somewhat different form of Western creativity.

On the opposite side of the world from Washington, DC, at 102 degrees East, we have the central longitude of the Eastern Hemisphere, going through today's Singapore and central China (Fig. 43a). While at the current time this line does not traverse a major power center, we may notice the rough distribution of today's "Tiger economies" around this line. Historically speaking, a few things also stand out about this line as a military, political, and religious power center. The centers of the mighty Khmer and Mongol Empires were, for instance, both located on this longitude. Hence, Angkor Wat, the capital of the Khmer Empire, abounding with eight-partitioning symbols and temples aligned with the four directions, is believed to have been the largest city in the world in the sixth DAY of the Sixth Wave.[23] Nonetheless, as the sixth NIGHT began Angkor would start to decline at the same time as Karakorum, located much further to the north in the Gobi desert, rose to become the capital of the Mongol Empire. Returning to the present day, we may notice that the practice of the religious philosophy of Buddhism (Fig. 43b) is roughly distributed around this central line of the Eastern Hemisphere. This could mean that Buddhism is the religion most typical of the smooth thinking of the Eastern Hemisphere.

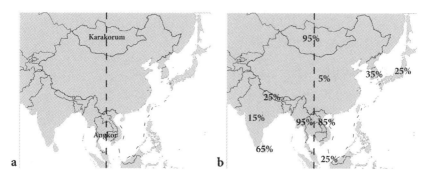

Figure 43. (a) The central longitude of the Eastern Hemisphere at 102 degrees east. (b) Buddhism in the modern world with approximate (± 5%) percentages of adherents in the population of different countries.[24]

Because the discovery of the polarity between the Eastern and Western hemispheres of the Earth's inner core was based on an a priori hypothesis, the conclusions we can draw from this must be regarded as very solid. This polarity provides a profound explanation as to why for so long our planet has appeared divided into an Eastern and Western civilization, each with its own mentality.

Also through this it seems clear the human mind is connected to the Earth's inner core. We have already seen that the general associations between our brain frequencies and the Earth's system point to such a connection, but the association of human history with the midline at 12 degrees East is so specific that it makes such a connection between the human mind and the global mind even more compelling. The human mind is simply not something that originates in our heads. Instead, it is a metaphysical or divine phenomenon that over the millennia has evolved through the resonance of our brains with the Earth's atmospheric-geological system according to a preset time plan.

Despite the apparent verification of my model to explain the East-West polarity, a complicating factor has also emerged from these new scientific articles, which deserves to be mentioned. This is that the longitude of the boundary line between the hemispheres seems to vary somewhat depending on at what depth in the inner core we determine it. Closest to its surface, corresponding to 40 Hz, as predicted it follows a line corresponding to Rome and Berlin along the 12th longitude East, but at deeper levels it seems to move further east up to the 20th longitude.[25]

Regardless, the planetary midline, around which the world to a large extent has been organized in the second half of the Long Count (Fig. 16), can now be seen to have a real foundation. This means that the statement made in the first chapter of this book—that there are no straight lines in nature—needs amending. There may indeed, and the evidence points in this direction, exist straight lines on the level of the Earth's inner core. Our interactions with these straight lines would then have a lot to do not only with the geometrical structure of the human mind, but also with the dawn of civilization 5,125 years ago. Through this connection the disciplines of psychology and history are now being unified within the same framework of understanding.

The 12th longitude East would then also be the chief line of the eight-partitioning of the Earth as described in the Mayan creation story in Palenque and shown in the cosmograms in Figure 3. It divides the world into two hemispheres, carrying the Oriental and Occidental civilizations, respectively. Moreover, as mentioned, we can track the movements in Figure 16 related to this line back to the Greco-Persian Wars when people first became aware of this civilizational polarity. Certainly, the Thirty Years' War, World Wars I and II, as well as the Cold War are also intimately related to this midline (Berlin is located very close to it). Several thousand years of fighting, sometimes religious, as well as differences between East and West in the ways of thinking, acting, and being have now been given a logical explanation.

The diversity of all cultures may, according to this, be partially explained by the eight-partitioning and the polarities this creates along the associated longitudes. The eight-partitioning, in other words, explains why there will always be diversity within the human race, despite the unity provided by the common framework of the global mind. In a time when many emphasize that we are all one, I feel there is also a need to emphasize this persistent diversity. Thus, we may ask, if we were not different individuals would life really be worth living? Fortunately for us, because of the partitioning of the global mind there will always remain diversity in the unity to keep us individually engaged in life.

The demonstration of our connection to the Earth completes the model for how the global mind has been partitioned as shown in a series of images (Figs. 11, 12, 14, 15, and 41). It is a curious fact to me that only two months after the thirteenth baktun of the Long Count came to an end on October 28, 2011, scientific information that conclusively verifies the Mayan calendar describes the evolution of the global mind, was published. This information thus seems to be a crucial component of the current paradigm shift and, in my opinion, the demonstration of the hemispheric polarity of the Earth's inner core is something that should be headline news all over the world.

Previously we saw how an individual human mind sphere could be anchored in a human brain at the pineal gland in an unambiguous way. Now we are also able to see that the global mind similarly is unambiguously anchored to the center of the Earth. As a result of these parallels the individual human minds are in resonance with the global mind in a very precise way. Consequently, this is not a vague and general holographic relationship of "As above—So below," but a resonance between two precisely defined spatial structures that plays out in history in clearly defined ways. This resonance is thus in effect the cornerstone for understanding the Mayan calendar, and the very reason that in ancient times this calendar was considered as prophetic. It is for this reason the Mayan calendar has been the basis of predictions that were later verified. For instance, at an early point I used it for predicting the shift now taking place towards Asia in the world's economy.

WHAT HAPPENS WHEN OUR RESONANCE WITH THE EARTH IS DISTURBED?

We have now seen how human beings develop their minds through resonance with the global mind and that, when these are in resonance with the surface of the inner core of the Earth, their brains display waves that oscillate with the frequency of 40 Hz. We should now probe this resonance between the individual human brain and the Earth's inner core somewhat more deeply. We know that the gamma 40 Hz coherence brain waves correspond to a number of mental faculties, such as attention, face and linguistic recognition, visual awareness, and task performance.[26] Francis Crick, the co-discoverer of DNA, called 40 Hz the neural correlate of consciousness. An obvious reason for this is that the gamma waves will disappear from EEG measurements in anesthetized, unconscious persons.[29] Some, who work with neurofeedback of brain waves, in fact call the 40 Hz brain frequency the Insight Wave.[27] The reason for this seems to be that it is within the sphere of the inner core that the "aha" moments are generated as new connections are made.

From our perspective what is also important are the implications that 40 Hz brain oscillations are related to cognitive functions and memory.[28] This is because it would explain why, as the ancients at the beginning of the Long Count began to download a spherical boundary in resonance with the Earth's inner core, their minds would gain proficiency in exactly these functions. Hence, it was only after this point in time that cognitive mental functions would be able to favor the development of civilization and we actually do not know to what extent people had a memory before this.

While it may appear as a sideline, it also adds to the evidence of the human connection to the global mind to study what happens with the 40 Hz gamma frequency in individuals with different mental disorders or psychiatric conditions. Over the decades since the introduction of EEG measurements, a multitude of studies have been performed focusing on anomalies in brain wave patterns. It has, for instance, been shown that compared to controls, children with learning disabilities have a deficit in 40 Hz gamma waves.[30] A deficiency in these gamma waves was also found in dyslexic children with reading and writing difficulties.[31] This finding is especially interesting in this context as it is consistent with the view that writing (and obviously then also reading) is a crucial aspect of civilization, and that writing only emerged as a resonance was established with the spherical 40 Hz boundary of the inner core. This in turn would mean that the emergence of writing in human culture is a product of the evolution of the global mind, something that we will verify in the next chapter. We would then also expect that the ability to read and write would suffer in an individual whose resonance with the inner core of the Earth for some reason is less than optimal. Judging from the aforementioned gamma wave measurements, this is indeed also what we find in dyslexics.

The finding that children with memory impairment display a deficit in 40 Hz gamma waves, however, takes our reasoning one step further. The reason being, it implies that the Earth's inner core in some sense plays a role for storing our memories, or at least plays an important role for memorizing. We would then expect people with impaired resonance with the inner core to also exhibit memory failures. Not surprisingly then, we actually find abnormalities in gamma waves in a whole range of adverse mental conditions, such as Alzheimer's disease,[32] autism,[33] and schizophrenia,[34] where the patients are known to suffer from memory loss. Even if memory failure is caused by some abnormality on the level of the individual brain—such as clearly seems to be the case in Alzheimer's disease—we no longer always need to conclude such an origin.

The point is then that most, if not all, mental disorders, even if they manifest in widely different ways, have a significant thing in common. This is that they display altered levels and, most commonly, a deficit of 40 Hz waves.[35] As we have now seen here, this seems to mean that the resonance of the individual brain with the inner core of the Earth, or at least with its surface area, is somehow disturbed or was not appropriately established to begin with. Disturbed resonance with this inner core may even be the fundamental origin of all mental disorders, including those with memory failure.

Sometimes a disturbed resonance may be caused by damage to the brain, such as, for instance, in stroke patients who have lost their ability to speak. However, the maybe shocking conclusion from the new perspective is that a mental disorder does not have to have its origin on the level of the brain. A disturbed resonance may instead imply that an afflicted individual has not established an optimal resonance with the inner core and so the global mind may be affecting his or her mental sphere differently. He or she may also be downloading something out of the ordinary and so become different from everybody else like for instance in schizophrenia.

THE BRAIN AS A RECEIVER FOR THE GLOBAL MIND

Making the analogy of the brain to a radio receiver, if there is a tortured sound coming out of it, it may be that its battery is failing or a component in it no longer functions. But it may also be that the antenna is not properly tuned in to the particular broadcasting station, or that the sounds that this is broadcasting are distorted to begin with. Maybe we cannot find the right frequency. An impaired reception thus does not necessarily mean that there is something wrong with the radio, or, to end the analogy, a mental anomaly does not have to mean that there is something wrong with the brain, which many pharmaceutical treatments take for granted. The way we have been thinking about mental disorders as always originating in the heads of people is thus most likely misleading. The new theoretical basis presented here thus deserves to be explored regarding how to treat a whole range of mental conditions.

It seems in fact that neurologists have not made it adequately clear that the premise that they have based their work on—that the frequencies of the brain waves find their origin in the brain—is an unproven assumption. Some have, for instance, suggested—based on this assumption—that 40 Hz would be the frequency of the brain's "operating system."[36] That such a parallel with a computer's operating system is at fault becomes immediately apparent when you consider that the clock rate, or operating frequency (for instance, 1.5 GigaHz), of a central processing unit of a computer does not just end up having its value by accident. Instead, an oscillator crystal determines the frequency of the operating system of a computer. No corresponding crystal fundamental to the theory about brain waves has, however, been discovered within the human brain. What this chapter has shown is that the oscillator crystal of the human brain exists outside of the brain, and that for the special case of gamma waves the Earth's inner core provides this crystal.

Much of the literature in the disciplines of neurology and psychiatry may therefore be hard to follow for someone who has gained the insight that the mind is a resonance phenomenon with the Earth, since the whole science of neurology is based on the premise that the mind is a product of the brain. The conventional belief today is that the sources of brain wave frequencies are localized inside of our heads, which when considering the evidence presented here seems to be a flawed premise. If instead we see the brain as an interface with the mind, then the interpretation of EEG measurements takes on a completely different meaning, which also may bring us forward in understanding how the brain actually works.

To give the full picture of the connection between the mind and the gamma waves it should be pointed out here that higher animals also display gamma brain frequencies, so the fact that the human brain displays these frequencies does not automatically prove that they are mental processes. Yet, if it is only in humans that the pineal is located in the center of the brain, then this might explain why animals may also resonate with the inner core and yet not have a compartmentalized mind with cognitive functions and an equally powerful memory as ourselves.

To summarize, then: Several lines of evidence now show that our individual minds gain their capabilities through resonance with the global mind. First, there are a number of global synchronicities, which become apparent especially when we study human history within the framework of the Mayan calendar. Included among those are the emergence of diversified stone tools (50,000 YA [years ago]), cave paintings (40,000 YA), agriculture and the extinctions of large mammals (10,000 YA). These phenomena occurred concurrently and independently on different continents, and so they all point to a common origin of these phenomena in the global mind. When it comes to more recent history there is a high number of examples of other synchronized activities, such as pyramid building in different parts of the world. Second, there is a correspondence between brain wave frequencies and the corresponding frequencies of the shells of the Earth's atmospheric-geological system. This implies that brain activities are connected to the Earth. Third, there is a connection between the internal structures of the shells in this system and the various mental states, which in turn suggests that the natures of our mental states are related to the earthly structures that our individual minds are in resonance with. Fourth, there is a connection between the brain wave frequencies and the increasing localization in the brains of these waves, indicating that at higher frequencies the brain is in resonance with a more compartmentalized structure in the Earth's system. Fifth, there is a connection between human history in relation to the 12th longitude East (and to some extent other longitudes) and the plane of separation between the melting and the crystalline hemispheres of the inner core. This again implies the people that created this history did so based on their resonance with the inner core. Sixth, mental disorders with cognitive or memory impairment are associated with abnormal levels of gamma waves, suggesting that the optimal mental functioning of an individual, at least from a social standpoint, requires a fully functioning resonance with the inner core of the Earth.

There is then already much support for the notion that civilizations were created by the global mind, which is intimately connected to the notion that the human mind does not originate in the brain. Still, rather than just pointing out the strong points of this argument, we should also ask what would be the alternative answers to a number of questions: "Why are historical phenomena globally synchronized?" "Why are the brain wave ranges of different mental states so strongly correlated with the spherical shells of the Earth's atmospheric-geophysical system?", "What is the explanation to the consistent historical separation into an Occidental and an Oriental civilization?" and "Why did Europe become a chief exporter of civilization?" It seems the theory proposed here provides answers to all four of these questions and if there are alternative answers they are yet to be provided. It is in fact doubtful if there currently exists any alternative theory at all to explain what the mind is and where it comes from. The new understanding of the mind thus opens up a host of new phenomena for study in a novel framework that unifies several disciplines. This pertains especially to the phenomena associated with the sudden rise of civilization about 5,000 years ago. In the next chapter we will therefore examine a few of the abilities conferred on human beings through their downloading of this global mind.

CHAPTER 6:

SOME CONSEQUENCES OF THE GEOMETRY OF THE MIND SPHERE

THE NATURE AND DEFINITION OF THE HUMAN MIND

The first four chapters of this book demonstrated that the rise of civilization is synchronized with the evolution of the human mind. From chapter five, we may now understand why the different human cultures and civilizations have so many similarities, their mythologies included. The reason is that they all have part in the same global mind and share their resonances with the Earth. We then also saw that the human mind finds its origin in a spherical geometric structure endowed to the humans through their resonance with the Earth's inner core. This geometry explains some of the phenomena we associate with the rise of civilization, such as major constructions and monarchy (discussed in chapter one) and mathematics (chapter two), as well as other aspects of technology such as the wheel (chapter four). In order to close the case as to how civilization rose on our planet, we need in the present chapter to look at how this geometry is at the origin of some other phenomena typical of civilization.

On the individual human level, a significant part of the geometry of the mind is a coordinate system defining three dimensions of space with the pineal at its center (Figs. 12, 26, and 36). This is the geometry that gives rise to the dimensionality of the mind, but as we know from the previous, this dimensionality is not static and is subject to the shift points marked by the Mayan calendar. The mind has, for instance, made evolutionary leaps at shifts between NIGHTS and DAYS or when going from one wave to another. As we will see in the present chapter, the geometric nature of the mind fully explains why we experience space and time the way we do and how this experience has evolved with the development of the waves, with wide-ranging consequences for human life. We will especially explore how the evolution of the dimensions of space and time of the mind gave rise to some capabilities we associate with the rise of civilization, such as writing and methods for measuring.

Since the mind, in contrast to consciousness, is largely something separate from ourselves, we can to some extent be objective about it. Yet, to discuss such a matter as the mind, a word that has all kinds of connotations in our everyday lives—"I don't mind," "mind the step," "What did you have in mind?" "In my mind," mindfulness, mindlessness, "the mind is powerful," "I can't get him out of my mind," etc.—presents a certain kind of challenge. Because of the variation in how the concept of the mind is used colloquially it may be difficult to use objectively.

To some extent, we also use terms such as soul, consciousness, psyche, personality, self, and ego interchangeably with mind. For this reason, in order to facilitate a precise discussion, the mind is here given a geometric definition: the mind is the partitioned metaphysical sphere that can be downloaded from the Sixth Wave. With this definition, it is the sphere shown in Figure 36 that is the human mind and creates its properties. In principle at least, it should from this then be possible to verify the existence of all of the properties of the mind from historical changes taking place in the seven DAYS and six NIGHTS of the Sixth Wave. This definition of the mind may not always coincide with how we use the word in our daily language. Nonetheless, this geometric definition has the advantage of being precise and to allow for a meaningful discussion about the emergence of the mind.

This definition highlights the roles of the dimensions of space and time for how the mind creates our experience of reality. While it may seem like a very simple or even simplistic definition of the mind, we will find that it is all we need to explain the role the mind has played in creating human civilization and its continued evolution. The spherical boundary and finite radius of the mind sphere, as we will also see, creates a basis for comparisons, which in turn is the basis of all analytical thinking. Consequently, all of science and all development of technology relying on such thinking are largely products of this mind.

Before looking into some of the more specific capabilities of the human mind, it may be in its place to recognize the aspects of human nature that are *not* mental. These are then all the aspects of our beings that are created by the five lowest waves of the Mayan calendar system (see Fig. 23 and appendix II) and include our emotions, sexuality, experiences of the senses, and physical bodies. These aspects cover essentially everything that we call natural in ourselves. Especially today, such experiences are rarely purely natural as the modern person's mind and its veils tend to modify them. While, for instance, sexual desires may not have their origin in the mind, their expressions can be influenced by the particular polarity of this and therefore take a special form. Spirituality, finally, is another thing not created by the mind and is actually, as we will see in Volume 2, more like an original aspect of nature. Broadly speaking, spiritual experiences are thus weaker the more dominant the mind is. We can also see religions, and especially religions based on Holy Scriptures, as the outcomes of spiritual experiences transformed and compartmentalized by the mind.

The properties of the mind define our ways of perceiving, understanding, and creating reality at any given time, meaning that whenever there is a mental shift history changes its course according to "As inside—So outside." However, the way human beings create their history under the influence of the evolving mind should not be looked upon in a mechanical way, and its expressions are not without certain irregularities. Yet, in the big scheme of things, the quantum shifts of the mind at specific points in time defined by the Mayan calendar are ultimately what are behind all evolution of history. At such shifts in the geometry of the mind, human beings will alter the focus of their creativity and over time change their external physical reality accordingly.

In this chapter we will then look at some additional examples of how the geometry of the eight-partitioned mind of the Sixth Wave created the civilization we now live in. The role of the geometry of the mind for the development of monarchy, division of labor, mathematics, and construction has already been pointed out, but many other phenomena are also of interest. Crucial among such phenomena related to the rise of civilization are writing and measurements. However, to study those capabilities we first need to verify that the mind of the Sixth Wave endowed people with the dimensions of time and space. As we will come to see, the development of civilization depends entirely on the invisible boundaries of the geometry of the mind.

HISTORY OF PAINTED ART: MOTIFS AND REALISM

In previous chapters, we could see that unless we are unconscious, our individual brains are always in resonance with the Earth's geophysical system and that the individual human mind is related to the global mind in a very precise way. Can we then study the geometry of the human mind directly in order to see if it has an invisible coordinate system that has evolved in accordance with the Mayan calendar? One conceivable way of directly studying the evolution of the three dimensions of space in the minds of people would be to follow the development of geometry during the past 5,125 years. Figure 17 shows that this indeed seems to be possible. In this table we can see significant steps in this evolution were taken by the early civilizations of DAY 1, another with the Greeks at the midpoint of the fourth DAY, and yet another with the analytical geometry in the seventh DAY. These leaps within the science of geometry are all reflections, according to the principle of "As inside—So outside," of the mental evolution of the three dimensions of space.

For the sake of variation, I have chosen to focus on how the three dimensions of space are expressed in painted art throughout the same evolutionary wave. The focus on art has the advantage that it allows us to continue the research line we started with the cave paintings. Art highlights how humans, in this case under the influence of the evolving three dimensions of space, experience reality in the different eras dominated by different states of the mind. Consequently, art will be looked at here, not only as a reflection of how reality is seen through the mind of the artist, but also as an externalized projection of the three dimensions of space.

Our analysis of the evolution of art (here only painted art in two dimensions) will be quite brief. As with so many other topics in this book, the study of art would require a book of its own for all the enriching and complicating factors of its evolution, geographical and otherwise, to be adequately covered. The new way of looking at history expressed in this book is so profoundly different from the conventional that it affects our understanding of all aspects of reality, but regrettably it is not possible to cover them all in detail. Therefore, I will limit the study of art to a few examples from the Mediterranean/European region that are reasonably comparable with each other.

If for studying mental evolution we begin by looking at the examples of art in Figure 45 from some later periods of the Sixth Wave, we may notice how much they collectively differ from the cave art of the Fifth Wave (Figs. 29–30). The difference between The Sorcerer at Trois Frères (Fig. 30) and a painting by Rubens (Fig. 45e) may, for instance, seem so striking that it hardly seems worth mentioning. Apart from the technical prowess of the respective artists, there are differences in the techniques and materials used, such as cave wall vs. canvas or ochre vs. a palette of oil colors. It cannot be denied that such material factors play a large part for explaining the differences between these two pieces of art. Yet, the point here is to recognize that the artists have created the two paintings in different states of consciousness. The Sorcerer was created in the spirit world of the Fifth Wave without a mental cage, while Rubens' painting reflects how reality was perceived through the three dimensions of space provided by the mind sphere of the Sixth Wave, and in particular of its seventh DAY.

Figure 44. Weighing of the heart scene with the fourteen gods of Egypt at the top.

One result of this difference between the Fifth and Sixth Waves is the choice of motif. Rubens' is obviously more reflective of the male dominance typical of the duality of the Sixth Wave (Fig. 26), whereas The Sorcerer reflects the preceding unity with nature and spirit. However, more interesting than motif, in light of our focus on boundaries and three-dimensionality, is the composition; all examples of paintings from the Sixth Wave are composed as *scenes* where the people form part of a common context. Such a context is obvious in the paintings in Figures 44–45 for the reason that the mind of the Sixth Wave has boundaries and a center around which the context and scenes are organized. The cave paintings of the Fifth Wave, in contrast, never have boundaries, borders, or frames, and with some exceptions do not portray scenes.

It is, however, not necessary to go back to the Upper Paleolithic to see the dramatic influence that the boundaries of the eight-partitioning have had on art. In *Genesis of the Pharaohs* Toby Wilkinson investigated cliff paintings from the Eastern desert of Egypt that are only 6,000 years old. Only a thousand years before the beginning of the Long Count the figures portrayed in these could easily be taken for people from another planet. Moreover, similar to in the much older Paleolithic cave paintings, no sun wheels or eight-partitioning stars are known in the pre-dynastic Egyptian rock art.[1] Then, suddenly with the first dynasty beginning around 3100 BCE, straight lines appear in the art. In terms of realism, the earlier cliff paintings do not come near what would later be

Beginnings of days   **Beginnings of nights**

Figure 45. Examples of painted European art from the Long Count.
(a) DAY 5, upper left. (b) NIGHT 5, upper right. (c) DAY 6, lower left. (d) NIGHT 6,
lower center. (e) DAY 7, lower right. The individual pieces of art are identified in
the illustrations list.

created in the New Kingdom with straight borders and much detail in the art (Fig. 44). Wilkinson's study actually provides for a direct comparison between "before" and "after" the eight-partitioning that allows us to see the immense effect it had on the art. This is because the religious motifs of the Egyptians often stayed the same into dynastic times even if the techniques used in creating the art and its realism underwent a quantum leap. The motif of souls being dragged to the afterlife in boats is, for instance, still kept, although it suddenly (a thousand years is a short time here) became more accurately portrayed when the Sixth Wave began.

HISTORY OF PAINTED ART: THE THREE DIMENSIONS OF SPACE

In the early phase of the Sixth Wave the Egyptian and Sumerian art may already be distinguished from that of the Neolithic, simply based on the presence of frames. Even if it did not have physical frames, most art from this early civilized era has sharp borders that, as we can see in Figure 44, provided perpendicular boundaries. These borders for the Egyptian art presaged the solid frames for paintings, the oldest of which are from the 2nd century CE (fifth DAY).[2] By the time Rubens made his paintings in the beginning of the seventh DAY, the making of wooden frames had in Europe even become an art in its own right. Therefore, the history of the framing of art by itself provides a strong argument that the art (Figs. 44–45) is a product of a mind created by boundaries and perpendicular lines. We may then argue the development of frames in painted art exactly follows the pattern you would expect from Figure 24, and the framing of the art may have as much to tell us about the mind that created it as the art itself.

From the few examples in Figures 44–45 it is clear that in contrast to many of the cave paintings (such as in Fig. 29), the art in the Sixth Wave is organized in relation to the horizontal and vertical lines. This is already evident in the painted Egyptian art from the beginning of the Sixth Wave. Yet, in this early phase the third dimension of depth seems to have been completely missing (Fig. 44). All that Egyptian artists then were able to do in order to convey a dimension of depth was to paint something partially in front of something else. What I think this tells us is that early in the Sixth Wave, in Egypt and elsewhere, the inner three dimensions of space (Fig. 36) had not yet gained their full power in the humans. This is not to imply they experienced the world completely as two dimensional, but their paintings do indicate that their inner spatial organization of the world was not yet fully developed. Hence, during the first half of the Sixth Wave, artists created reliefs without a true perspective of depth (see also Fig. 6).

At later points in the Sixth Wave (Fig. 45), the depth perspective, or third dimension of space, became increasingly evident in the art. From about the midpoint of the Sixth Wave persons are, for instance, no longer always painted in profile, but also as facial portraits, which attests to an increased ability to reproduce the dimension of depth. There is an interesting parallel to this in that before the beginning of the second half of the Sixth Wave it was not possible to see the direct effects of the planetary midline (Fig. 16). Possibly then the experience of three, rather than just two, dimensions of space is directly related to the existence and activation of this midline on the global scale and the resulting separation of the left and right halves of the human brain.

What we may also see from the examples in Figure 45 is that the depth perspective became most apparent in the time periods that are DAYS (a, c, and e) and by the beginning of the seventh DAY (e) this had become fully developed. There is a general agreement that the early Baroque art from this time, especially from the Netherlands, is among the most photographic art ever created, and Rubens' painting is certainly no exception in this regard. The painting in Figure 45e typically has a very well developed three dimensionality, in this regard surpassing what had been created in previous eras.

If we instead look at the examples of paintings from NIGHTS (b and d), when the global mind is deactivated, these seem markedly more flat and much closer to a mere two-dimensional perspective. From the era of the fifth NIGHT it is in fact very difficult to find art from Europe that has any depth perspective at all. The Aztec god of darkness (Fig. 28) ruled the fifth NIGHT, corresponding in Europe to the aptly called Dark Ages, which in many respects was a low point, not the least when it came to its art. If, however, we move to the painting from the sixth NIGHT taken from a French Bible, we may note that this displays many steps forward regarding the reproduction of details and the use of colors compared to the earlier art. Nonetheless, and this is the main point here, this picture also lacks the depth perspective of the art made in the DAYS, and the persons in it seem to exist in a flatland out of reach.

Based on the above examples of how art alternates between DAYS and NIGHTS, we can see that the depth perspective of painted art exhibits a wave movement. The three dimensions of space are more strongly expressed in the periods of the Sixth Wave that are DAYS and less so in the periods that are NIGHTS. This is then exactly what you would expect if the three dimensions of space were inherent properties of the global mind, generated by the eight-partitioned sphere and developed by the process of seven DAYS and six NIGHTS of the Sixth Wave. The reason that the appearance of art, and especially its depth perspective, undergoes such a wave movement should be clear from Figures 14a and b, which show how the polarity fields of the Earth alternate between DAYS and NIGHTS, respectively. Hence, a global mind with three dimensions of space is activated in the DAYS and deactivated during the NIGHTS.

The fact that we now know the polarizing midline in Figure 14 to be real only adds further to our understanding of the introduction of the depth perspective. Therefore, the particular field of the global mind that an artist is in resonance with will determine to what extent he or she will fully recreate the three dimensions of space in different eras. What this tells us is that the organization of our perception of the world through three dimensions of space is not something to take for granted. It is something that has been generated for us by the wave movement of the Sixth Wave. Certainly, this also demonstrates that the mind modifies what we experience through our senses, a fact that incidentally any student of witness psychology can attest to.

HISTORY OF CALENDARS AND CHRONOLOGIES: THE LINEAR DIMENSION OF TIME

In addition to the three dimensions of space, the mind sphere also provides the human beings with a linear dimension of time, which we will look at in the present section. The question we will then ask is to what extent an experience of long-term linear time, and the sense of time having a "direction," develops in the humans through their resonance with the global mind of the Sixth Wave. The next volume will discuss in detail how the mind interacts with the bodily rhythms to create our experience of time. This will then be in the context of altered states of consciousness created by altering these rhythms.

Here we will track how the experience of linear time generated by the mind has evolved over the course of history. For this, we will again need some external correlate to follow. The most direct way of studying how linear time has evolved is to make an overview of the history of timekeeping as this is reflected in calendars and chronologies (Fig. 46). Throughout the course of the Sixth Wave, the latter have reflected how people experienced time. As far as we know, there were no calendars in use before the activation of this wave in 3115 BCE, even though some megalithic structures in the pre-Long Count might have prepared for them.

What I propose is that with the downloading of the eight-partitioned mind, with its three linear dimensions of space, the experience of linear time also emerged. Thus, in the beginning of the Long Count calendars were invented independently at approximately the same time in Egypt and Sumer.[3] As we may see from Figure 46, ever since the experience of a dimension of linear time, it has continued to evolve as part of the individual mind spheres. Because of this dimension of time the mind of the Sixth Wave has increasingly created an experience of time as having a direction and as moving from the past into the future. Since this experience presumably was much weaker prior to the Sixth Wave, humans in general then saw no reason to use calendars. (We saw, however, in chapter four that an early experience of linear time in the pre-Long Count contributed to the emergence of agriculture.)

Step in Wave	Calendars and Chronologies
DAY 1 3115-2721 BCE	Yearly Sothis calendar based on the rise of Sirius (Egypt, 3000), Calendar of 12 x 30 days (Sumer, 3100)
NIGHT 1	
DAY 2 2326-1932 BCE	
NIGHT 2	
DAY 3 1538-1144 BCE	
NIGHT 3	
DAY 4 749-355 BCE	Count of Olympiads (776), Era of Nabonassar (747), Roman Consuls, Babylonian calendar in Persian Empire (539)
NIGHT 4	
DAY 5 40-434 CE	Mayan Long Count (32 BCE), Julian calendar (45 BCE)
NIGHT 5	
DAY 6 829-1223 CE	Chronology based on the birth of Christ (ca 800 CE)
NIGHT 6	
DAY 7 1617-2011 CE	Gregorian calendar (1582)

Figure 46. The evolution of calendars throughout the Long Count.

To understand the evolution of the linear dimension of time from Figure 46 we first need to make a distinction between short-term calendars of a year or less, and long-term calendars, or chronologies that may span millennia. Short-term calendars usually serve to divide the solar year into shorter time periods such as months or weeks and are useful for agriculture and the observation of yearly religious holidays. Since the duration of the year of 365.2422 days is not evenly divisible with the duration of the full moon cycle of 29.53 days, there is no obvious way of combining the two in a joint calendar. Different cultures of our planet have thus used many different combinations of astronomical time cycles to form calendars. Most of these are not included in Figure 46 since they represent a variation on a theme rather than evolution. Regardless, the emergence of such short-term calendars at the beginning of the Sixth Wave shows that an early experience of linear time was emerging then.

Chronologies are instead used for following the long-term passage of linear time and for distinguishing between different years in history. The chronology most of the world uses today is the Gregorian calendar, where years until recently were given as *Anno Domini* (AD) based on the accepted year of the birth of Jesus. The Muslim chronology starting in the year 622 CE, when Mohammed fled from Mecca to Medina, is also used by a large number of people.

At the time of the beginning of the Sixth Wave, no chronologies were in existence and early civilizations identified different years by counting from the year when a new ruler ascended to the throne. Expressions such as "The tenth year in the reign of King Kalibum" then provided a rudimentary chronology, at least if it could be related to a reliable list of kings. However, since each city or country counted years based on its own kings, it is in general difficult to accurately date events from the first half of the Sixth Wave. Many cities and nations with different king lists would rise and fall over the centuries, and to make things worse, many of the listed kings seem to have been mythological.

Incidentally, the mythological kings mentioned in Sumerian and Egyptian lists, living before what we know to be the beginning of the Long Count were said to have become tens of thousands of years old. Similarly, the Biblical patriarchs before the Flood were assigned ages of more than nine hundred years. This provides a further indication that before 3100 BCE a mind with a linear dimension of time could not be downloaded. It seems that before the existence of such a dimension, or even numerals to count with, no one would have been able to keep track of the years. Presumably, from the perspective of those who several hundred years later had written down the ages of such kings and patriarchs, they appeared as larger than life. These early god-like individuals who were never subjected to the limiting constraints in space and time of the mind would later be seen either as giants or men of very high age.

It was then not until the fourth DAY, and the midpoint of the Sixth Wave, that true chronologies started to appear. As always, the exact midpoint of the Sixth Wave in its entirety, 551 BCE, meant a very significant shift in the human mind, profoundly affecting the linear dimension of time. Shortly after this midpoint, the Roman republic that was instituted in 509 BCE[4] established a chronology based on the names of its various ruling consuls. This was a chronology that could be used for identifying years in the long-term passage of time, going as far back as the founding of Rome in 753 BCE.[5] Similar systems of unambiguously identifying years began to be used in Greece by counting Olympiads from 776 BCE.[6] From Mesopotamia, the Era of Nabonassar taking its beginning in 747 BCE[7] can be similarly used. Based on these chronologies it is generally considered that from 680 BCE and onwards, significant historical events can be dated with accuracy.

Following these significant changes taking place in the fourth DAY, the Julian calendar and the Mayan Long Count were introduced shortly before the beginning of the fifth DAY (Fig. 46). The Julian calendar then introduced the leap day correction throughout the Roman Empire, making its calendar more astronomically exact than previously. An even bigger step was taken in the left hemisphere of the global mind (that is to say the West) as the Mayan Long Count came into use (the oldest inscription of this is from 36 BCE).[8] This Long Count was a metaphysical calendar and was in fact the first chronology of our planet that was based on the notion that time was running by itself, tun by tun, from its beginning. With this change, timekeeping became independent of who happened to be the ruler at a particular time. From this global perspective on the evolution of chronologies, we may understand how important a breakthrough this actually was.

a   b

Figure 47. Parts of Mayan inscriptions of the end of thirteen baktuns of the pre-Long Count (left, from Stela C in Quirigua) and the thirteen first baktuns of the Long Count (right, from Tortuguero Monument 6).

The synchronicities between the times of emergence of different calendars and chronologies alone tell us that we are all part of one evolving global mind. We can again note how steps taken in different parts of the world are part of the same evolutionary process of the mind. For example, seen in such a larger perspective the Mesopotamian, Greek, and Roman chronologies that all emerged independently, took their beginnings at approximately the same time in the fourth DAY. Even more notably, the Julian and Long Count calendars also emerged independently shortly before the fifth DAY. Since these respective timekeeping systems are entirely different in their details, it is quite clear that people did not cross the Atlantic to share their calendrical knowledge. Instead, similar to many other examples presented previously, they attest to synchronistic innovations based on a shared resonance with the evolving global mind. In this, the more analytical Western minds of the Maya played a special role for developing a sequential linear timekeeping.

While what happens in one culture in one part of the world may not be due to a direct influence from another culture elsewhere, the expressions of different cultures are still related to the same global wave movement of mental evolution. *Even in the case when direct contacts between cultures do take place, the reason that something is picked up from another culture is that this is something "whose time has come" according to the time plan for the evolution of the global mind.* The mind of the planet, compartmentalized by the north-south and east-west lines, evolves like one entity even though it may express itself in somewhat different ways in its different parts.

It is also noteworthy that the great steps forward in the standardization of calendars and chronologies took place in the beginning of (or admittedly, sometimes slightly before) the DAYS of the Sixth Wave. Thus, in the Old World the fourth DAY brought the Babylonian calendar on a wider scale (standardized throughout the Persian Empire)[9] and the fifth DAY, the Julian calendar (Roman Empire). It was, however, only in the 800s,[10] with the sixth DAY that the latter became a chronology based on the birth of Jesus rather than on the founding of Rome. Shortly before the seventh DAY, the Gregorian calendar (Catholic Church and worldwide) with its even greater astronomical accuracy was implemented (Fig. 46). The long-term experience of linear time has thus become more prominent with every DAY of the Sixth Wave, as the dimension of linear time is indeed a part of the global mind. As the previous section demonstrated, the three dimensions of space are increasingly developed in the same DAYS, and so most likely the development of linear time is created by the same geometry of the mind.

THE HISTORICAL ROLE OF THE WRITTEN LANGUAGE

From the evidence so far, we may conclude that the mind is an integrated space-time organizer for humanity, which creates a framework for how we experience reality. We can see this because phenomenon after phenomenon that we associate with civilization—construction, mathematics, art, timekeeping, etc.—can be tracked DAY by DAY as evolutionary processes of the Long Count and understood as originating in the geometry of the mind that this made available.

Among the phenomena of civilization, writing, which accounts for the accumulation and communication of knowledge, has played a role second to none. Therefore, the origin of writing deserves some special attention. We may then first want to consider why it is that the written language has played such a significant role for the development of civilization. This is in essence because a written language allows a society to conserve and accumulate knowledge, thus allowing for very specialized capabilities. These capabilities will then, in turn, even further foster the development of civilization. While literacy is a product of civilization, it also expands civilization and is a prerequisite for its further evolution.

To demonstrate the power of literacy we may as an example take someone today studying to become a medical doctor. It is then only because of the existence of a written language that he or she does not have to generate vast amounts of basic knowledge concerning the functioning of the human body by repeating hundreds of thousands of experiments and autopsies made by others. Instead, he or she only needs to spend some five years reading textbooks synthesizing the existing knowledge of medicine, based on countless studies, each of which may have taken five person-years to produce. Thus, without a written language the medical students would have to base themselves solely on their own experience, or on that of their mentor. Considering that there are thousands of different diseases, this would often not be sufficient. Without medical literature and literacy, how would a doctor know how to diagnose, let alone treat, a disease he or she has not encountered before? The knowledge and practice of medicine is completely dependent on the existence of a system of writing. In fact, none of the specialized activities of a civilization can emerge without a system of writing that allows for the conservation and accumulation of information from past generations as well as communication within the present. Moreover, the role of written laws, contracts, and treaties for the regulation and maintenance of civilized societies can hardly be overestimated.

Step in Wave	Means of Written Communications
DAY 1 3115-2721 BCE	Undeciphered (Indus Valley, 3200), Logograms (Sumer, 3200) Hieroglyphs (Egypt, 3100)
NIGHT 1	
DAY 2 2326-1932 BCE	Development of Mesopotamian Cuneiform
NIGHT 2	
DAY 3 1538-1144 BCE	Consonant Alphabet (Canaan, 1600)
NIGHT 3	
DAY 4 749-355 BCE	Complete Alphabet (Greece and Etruria, 750 BCE)
NIGHT 4	
DAY 5 40-434 CE	Papyrus Codices (Rome, 70 CE) Paper (China, 105 CE)
NIGHT 5	
DAY 6 829-1223 CE	Book printing (China, 868)
NIGHT 6	
DAY 7 1617-2011 CE	Daily newspapers (Amsterdam, 1618) National mail service (Denmark, 1624)

Figure 48. The evolution of means of writing throughout the Long Count.[11]

Then, why and how did the first systems of writing emerge? In their myths the early civilizations saw writing as another gift of the gods, and we might note that Thoth, the Egyptian god credited with the invention of writing, was also the scribe of the underworld (inner core of the Earth). What we know more firmly is that on the surface of our planet Sumerian logograms and Egyptian hieroglyphs appeared independently approximately at the time of the beginning of the Long Count (circa 3200–3000 BCE). Clay tablets from the Indus Valley are probably from about the same time, give or take a few hundred years as with all such early dates, but this script has yet to be deciphered. A few other contemporary scripts have also been discovered from the same general area and time, such as those of the Minoan, Elamite, and Jiroft civilizations.[12] The independently arising Chinese[13] and Olmec/Mayan scripts,[14] however, came into existence at later points in time. The only known written symbolic system clearly preceding the beginning of the Sixth Wave is the one from the so-called Vinča culture in current day Serbia, dated to about 5500–4500 BCE.[15] However, most experts doubt that its symbols, many of which are actually early perpendicular forms, are part of a system of writing that reflects a spoken language.

WRITING AS A COMBINED EFFECT OF THE LINEAR DIMENSIONS OF SPACE AND TIME

In conclusion, written languages do not seem to have existed before the downloading of the Sixth Wave mind sphere. Why this mind sphere is necessary for writing is something that I will attempt to explain here. Any serious theory proposing to explain why civilization arose on our planet will have to provide an outline of how and why a system of writing would emerge as part of it. We have seen that civilization comes as a kind of package, but it is still not immediately clear why the emergence of writing was synchronistic with the rise of monarchies and the building of pyramids. To explain this within the present theory would mean outlining how the emergence of writing depended on the activation of the linear dimensions of space and time, which we saw in the previous sections happened at the same time. It, however, does not seem possible to point out a singular mental factor that explains the emergence of the written language. Instead, the dimensional shift at the beginning of the Long Count may have facilitated the emergence of a written language through combining several different factors.

To understand this, we should remember that written languages came out of spoken languages, whose evolution for obvious reasons might be difficult to follow. Anatomically, most anthropologists believe *Homo sapiens* have been able to speak throughout most of its existence.[16] Some kind of advanced signaling system likely existed ever since the beginning of the Fifth Wave about 100,000 years ago. The indications from the present study, however, are that an actual spoken language, which made use of concepts, is a more recent innovation than has previously been thought. The diversification of Indo-European languages, outlined in Figure 7, tracks the origin of these back to the beginning of the pre-Long Count about 10,000 years ago when the first boundaries of the human mind appeared (Fig 2). This leaves the question open as to what a spoken language would have been like before the Anatolian. We may even wonder if before there were boundaries to the human mind, people would have been able to create and communicate concepts through their language.

Still, there is nothing new under the sun, and the demarcation lines provided by the Mayan calendar are rarely absolutes. Even so, considering the diversification of the Indo-European languages, it seems that a spoken language also may depend on a compartmentalized mind for its existence. This is because all sentences describe something happening in space and time. A noun, for instance, always describes something defined, or compartmentalized by the three dimensions of space, whereas a verb describes an action related to the dimension of linear time. Hence, for a fully developed spoken language to emerge it would be a prerequisite that a mind with those dimensions had already been downloaded. Therefore, spoken languages, in contrast to simpler signaling systems, could have emerged around 10,000 years ago, but not much earlier.

If we then continue to the written language, we may note that one of its inherent properties is that it serves the preservation of information to the future in a more unambiguous way than oral traditions. Already the very earliest Sumerian clay tablets (Fig. 49), with their information of taxations, etc. served to preserve information to the future. We may then realize that only a person with a mind with a linear dimension of time will see a need to develop a script. Only as people started to distinguish between past, present, and future (which animals presumably do not) was a need created for means of storing information. Therefore, only at this point was there an impetus for developing a means of writing. From this it would then be logical for writing to emerge and develop in parallel with the linear dimension of time of the mind, which is in fact what we find if we compare Figures 46 and 48.

Moreover, the written language, in contrast to the spoken, requires a mind with the geometry of at least two dimensions of space, the horizontal and the vertical. This is because the use of written communication mandates that visual symbols, in order to be unambiguous, have relatively fixed appearances in relation to the two planar dimensions. The two planar dimensions of space we saw reflected in the painted art from the beginning of the Long Count are then necessary to provide such a framework for visual symbols, whether they are letters, syllables, or logograms. Consequently, only a mind with those dimensions will be able to develop an unambiguous system of symbols and a definite organization of these in relation to one another (reading from left to right or from right to left, etc.). To realize this, you may recall when you first learned to write how important it was to have a paper with lines and write the letters properly in relation to the vertical and horizontal directions. The ancient Sumerians did the same (Fig. 49).

*Figure 49. Sumerian cuneiform text from the 26ᵗʰ century BCE.
Note how it is organized in relation to perpendicular lines.*

The emergence of a written language, however, does not only require a dimension of time (for conservation and for hearing the sounds in a word in a specific order) and two dimensions of space (for visual symbols), but also a mind able to combine these unequivocally. What a written language does is to connect the audible signals in a spoken language with visual symbols. That we can establish such unambiguous connections between sound and sight is indeed the basis for a true system of writing and demonstrates a very remarkable ability of the mind. Think about it a second: Why is it that when you see a certain letter you associate it with a specific sound? How can sounds be connected to sights in a specific way as they are in a written language? This crucial connection must primarily have depended on the emergence of a mind not only with the dimensions of time and space, but also with the ability to connect these in a very precise way.

Psychologists call the combination of the perceptions by two different senses, such as hearing and seeing, cross-modal sensory processing. What is interesting about this is that when such cross-modal processing takes place the brain displays gamma waves.[17] This implies that for the connection between sight and sound to take place, such as when we learn to write, we need to have developed a 40 Hz (Fig 39) resonance with the Earth's inner core. Therefore, the emergence of writing at the beginning of the Long Count is dependent not only on the dimensions of space and time, but also on the cross-modal sensory processing taking place because of our resonance with the inner core of the Earth. Maybe we can then understand that it was Thoth, the Egyptian scribe of the underworld that was credited with the invention of writing.

Even if a spoken language is also dependent on the existence of a mind, we should note that this is much more markedly the case for a written language, which requires a more advanced mind capable of exact cross-modal sensory processing. For the development of writing, the dimensions of space or time in isolation are thus not sufficient. What is required is that these dimensions exist within the context provided by the spherical boundary of the mind. This is presumably the reason that the written language emerges at the beginning of the Long Count, about 5,000 years ago, and only after the spoken language has been in existence for some time. It seems for the generation of a written language the more advanced mind of the Long Count proper was needed. Part of the reason that the cave painters of the Upper Paleolithic (and no other culture before the beginning of the Sixth Wave, for that matter) were unable to develop a system of writing was then that they did not have minds with boundaries yet.

If the mental dimensions of space and time are prerequisites for the origin of writing, we would also expect that at certain points in time, not only at the very beginning of the Sixth Wave, but also in all of its DAYS, steps forward would be taken in the development of writing. This is what we may see in Figure 48, where step by step we can follow the development of written communications, from the earliest symbols in clay tablets in the first DAY to the complete alphabet in the beginning of the fourth. The second half of the Sixth Wave, however, seems to be more about producing books that treat topics comprehensibly and developing means of rapidly disseminating information. In this development, we again see a process from seed to mature fruit typical of the seven DAYS. With this logical understanding of the origin of the written language, we can see how it directly depends on the mental dimensions of space and time. Therefore, step by step with every DAY, the amount of accumulated information has increased, which in turn has been a critical factor for the continued development of civilization. It is all dependent on the evolution of the global mind.

HISTORY OF MEASUREMENTS:
THE FINITE RADIUS OF THE MIND SPHERE

We now need to examine one more factor in order to understand how the geometry of the mind of the Sixth Wave created civilization. This is the phenomenon of measuring, or, in other words, to compare different properties of physical objects, such as length or weight to some standard. As a science, this sometimes goes by the name metrology.[18] Measurements also relate to the famous Mayan symbol of the eight-partitioned Hunab-Ku deity (shown in Fig. 50 in its Aztec variety). This symbol actually describes the good and evil aspect of the Tree of Life, and was called "The One Giver of Movement and Measure."[19] The name for this symbol of the eight-partitioning implies that a characteristic property that the global mind conveys is the ability to measure.

Figure 50. Aztec symbol of the eight-partitioning often referred to as Hunab-Ku, the One Giver of Measure and Movement.

The development of measurements may have played a role for civilization, whose importance can only be compared to that of writing, and its consequences may have been equally far reaching. For instance, straight and perpendicular buildings made from blocks, such as the Egyptian pyramids, could hardly have been built without standardized measurements. Likewise, the later sciences of electroengineering or chemistry in our own time could never have been developed without means of measuring and much of mathematics and physics have been developed from practical applications of measurements. It is thus inconceivable that the modern technological civilization could have arisen without metrology.

In Egypt, the use of measurements took its beginning around 3000 BCE, when for instance the royal cubit, the distance from the elbow to the fingertips, was introduced as a standard for measuring lengths. This unit was 523 to 529 millimeters long, and there is evidence that it was already in use at the building of the first major pyramid, Djoser's Pyramid.[20] Thus, as far as we know, people only started to make measurements after the Sixth Wave mind sphere had began to be downloaded. We saw already in chapter two that numbers and geometry was based on this sphere, and it was only with a mind with lines of a finite length that the idea of measuring by comparing with a standard, such as the Royal Cubit, would arise. What I am proposing here is that the idea of measuring lengths only came as people had integrated the existence of the radius of the mental sphere (as we saw in Fig. 36).

We do not know exactly how long the radius of the mind sphere is, but presumably it is in the range of a few decimeters (or perhaps a cubit or a foot). The point to realize, however, is that based on its resonance with the Earth's inner core, this radius of the mind sphere must have a precise length (albeit of a metaphysical nature). Accordingly, only as people downloaded a mind sphere with a finite radius would they start to measure the blocks they used for constructions. Thus, the idea to compare and measure things arose only as spherical boundaries came to define the minds of people. There are no comparisons in nature. Only the mind compares, and this is one of its predominant traits.

Measurements of time, through sundials or water clocks, also started at about the same time. However, the techniques of measuring time always go back to comparisons of lengths. Lengths and movements in space, for instance form the basis for measuring the full moon cycle. The same applies to the timekeeping of the day, or the solar year where we can make measurements of the position of the sun in relation to the Earth through measuring distances. Hourglasses and later pendulum clocks also use measurements of spatial changes, as do the atomic clocks providing the modern standard for the second. Incidentally, measuring time as lengths is the reason only someone who has a mind with three dimensions of space experiences linear time, and it also means that only as the idea of measuring lengths had dawned would humans start to measure time. This, in turn, would only happen after the mind sphere with a finite radius had been downloaded and brought one more thing in the package of civilization.

MONEY: HISTORY OF MENTAL COMPARISONS

Based on this, it seems the very idea of measuring or comparing—anything— came with the downloading of the mind sphere and its radius, where the latter could serve as an inner standard for measurements of lengths. Measurements of weights also go back to comparisons of lengths, for instance, when using balances and looking at a scale. Such measurements of weights, arguably first developed in the Indus Valley,[21] have several applications. One that has had long lasting consequences into our own time is the weighing of noble metals, which began the evolution of increasingly abstract means of tender.

In Figure 51, we can see the development of the means of tender throughout the various DAYS of the Sixth Wave. From this, we can understand that the development of money is also a direct product of the evolution of the mind. Around the time of the beginning of the Long Count a monetary economy thus started to replace what previously had been bartering or gift economies. The first unit we know of going beyond this was the so called Shekel used in Mesopotamia already around 3000 B.C.E.[22] This was a unit that at the same time corresponded to a certain weight of barley and a certain weight of copper, silver or gold and could thus be used more generally as a basis for trade.

Step in Wave	Means of Tender
DAY 1 3115-2721 BCE	Shekel (Mesopotamia, 3000)
NIGHT 1	
DAY 2 2326-1932 BCE	Noble metals with stamps
NIGHT 2	
DAY 3 1538-1144 BCE	Cowry shells (China, India), Bronze coins (China)
NIGHT 3	
DAY 4 749-355 BCE	Gold + silver coins (Lydia, 650), Gold coins (King Knoisos, 560-546)
NIGHT 4	
DAY 5 40-434 CE	Standardized coinage system (Roman Empire)
NIGHT 5	
DAY 6 829-1223 CE	Paper bills without set denominations (China, 860 CE)
NIGHT 6	
DAY 7 1617-2011 CE	Paper bills with set denominations (Sweden, 1661)

Figure 51. The evolution of the means of tender throughout the Long Count.

The idea of abstracting value, based on weighed pieces of silver and gold, thus relied not only on the emergence of numbers (Fig. 17), but also on the means of measurements that were introduced with the first DAY of the Sixth Wave. From this point we know that in Mesopotamia step by step, the means of tender became more standardized and strictly comparable. As usual, around the midpoint of this wave in 551 BCE very significant changes manifested, also regarding the means of tender. Then, for the first time, real gold coins started to be used in Lydia on the west coast of Asia Minor. As another reflection of the global nature of the mind, the use of coins started almost simultaneously in India.[23]

The Sixth Wave completed this evolution in its seventh DAY through the introduction of paper bills, a completely abstract means of tender that had no value by itself. This initially happened in Sweden, with the institution of the world's first central bank and the decision to replace the heavy copper coins that previously had been in use there. Not surprisingly, this first experiment with paper notes failed as people's instincts made them question why they would exchange their iron or produce with someone who had nothing to offer in return but a piece of paper with some numbers and a name on it. Because of this resistance inflation went rampant, the experiment failed, and the head of the central bank was thrown in prison in 1667.

Nonetheless, the idea of paper bills was one whose time had come, as the comparing mind had now come to its seventh DAY and developed a thinking much based on comparisons and measurements. As a consequence of this new mentality, not long thereafter the Bank of England took up the idea of using paper bills and introduced it to its colonies in America. Under the dominance of the same global mind, paper money has later been introduced all over the world and is at the present time increasingly replaced by digital money in cyberspace. As I have described in an earlier book,[24] in recent times the world's economy has become a house of cards completely based on mental agreements and with no actual values to back it up. This is a long story, but I believe the point to realize here is that such comparisonsof economic values are created by the mind.

SOME ALIENATING ASPECTS OF THE MIND

Ever since the beginning of the seventh DAY of the Mayan Long Count in 1617, we have been living in a world increasingly dominated by the mind. This dominance of the mind has been at the expense of the yearnings of the soul, the divine presence and everything natural. Today, measurements and comparisons follow us everywhere in life. Our length and weight are determined through measurements immediately after birth, and then in school we receive grades comparing us with other children on a regular basis. When we reach adulthood, our income and wealth is compared based on the monetary system, and from this we receive a credit rating.

Comparisons have already dominated the huge sports industry for a long time, but at present the measuring and comparing aspect of the mind is turning all culture and entertainment into competitions, such as talent searches and reality shows. Popular music is compared based on the ranking of hit lists and, similar to in the movie industry, its products are compared based on sales. We no longer listen to someone singing a song, but to a video clip on YouTube with a hundred million viewers. We no longer appreciate the athletic achievements of a person, but feel admiration that he was sold to another team for the sum of a hundred million dollars. From such phenomena, we may also be able to see several negative consequences of the modern mind. It prevents us from being present with what is and instead leads us to judge and evaluate it.

In our own time the mind has then largely come to dominate all aspects of human life, and through measurements and comparisons it tends to deprive us of our direct natural experiences. Meanwhile, due to the exploitation of its resources, we witness the destruction of our natural environment, the Earth. This is because its resources generate measurable numbers in bank computers, which allows some to compare their values to other things that on this basis can be "bought." Much of the threat to the human environment comes from a narrow-minded focus on such comparisons. Today, not only corporations, but politicians, and large sections of the public, are focused primarily on the measureable growth of the economy rather than on meeting natural human needs.

The emphasis on measurements also plays a significant role in the ideology today often associated with modern science, where some believe that if something cannot be measured then it does not exist. This philosophy is a result of the fact that for a whole baktun—ever since 1617—the measuring aspects of the mind have guided much of science and, especially in the past 150 years, it has come to promote a materialist philosophy. Yet, there are many things that exist that cannot be measured. This is true for many subtle phenomena associated with the soul, spirit, and consciousness. As we have seen, the human soul has evidently manifested in matter for at least the past 100,000 years, and yet it is not directly measurable or directly observable. To deny the existence of the human soul and spirit on this basis amounts to likening us to machines. This is the consequence of much modern brain research and remains the official philosophy for much of science.

The mind then also has a tendency to exclude certain phenomena from the experience of humans, hence the metaphor of a mental cage. While the mechanistic worldview has been very helpful for the development of technology, it has also been detrimental regarding subtler qualities of the human soul. At the current time, the powers that be seek to deny the existence of the human spirit by giving a monopoly to the atheist-Darwinist ideology. We see this in science as well as in the educational system, despite the many objections that may be raised against this view. The year 2014 has thus been declared as the European Year of the Brain, and President Obama has called on the US Congress to devote 100 billion dollars of this budget year to research on the brain.[25] Yet, one might ask, how can such a project be successful if the basic assumptions upon which it is based are flawed?

Because of the dominance of the mind in our current era, all human activities have become wrapped up in a materialist consensus. In the end the materialist view that the human being does not have a soul or a spirit limits and disempowers everyone. Therefore, at least in the Western world there is an increasing divide between "people of the mind" and "people of the spirit". The political and economic power then resides with those of the mind. As we have seen in different ways in this volume, the mind is very powerful and so there will likely be a strong resistance against a retrieval of spirit. This is because a shift towards a truer and more encompassing worldview, and especially putting this into practice, would adversely influence a large network of connected power structures as well as the egos of many people. Yet, the ego-based mechanistic worldview ultimately threatens the existence of our planet as it blocks the emerging understanding that we are all one.

Hence, not everything that comes out of the mind is "good," at least not in my own particular value system. This will become even more evident as we look at the things that are the products of the particular yin-yang duality that colors the mind of the Sixth Wave. Together with a judgmental attitude and a system of law, the mind has in fact also generated the inequalities between social classes and genders. These aspects, together with the transformation of spirituality to religion that began 5,000 years ago, will be looked at in the next volumes, in the context of the higher waves and the shifted polarities of the mind these bring. We will then also ask the question what there is to do, if anything, with the mind. In this volume the purpose has instead been to understand the origin of the mind and describe its nature. We have thus now covered how many expressions of civilization; monarchies, mathematics, calendars, art, money, constructions, measurements, technology, writing and language, and the division of labor, find their origin in the Sixth Wave mind. Based on this evidence, I will in the last chapter discuss the broader consequences of these discoveries.

CHAPTER 7:
CONCLUDING PERSPECTIVES

A PARADIGM SHIFT AT THE END OF THE THIRTEENTH BAKTUN OF THE LONG COUNT

We are living in a time of a very significant paradigm shift, which is to say a fundamental shift in our way of looking at reality. In significant regards, this means leaving the past behind. Hence, as of October 28, 2011 the thirteenth baktun (beginning in 1617 CE) of the Long Count (Sixth Wave) was completed, by itself marking an important mental shift. More importantly, the sum total of the thirteen first baktuns of this Long Count (beginning in 3115 BCE) has been completed. The present time may then be the first when it is possible to synthesize and integrate the entire evolution of civilization that has taken place during these thirteen baktuns.

It is because all human thinking, philosophy and religion are the products of the mind, and go back to shifts in the waves described by the Mayan calendar, that the current time becomes very special. It may allow us for the first time to integrate all of the thought systems that throughout its existence the human mind has produced, and develop a new paradigm based on this integration. Usually at such significant shift points, a wide variety of new and old viewpoints, sometimes also superstitious or reactionary, compete for attention because of the prevailing sense that something new is coming. Eventually, however, some new way of thinking emerges that generates a broader consensus by including many different view points, and hopefully the insights presented here will be part of this paradigm shift.

Paradigm shifts within the thirteenth baktun (1617-2011) mostly came out of the mind understanding nature (natural science and technology), but the current paradigm shift, based on the sum of all the thirteen baktuns (3115 BCE -2011 CE), not surprisingly must be expected to go deeper. Because we are now able to synthesize the entire wave of the very mind that developed this natural science and technology, we may expect that the current paradigm shift will mean a new understanding of the mind and what consciousness is.

Nonetheless, paradigm shifts do not manifest overnight, and we have yet to see what will crystallize and have a lasting impact. To recognize that this change may come slowly, we have only to look back at the most recent baktun shift in the Sixth Wave in 1617 CE that brought the scientific revolution. Thus, subsequent to this shift point, Kepler published *De Harmonice Mundi* with the mathematical laws for the movement of the planets in 1619; Galilei published *Dialogue on The Two Chief World Systems* in 1632, arguing for the heliocentric worldview; Descartes published *Discourse de La Methode* with the new philosophy of science in 1637; and Newton published *Principia Mathematica*, laying the foundation of mechanics in 1687. These pioneering works reflected the activation of the global mind that took place at the time and, following this, over time an ideal of approaching reality rationally spread to the entire population in all areas of the world. Yet, ultimately, this intellectual change originated in the activation of the mind in 1617. It then took about seventy years until this paradigm shift was fully established. Even if a paradigm shift today for a variety of reasons is not likely to take such a long time, the delay at earlier times in the manifestation of mental shifts is still something to be aware of.

The current volume of this trilogy about the origin and evolution of the mind presents at least five major potential paradigm shifts for our own time. Accordingly, evidence has been provided that: 1) Civilization is a product of the evolution of the human mind. For example, the Egyptian pyramids were built as a reflection of the new eight-partitioned, compartmentalized mind emerging at the beginning of the Long Count, based on a metaphysical imprint. 2) The mind is divine in nature and does not originate in the brain. It instead follows a rhythm of evolution determined by the Mayan calendar. Human history is a function of mental shifts and from this a very wide range of historical phenomena and synchronized occurrences may be understood. 3) The polarity between East and West, which is also at the origin of the separation of the left and right brain halves, finds its origin in the hemispheric polarity of the Earth's inner core. 4) Consciousness is a state of "knowing with" something else and is not something that can exist in isolation. In particular, it emerges in relation to the Earth's atmospheric-geophysical system created by the Tree of Life. 5) Human mental faculties emerge from a resonance with the inner core of the Earth and disturbances in this resonance may generate mental disorders.

These shifts in understanding are all interconnected and cannot be looked upon in isolation from each other. For instance, it is not possible for someone who thinks thoughts can be reduced to brain chemistry to understand the independent evolution of the mind. Similarly, it is difficult for someone who rejects the idea that the Mayan calendar provides a time plan for the evolution of the mind to understand why the Egyptian pyramids and other ancient monuments were built. Everything is connected with everything else, but in the end what it all comes down to is the realization that the mind is not a product of the brain. This was substantiated in chapter five as it was demonstrated that we are all part of the same global mind and, through our thought processes, connected to the inner core of the Earth. The proposal here then amounts to a very fundamental reappraisal of what it means to be a human being including the origin, evolution, and future of our minds. It also makes it clear that we are connected to a reality beyond the mind that created the mind in the first place.

In Western culture, however, we have become used to thinking according to a materialist philosophy that our brains generate the mind and to view the mind almost like private property. According to Webster's, materialism "is the philosophical doctrine that matter is the only reality and that everything in the world, including thought, will, and feeling, can be explained only in terms of matter." In contrast to this, what is coming forth here is a view where the global mind is a nonmaterial entity originating in the Tree of Life, which we may regularly access through our connection to the Earth's atmospheric-geophysical system. In reality, the mind is more like a shared resource made available to us through the Earth and its connection to the larger cosmic hierarchy of mental systems (Fig. 13).

Despite this common source, however, we craft our individual minds depending on what particular resonances we establish with the global mind. These resonances we establish at birth, and later further through developing different kinds of habits and, sometimes, intentions to change. To be conscious is then always about "knowing with" something else, even though we constantly tend to delude ourselves into believing that our individual minds are isolated and personal. In reality, we cannot escape our connection to the global mind if we want to stay conscious, but since our connection to it is so much a part of ourselves we tend to be oblivious to the fact that the global mind has an independent existence.

Depending on our individual experiences and the particular worldviews we embrace, it may be more or less easy to accept the existence of such a global mind, even if the evidence presented here is, intellectually speaking, quite unambiguous. However, for many people who experience "receiving" information of a spiritual nature from sources outside of themselves, it may make perfect sense that their minds are not personal and that they are sometimes in contact with "something greater," which inspires and guides them in whatever way they may conceptualize this. Certainly, such inspiration would have been present for all mystics, prophets, and founders of religions in earlier times.

THE INDEPENDENT ORIGINS OF THE MIND AND THE BRAIN

As we have seen here, a theory about the rise and continued evolution of civilization generated by the mind needs to be backed up by evidence that the mind does not originate in the brain. To realize that the origin of the mind is independent of the brain, it may suffice to consider how the two have developed timewise. The brain, as a physical or biological organ, has stayed much the same since the first appearance of *Homo sapiens* 160,000 years ago. The mind, on the other hand, has basically only evolved in the past 5,125 years (although, as we have seen, there existed some preparatory forms) and has in this time generated many of our current mental abilities. Already from the difference between these points in time we can conclude that the mind is not a secondary phenomenon generated by the brain. Instead, for the past 5,125 years the global mind has transformed how our brains function. In the different evolutionary processes of the mind that we have followed, for instance in chapter six, it was thus not the development of our brains that caused steps forward in the DAYS of the Sixth Wave.

This is an important thing to note because of what it teaches us about the relationship between mind and brain. Our thinking is generated by a particular compartmentalization of our minds and it is because of this, which may vary individually, that we have the particular thoughts that we do. *The brain thus creates nothing by itself* but depends on the mind for thinking to occur. Without the mind, our brains will not engage in thought processes, and even if the mind has correlates in brain activity and is anchored in the brain, as we saw in chapter five, this does not mean the brain can generate thoughts in isolation from the mind.

To take this one step further, we now know generally speaking that the mental faculties of human beings are not hard-wired into our biological systems. Our mental abilities do not come from our brains and are not programmed into our genes or our DNA. In a sense, this seems obvious already from the fact that the coding DNA from a chimpanzee is practically identical (99.4%)[1] with that of a human being, despite the enormous difference in mental capacity between these two species. I might add then that shifts in consciousness are not generated by any DNA activation, but are generated by resonance with the global mind. Hopefully then the present theory may provide the final nail in the coffin for all forms of racism and all the genetic ideologies that have been derived from this.

We can thus never understand the mind if we look upon it merely as an expression of the chemistry or biology of the brain. However, even though the brain has a secondary role for our language and our thought processes, it is not unimportant. The brain is obviously necessary for the performance of mental activities, and we know that certain forms of physical damage to the brain cause a more or less serious mental disability, for instance, in stroke patients. We also know that if the normal brain chemistry is disturbed by heavy metals, such as lead or mercury, this adversely influences our intelligence. Yet, this does not prove that the brain generates the mind any more than music stopping when a radio is smashed proves the music was generated inside the radio. The brain functions as a receiver, relay, and resonance unit for the global mind, and for this to function properly it must be intact.

Moreover, and this may be the most difficult for our egos to bear, the mind is not only not created by our brains, it is not even personal! It is global (actually also solar, galactic and cosmic, see Fig. 13) in nature and is developed on a large scale according to a metaphysical pattern beyond our own control. Maybe the global mind can best be likened to a "cyber cloud" we may connect to and which exists independently of ourselves. If the global mind is like the Internet, we may liken our individual minds to a combination of our favorite websites. Depending on what "websites" in the global mind we choose to visit, our individual minds will develop in special ways. Therefore, we create habits of connecting to this global mind in individual ways, which in turn will craft the brain in a special way to facilitate specific resonances. As we focus on certain intentions and goals, we activate particular channels of resonance with the Earth's system, and our brains' neural network will be molded to accommodate these. Because of this individual crafting of our resonance, we will not all think the same way, even if we will always all think within the overall framework of the global mind as this exists at a given point in time. Hence, we are individually responsible for what we think and how we use our thinking in the world. Our individual minds are not hardwired into our brains and so we will always have free will regarding how we craft them.

However, as we saw in chapter one, the evolution of the global mind was not initiated by the human beings themselves, but by the nonphysical eight-partitioning event in the north. The ancient Egyptians, Sumerians, and Mayans symbolically expressed this event, which was of supreme importance to them, in the building of their pyramids. On my own part, I look upon this event as part of a "divine plan," where for reasons we may not be able to understand spiritual waves are activated at preset points in time. Because the metaphysical realm is beyond the mind, I believe we are here coming to the limits of what our minds may grasp.

That the eight-partitioning happened in accordance with an already established time plan, going back to the very beginning of the universe sixteen billion years ago is an important point. It means that our minds are not accidental by-products of a lump of grey matter—the brain—but are conceived of at a high metaphysical level. We presumably have reasons to be grateful that evolution is such a precisely timed and coordinated process. Yet, as stated, it seems as if we are here coming to the limits of what our minds may grasp intellectually, namely to what caused them to exist in the first place. Thus, the mystery of life still remains, and the mystery of the nature of the divine and the metaphysical realm will probably stay with us mortals forever. Or maybe, as another possibility, the mystery is that there is no mystery and things are just the way they are.

THE SACRED GEOMETRY OF THE GLOBAL MIND

We have now come to a point when we should look at how the eight-partitioning is related to so-called sacred geometry, as well as how this form of geometry is related to the global mind. After all, the compartmentalized mind, which gave rise to the first pyramids, was created from a particular geometric structure. In *The Purposeful Universe* I demonstrated how certain aspects of sacred geometry, such as the Golden Mean, underlie the evolution of the anatomy of biological species and are thus intimately related to the Mayan calendar. The current book has instead essentially dealt with the evolution of the mind, but the source of both biological and mental evolution, the Tree of Life, remains the same. The origin and evolution of the mind, whether global or human, is thus intimately related to sacred geometry, and what is proposed here, perhaps for the first time, is that the mind fundamentally has a geometric nature that drives all of history.

Therefore, this divine mind, and its geometry, is evolving, and us along with it. It is then simply not meaningful to study evolution in light of the Mayan calendar in the absence of geometric concepts, since what this calendar actually describes is the timing with which certain aspects of sacred geometry are activated.

When we hear the term sacred geometry, we usually tend to associate it with relatively advanced geometric concepts, such as the Platonic bodies, the Golden Mean, or the Flower of Life. However, in respect to the mind, already the very simplest concepts of sacred geometry, such as the point, the line, the cross, the circle, and the eight-partitioning, which are also all products of the divine mind, are intimately related to its evolution. Among these, the cave painters in the Upper Paleolithic depicted points, short lines, circles, and sometimes even rudimentary perpendicular lines early on. However, sun wheels or eight-partitioning stars are not found in cave paintings earlier than 10,000 years ago[2] or even in pre-dynastic Egypt. Later, especially after the beginning of the Long Count 5,125 years ago, sun wheels became commonplace on cliff paintings. Assuming, then, that art also reflects the inner reality of the artists, there seems to be a strong case that we can correlate the sacred geometry of the mind not only with the Mayan calendar, but also with the rise of civilization.

Figure 52. Eight-partitioned religious symbols. Clockwise from upper left hand corner: Buddhist Dharmachakra: Ba Gua, yin-yang symbol surrounded by I Ching signs; Nordic Sun Wheel; Sumerian god of heaven; Celtic cross; eight-pointed Islamic star; Buddhist lotus flower; Hunab-Ku symbol. Center: Hindu Yantra.

Hence, it was only with the eight-partitioning event at the beginning of the Long Count that human beings gained a comprehensive mental structure with clear overall boundaries and the rest is, as they say, history. As we may see in Figure 52, many, if not all, religions and spiritual traditions spanning the 5,000 years of human history came to honor the eight-partitioned circle as a symbol. As a result, within the time frame of the Mayan Long Count of thirteen baktuns, the eight-partitioning is found on all inhabited continents. Based on the information presented here, one might say that human history is really the history of sacred geometry, because the geometric structure of the divine mind determines what we may create at any given point in time. It is with the unfolding of geometric structures in accordance with the Mayan calendar that certain possibilities and limits for human creativity to express itself arise. It is no wonder, then, that from the dawn of human civilization, for instance, in Egypt, initiates have been using sacred geometry for connecting with the divine mind, and growing spiritually through this connection.

The eight-partitioned lotus flower, for instance, which is now seen as a symbol of Buddhism, was an extensively used symbol for rebirth among the ancient Egyptians already at the very beginning of the wave. As such, it is an excellent symbol since its eight-petaled flower opens when the day dawns, much like in the larger scale of human history the DAYS of the Sixth Wave open with eight-partitionings.

In Buddhism, which among the world's religions may have the greatest focus on the mind, the eight-partitioning is referred to as the noble eight-fold path, which has become the very symbol of the religion itself. The eight-partitioning plays an almost equally important role in Hinduism as the wheel of karma. Moreover, the balanced cross in early Celtic Christianity was often an eight-partitioned symbol, although later this has mostly been changed to the cross of Golgotha. Through this modification the cross has become connected to the suffering of Christ, although the Star of Bethlehem and hence Christmas stars everywhere are still eight-partitioned, symbolic of their origin in the divine mind.

The number of adherents of Christianity, Buddhism, and Hinduism, religions which then have predominant symbols related to the eight-partitioning, currently includes more than half the population of our planet. In addition, as we can see in Figure 52, an eight-pointed star reminiscent of the ancient Egyptian Ogdoad is a symbol in Islamic art. This motif is formed from two squares aligned at 45 degrees to each other. If you add to this the Chinese traditions through the Ba Gua symbol, about 90 percent of the world would appear to be honoring symbols of the eight-partitioning of the mind. The Daoist eight-partitioning through the I Ching trigrams combined with the yin-yang symbol is, much like the Sumerian Dingir, a symbol of heaven. Interestingly, the Ba Gua symbol exists both in an "earlier" and a "later" form. Presumably, this refers to states before and after the downloading of the eight-partitioning. Like the spokes of the Buddhist Dharmachakra, we can see the sixty-four I Ching trigrams as partitionings that create the mind, associated with somewhat different and elaborate philosophies.

Moreover, there are cliff paintings from across the world from non-literate cultures, ranging from Australia and Scandinavia to California, that also have eight-partitionings as motifs (see, for instance, Fig. 32). When we include these, there are few religions or cultural traditions that have not recognized the sacred geometry of the eight-partitioning.

In the more secular era of the past few hundred years, Great Britain, the chief exporter of European civilization and language, has also notably had an eight-partitioned flag. Since 1606, and so essentially from the beginning of the seventh DAY that created the British Empire, its royal naval ships have flown the Union Jack. More recently, the emblem of the United Nations shows an Earth eight-partitioned from the North Pole, in principle identical with the model shown in Figure 11. In the modern world the eight-partitionings are also part of a large number of designs in clothes and architecture, which seemingly have little to do with their metaphysical origin. Therefore, if you focus on it you will find the eight-partitioning in many places you would not expect it. The eight-partitioning has become widely spread on our planet, the reason being it is the specific aspect of the divine mind that created human civilization. In modern times, these roots are, however, often unconscious, and it has become a symbol with little emotional or spiritual charge. Many may not recognize the divine origin of the eight-partitioning as it has now become fully integrated in the modern mind and seems like a self-evident part of reality.

Yet, in India the eight-partitioning is still at the heart of a certain kind of yoga where practitioners focus on a so-called Sri Yantra (Fig. 52, center) as a means of accessing the divine mind and by doing so balance their own minds. The practitioners not only focus on the central point of the Yantra, but also move their attention clockwise around the eight petals of the lotus flower surrounding it. The tantric traditions of the Indian religions thus see the wearing, depicting, enacting, and/or concentrating on a Yantra as beneficial. Naturally, the same is true for the mandalas of Tibetan Buddhism, which for the most part are also eight-partitioned. (The Sanskrit word mandala implies something that is circular and, as we have seen, the circular enclosure is a key facet of the mind.)[3] Maybe we can now start to see why it is that we refer to certain forms of geometry as sacred. The reason is that sacred geometry finds its origin in a global divine mind that exists on a higher level than the human beings themselves, and immersion in its symbols will generate a deeper contact with this mind.

It should be added here that the number of partitionings of the mind, judging from ancient symbols at least, is not limited to eight. In the Hindu tradition you will, for instance, see many wheels with sixteen spokes. The same is true on Sumerian seals. The imperial seal of Japan is not only sixteen-partitioned, but is then divided again into thirty-two partitions. Furthermore, the Chinese divinatory system of I Ching is sometimes presented as a sixty-four-partitioned circle. It is then possible that the mind gained its full compartmentalization only by being divided with the number two several more times.

AN ALTERNATIVE TO THE CONVENTIONAL VIEW OF THE RISE OF CIVILIZATION

The suddenness, a quantum leap in fact, with which the earliest civilizations of our planet emerged is staggering. Moreover, the degree of diversification of their societies, and the scope of their building projects seem, as previously mentioned, incompatible with the notion of a static mind or one that would have to guide itself. Modern science with its materialist bias is thus not without theoretical problems in its attempts to explain what happened, and the sudden rise of civilization has baffled historians and the general public alike for a long time. Why would cultures appearing around the beginning of the 3rd millennium BCE, apparently preceded by very few preparatory forms, suddenly exhibit the whole range of phenomena we associate with civilization? And why would several phenomena, unrelated from a materialist perspective, such as building, writing, numbers, and monarchy appear at approximately the same time?

Modern academic science remains at a loss to answer these questions. It simply refrains from addressing the issue why civilizations emerged, seeing its task to describe these civilizations rather than explain what gave rise to them. This, as I have already pointed out, means ignoring, or at least not taking seriously, the accounts of the peoples living at the time. Although the ancient peoples themselves described divine intervention as responsible for the phenomena of civilization, most modern researchers, who look upon the ancients as confused regarding their own experiences, flatly deny this notion. But how much sense does it make to ignore the actual witnesses of an event and instead try to reconstruct it based on the belief systems of those that lived 5000 years later?

For many people outside of the academic community, something has thus seemed amiss in an approach that merely aims to describe without providing any context or understanding. Few people can, for instance, view the Egyptian pyramids without wondering why and how these were built. It is also natural if we wonder why other cultures, such as in Greece, Peru, and Mesopotamia appear to almost simultaneously, and independently of each other start to build pyramids and cities linked to them. The global eight-partitioning mediated by the Earth's inner core may, as suggested here, provide a deeper understanding of this phenomenon, which has the virtue that it conforms exactly to what at least the Maya were saying. However, from the materialist perspective, which does not consider the existence of spirit or the evolution of the mind as real, the rise of the early civilizations will always remain enigmatic.

Because of these shortcomings characterizing the "official" view of archaeology, dozens of theories have been proposed to explain the reason for building the pyramids, especially the Egyptian. The theory proposed here stands out in that it does not look upon the building of these in isolation from the continuation of human history. (It is for this reason that the message of the pyramids is primarily about us and not just about the Egyptians.) Thus, in this view the building of the Egyptian pyramids came from the same mental power that led to the contemporary construction of pyramids in other parts of the world. It also came out of the same power from which the continued evolution of civilization would draw. In terms of its purpose, there is, for instance, little difference between the building of the Egyptian pyramids in honor of the divine eight-partitioning and the building of the European cathedrals in honor of the holy cross. These are simply expressions of sacred geometry marking different steps in the mental evolution of the Sixth Wave.

In this way, the model proposed here explains that pyramid construction and the rest of history finds its origin in the emergence and continued evolution of one and the same global mind. As demonstrated, by means of this theory about the mind, with its dimensions of space and time, it is now possible to explain one by one the emergence of all the other important novelties appearing with the early civilizations: nationhood, numerals, geometry, art, calendars, measurements, cities, means of tender, division of labor, and written languages. All further steps forward of civilization, and not only the initiating steps, also come from an inspired inner change in the human beings themselves. This inspiration is provided by the polarities and sacred geometry generated by the Tree of Life and is what has inspired people to download a new mind.

The different phenomena of civilization are hence directly connected, which is only logical if they emanated from the same global mind. They emerged simultaneously as part of a package and have since continued to evolve in synchrony in different locations. The downloading of the eight-partitioned mind sphere (Fig. 36) thus provides a remarkably simple explanation to all of the phenomena that are part of civilization. Downloading perpendicular mental lines of finite lengths limited by a spherical boundary has, in fact, had a very multifaceted and powerful effect on the lives of human beings. The absence of such a powerful compartmentalized mind prior to the beginning of the Long Count also explains why no higher civilization, meaning one with city life and a written language, has been found on our planet from any earlier point in time. Before human beings could access a mind based on the linear dimensions of space and time, they would simply not have been able to create the specific phenomena of civilization. With a slight exaggeration: *Civilizations do not build pyramids. Instead, the same inspiration that moves people to build pyramids may lead them to create civilizations.*

The downloading of the compartmentalized mind, however, was not just a one-time event at the beginning of the Long Count. It is something that would be repeated and reinforced with every new DAY in the wave of the Plumed Serpent bringing its eight-partitioning cross (Figs. 19 and 35) all over the planet. The emergence of the earliest civilizations was only the beginning of a process of transformation of humanity that would eventually lead to the current modern global civilization. What this means is that all aspects of human history are related not only in space, but also over time, and subordinated to the same wave movement of the evolving global mind.

While the theory about the rise of civilization presented here is not conventional, it deserves to be pointed out that none of the facts it builds upon are by themselves controversial. It is, for instance, not controversial that the Thirty Years' War started in 1618 or that brain waves in the range of 7 to 13 Hz have a distinct character qualifying them as alpha waves. Moreover, the Mayan inscriptions were interpreted by qualified epigraphers and the model of the

Earth's interior was taken from *Nature* magazine and most of the facts can be verified by Wikipedia. What may be unconventional here is the integration of non-controversial facts within a radically new framework that may make more sense to many people than to study the facts of life in separate disciplines. True paradigm shifts do not simply dismiss the previous knowledge, but incorporate a wider range of facts and relationships in a new and more encompassing framework, and hopefully this has been accomplished here.

WHY THE EARLY CIVILIZATIONS DID NOT EMERGE EARLIER

The evolution of the mind independently of the brain is a notion that has not previously been taken into consideration regarding the rise of civilization. This new understanding of the mind/brain relationship may then also come to affect how we look upon the timing of some events in the past. It may be that the acceleration of time has had stronger effects than previously thought. This acceleration of time is an inherent consequence of the cosmic time plan (Fig. 21) that was felt especially strongly in our previous decade. The consequence of such an acceleration of time is that significant manifestations of a wave tend to happen toward its end.

The Fifth Wave is no exception from this, and it is only toward its end that we may really follow what came out of it. Yet, if the emergence of a compartmentalized mind is crucial for the emergence of a spoken language and a tribal society, then, as I argued previously, these may be more recent phenomena than previously thought. Civilization, as we have seen is a result of the diversification of human life brought about by mental holograms emanating from the Earth and the timing of these emanations follow a strict time plan. Based on this theory, we may understand why no civilization older than about 5,000 years has ever been reported on our planet, at least not by professional archaeologists. The reason the early civilizations did not emerge earlier is then that civilization is not something that for no reason pops up in the brains of people. It appears because of the human resonance with the global mind, which ultimately is divine in nature and has a preset timing for its evolution. For the same kind of reasons, it seems unlikely that any megalithic monuments or agriculture much older than 10,000 years will ever be discovered.

Some may then ask, "What about Atlantis?"[4] or other ideas of an early "lost civilization" from which all others purportedly would have been spawned, an idea that has become very widespread in recent decades. As a myth, Atlantis and its purported destruction have fascinated the human imagination for a long time and may be discussed as a typical case of the idea of a "lost civilization." We find the origin of this purported sunken continent in some of Plato's dialogues. In these, he states that he got his information from Egypt, where Atlantis was said to have been destroyed 9,000 years before the life of Solon, or, in other words, approximately in 9600 BCE.[4] Later, there are few places on Earth (even Sweden in the 1600s)[5] that have not been suggested as the location of Atlantis. In modern times it has become a popular idea that it had both lasers and nuclear weapons.

When assessing the reality basis of these accounts, the first thing to consider is the reliability of the dating. We should then note that at the time of Solon, the Greeks had barely begun to use a long-term chronology based on the count of Olympiads, which went back to 776 BCE. We also know that the Egyptians never had any chronology to begin with (except for king lists). So we may immediately ask: If Atlantis had collapsed nine thousand years before Solon, who had counted the years? There is no reason here to question the intellectual integrity of Plato, who presumably did not know the Egyptians never had a chronology and no system of writing that went further back than to 3000 BCE. Therefore, "nine thousand years" with a realistic appraisal simply means "many thousand years," and probably only "some time before my own time." As shown in chapter six, long-term consciousness of linear time was a product of the midpoint of the Long Count and did not exist anywhere much before the time of Solon. Consequently, as far as I can see there is no reason to believe that we can assign any reliable age whatsoever to what Plato wrote about. I do not think that we can simply extrapolate our own compartmentalized consciousness of time to the past and assume that the mind then had the same properties as it does now.

Yet, aside from the dating, Plato's account may very well be describing a historic reality similar to Troy, which was also thought of as merely mythological until Schliemann discovered it in the 1800s.[6] Maybe one of the bases of the "Sea Peoples" that attacked Egypt and other parts of the Near East circa 1200 BCE was a place called Atlantis.[7] Since Plato described a war between the Atlanteans and the Athenians and Athens has a recorded history that goes back 3,400 years from our present time,[8] this would place it in a realistic historical time frame. Traces of a city, apparently destroyed by a tsunami, have in fact been discovered outside of Gibraltar,[9] which seems to meet several of Plato's descriptions, for instance, that Atlantis would be located "beyond the pillars of Hercules," associated with the Straits of Gibraltar. Hypothetically, this could have been the real "Atlantis" that at some point had also been engaged in a war with Athens. As the westernmost location in the world he was aware of, it may well have been rumored to have certain aspects that seemed advanced to Plato. This Atlantis would, however, have been a historical city-state and not one in any sense reminiscent of our own civilization with its advanced technology. Atlantis would have been a city in current-day Spain that was destroyed around 3,000 years ago. Why not?

If we recognize that the source of the early civilizations was truly the divine inspiration of structures of sacred geometry and that this inspiration was global in nature, there is no reason to believe that any civilizations existed earlier than those that we actually know of. The internal coherence, clear direction and strict timing for the evolution of consciousness of humanity would preclude this. Taken together, the evidence is simply massive that evolution follows the rhythm of the Mayan calendar, even if most people remain unaware of this. At a larger scale, this evolution always has a forward direction going from seed to mature fruit, stepwise creating more favorable conditions for the emergence of civilization. It is for this reason civilizations cannot appear at arbitrary points of time in the past, but only as the inner life of human beings has been duly made ready for the next step.

THE MESSAGE OF THE EGYPTIAN PYRAMIDS

Based on the knowledge we have accumulated, it may now be time to go back to where we started, namely with the Egyptian pyramids. According to the pyramid texts from the Old Kingdom, these pyramids reflected the so-called Benben, which was a name for the primordial mound of creation on Earth. Assuming then that the Earth's inner core is this original world mound (and it is not easy to see what else would qualify), it appears the ancient Egyptians described what they did in quite unambiguous terms as they built the pyramids. They created buildings, pyramids, in the image of the original world mound, and they did so because they actually experienced the eight-partitioning of the divine mind. Even if the earth's inner core is not actually pyramidal, but spherical, through the eight-partitioning anchored in its hemispheric polarity, it will transmit the metaphysical reality of a pyramid. By them, this was symbolized both by the Ogdoad and the lotus flower. It now makes perfect sense for us to identify this primordial mound, the Benben, with the Earth's inner core even if their knowledge of this was metaphysical and intuitive rather than based on physical measurements as it is now.

A pyramid was thus a very well-chosen symbol of how the mind is related to the inner core of the Earth on the Northern Hemisphere. if the new mind at the time actually was a projection of the Earth's inner core, this however raises a possible question regarding the calculation made earlier connecting the dimensions of the pyramid to the equatorial circumference. Depending on where it is measured the radius of the Earth's surface is however close to five times that of the inner core, and the circumference of the Great Pyramid would instead be close to 2.5 minutes of arc at the surface of the inner core of the Earth. Whether the Egyptians were actually in resonance with the eight-partitioned Earth grid as it was projected to the surface of the Earth or directly with the Earth's inner core is somewhat of a quandary. The Mayan inscription about a House in the North would imply that it was on the surface of the Earth, but I can see it both ways.

Some believe that the Egyptians, who built these pyramids, saw them as a message to our own time. I would prefer to say that they saw the eight-partitioning of the Great Pyramid as a message to people at *any* time, including their own. For them building the pyramids might have been a means of seeing the divine mind reflected through their own. Because of the consciousness shift at the beginning of the Long Count, and the eight-partitioning of the mind that then took place, I believe they simply felt a calling mediated by the Earth to build the pyramids. Yet, it may be only now after the end of the thirteen baktuns of civilizational development that we are beginning to see that the pyramids hold a significant message not only for ourselves, but also about ourselves. Whether or not this message was intentional by their builders, it certainly has a very profound meaning to us in our own materialist day and age. The message is that there is a global mind, connected to the Earth's inner core, that is divine in nature and which we are all in resonance with. Nonetheless, it deserves to be pointed out that this message could not have been retrieved without our modern sciences of archaeology, neurology, and geophysics. In this sense, we may at least look at the message of the Great Pyramid as one whose time has now come.

Any way we look at it, this message—that our minds are in resonance with a divine mind evolving according to a preset time plan—is an immensely significant message about ourselves and what makes us human. Yet, it is inconsistent with the materialist bias that dominates most of modern science, psychology and the modern world in general, which presume the mind is simply a product of brain chemistry that hardly inspires anyone to see the higher meaning of his or her life.

It is then maybe also part of this message for us now to reconsider this materialist bias. It is because of this particular modern bias that historians have not been able to see that there is an underlying time plan for the evolution of civilization or what is behind this. For instance, while modern archaeology has discovered that the Egyptians built their pyramids as reflections of the original world mound, so far it has not been recognized that this original world mound *actually is* the chief organizer of the human mind. This bias makes us look upon the notions of the ancients as inferior and so often prevents us from seeing that the ancients were literally telling the truth. I suspect that in the time ahead we will increasingly become aware that the overall perspective of the ancients was more reality-based than our own has been for quite some time.

I believe that now, at our current shift in consciousness after five thousand years, the Egyptian pyramids have finally given off their secrets and the alpha has been brought to the omega. Their "secrets," which probably never were meant to be secrets, are then about us and our relationships to the Earth and the divine mind. They concern our very origin or, in other words, what makes human beings human. This in itself is among the most profound knowledge that we can acquire. After seven DAYS and six NIGHTS of evolution of the Long Count, we are now able to understand what has occurred in human history on a deeper level than ever before. Now, at this momentous shift, the origin of the very mind from which we have understood and created the world is being revealed to us.

THE UNIVERSAL INSPIRATION FROM THE GLOBAL MIND

It is sometimes argued that the fact ancient peoples in different parts of the world had similar myths must mean that these myths were spread either by an earlier "lost civilization" or by extraterrestrials. Because we have shown here that all human cultures are connected to the same global mind, this argument completely loses its relevance. As we all share in the global mind it would, in fact, be very surprising if we did not also share many myths and other ideas about the metaphysical reality (see, for instance, Fig. 52), and there is no reason to assume that transoceanic journeys were necessary for their spread. In fact, similarities between myths are exactly what you would expect based on the common resonance of the Earth's peoples with its inner core.

Take the number seven, for example, recognized all over the world as sacred. This is not because someone travelled around the world to tell others that this is a sacred number. Instead, it is the movement of seven DAYS and

Figure 53. This rock carving from about 1000 BCE from Valcamonica in northern Italy shows a so-called Camunian Rose above a man. In my view, this depicts the downloading of the eight-partitioned mind in an almost overly explicit way. What may look like a helmet around the head I interpret as the mind sphere that is here being activated by the downloading.

six NIGHTS of the Long Count, which is behind the symbolism of seven. People in earlier times directly experienced these influences of the global mind. We know this because, as we can see from Figure 16, these alternating polarities propelled them into action. Since these influences came from the metaphysical realm, the number seven became sacred and associated with various religious themes. So why would they not see the number seven as sacred regardless of where they were living or what particular tradition they belonged to?

For me, at least, the global nature of the mind provides a very direct and easy way to understand why people in ancient times, even on different continents, similarly built pyramids, mummified their dead, and produced mythologies of serpents and trees. To do so for them was simply a matter of recognizing their own experience of the metaphysical reality, and this required no direct contact with any other culture. As an example, the reason the number seven was considered as sacred in so many traditions is that *objectively seven is part of the metaphysical reality of this creation.* The Drachenloch altar, the Plumed Serpent, the Jewish menorah, and the Great Seal of the United States all reflect this same metaphysical reality, even if the respective cultures that created these symbols arrived at them independently. The same would go for anything else, such as the Tree of Life that played a significant role in the creation of life on our planet.

In recent decades similarities in symbolism present in esoteric traditions and secret societies have gained much attention, notably through the books of Dan Brown, such as the *Da Vinci Code*. Some common numerology and sacred geometry expressed in the architecture of important monuments, such as in Washington, DC, or Rome, in fact, goes back far into antiquity.[10] Here, however, we have taken the study of such connections one step further by pointing out that the origin of this symbolism is not to be found in the heads of men, but in the nature of the global mind and how the evolution of the universe is actually designed. *It then follows that such symbols that truly have a metaphysical origin may have a powerful effect on people.* Whether we recognize it or not, we are all in resonance with the eight-partitioning of the global mind that created and centralized civilization, and so also its modern centers of power may want to express this geometry symbolically. It is then only natural that the architecture in modern cities with such ambitions will incorporate metaphysical symbols in their design. The earlier mentioned architecture of Bernini at Saint Peter's Square in Rome (Fig. 37) is, for instance, primarily an expression of the global mind, whether it was designed consciously as such or not. The discovery of this global mind has potentially huge consequences for the study of comparative mythology, by not merely telling us what different ancient peoples "believed," but also helping us through the discovery of parallels between the myths to reconstruct the metaphysical reality that inspires our lives.

What we have found here, in fact, turns many of the common assumptions regarding the rise of civilization upside down, including several of those that alternative historians base their work on. The assumption that a civilization "must have" existed before the first megalithic monuments were erected is not valid. Rather, shifts in consciousness, with associated metaphysical imprints simply compelled the ancient peoples to build monuments through the influence these had on their minds. For this reason civilizations would in many cases emerge almost simultaneously with, or even later than, the monuments. Again, civilizations do not build megalithic monuments, but the same inspiration that created the megalithic monuments may also lead to the creation of civilizations.

There is, in other words, no need to hypothesize the existence of any "missing links" or prior advanced civilizations in order for us to understand the advancement of the civilizations closer in time to ourselves. If there is a "missing link" it is the link to the global mind and the spiritual dimension of reality.

The main point is that no external influence, whether from purported Atlanteans or extraterrestrials, is actually needed to explain any particular aspect of the rise of civilization. This means that such suggestions can only complicate our understanding of our origins. The emergence of civilization is more coherently explained by the downloading of a compartmentalized mind (Fig. 53) with the dimensions of space and time. The evolving divine mind, as we have seen throughout this book, is then what has generated these inner changes in humanity at different points in time, and we can actually directly explain all the specific characteristics of civilization from such inner changes in the humans themselves. Accordingly, if we accept what the Mayans themselves described as the basis for their calendar, namely the erection of the eight-house partition, there is no longer any gap to fill in our knowledge about the rise of civilization. The simplest and most encompassing explanation seems to be that our ancestors created the early civilizations by themselves based on a very particular form of divine inspiration, or, if we like, sacred geometry downloaded from the heavens.

Our understanding of who we are, our place in the cosmos, and what the future may look like is in fact very intimately related to how we understand the original rise of civilization. Theories on such matters may thus have great consequences, and the issues involved must be approached carefully. Many theories of alternative history, such as that of Atlantis, postulate the existence of catastrophes in the past that may in fact not even have taken place, at least not on the scale proposed, so what is gained by promoting them? The risk of focusing on such events, or, for instance, ideas that speculate human beings were enslaved by extraterrestrials in the past, is that it creates a dark outlook on our past, which can needlessly then be projected onto our future. Moreover, if we do not recognize our real forefathers and foremothers for what they did, it is not necessarily obvious who we ourselves are and what our continued role in this creation may be. I believe that the theory presented here has the virtue of connecting us with our ancestors in a meaningful way and understand exactly the divine inspiration they were guided by.

Recognizing that the ancients created the early civilizations themselves, beginning 5,125 years ago, provides us with both great responsibilities and new opportunities. If, as I am proposing, they created the early civilizations with divine inspiration, then a very significant consequence in our own time of a great shift is to retrieve such inspiration. Essentially, the first phase of evolution of civilization, that of the initial thirteen baktuns of the Long Count, was completed on October 28, 2011. Very likely, this shift will stimulate us to create a new external reality, and it is then important to know what inspiration to follow and how to find this. Maybe, then, what we should really learn from the ancients is that change must come from inside and that divine inspiration can be projected outwards for a remaking of human society.

OUR CONNECTION TO THE EARTH

The paradigm shift mentioned in the beginning of this chapter does not only affect our view of our origins and human history. It also directly affects the overall modern frameworks for understanding medicine, psychiatry, theology, consciousness research, philosophy, and psychology. As we will increasingly find in the new paradigm, all things are related, and to be meaningful the old disciplines need to be integrated into a new whole. From the perspective developed here, psychology, for instance, is nothing but a cross section of the history of the mind made at our current time. It then more or less goes without saying that the global mind provides what is often referred to as the "collective consciousness" of humanity with somewhat varying definitions. Thus, already in the early 1900s Sigmund Freud recognized what he would call "archaic remnants" in the human collective, which Carl Jung, with his concepts of the collective unconscious and the archetypes, would develop further. Jung identified collective archetypes not originating in the actual life experiences of an individual and thought of these as having been inherited and so concluded that they must be part of a collective consciousness.

Through the theory presented here we may take the mystery out of this concept of collective consciousness. We may now realize that we did not inherit these archetypes by some unknown biological mechanism, but that these are part of the reality of the global mind. Accordingly, we collectively share archetypes because we are all in resonance with the global mind, and now know the very solid underlying reality to the concept of the collective consciousness of a culture or humanity at large. The rich work not only of Jung, but also of Joseph Campbell, who studied similarities in the mythology and symbology of different cultures, now gains a deeper meaning: the similarities between these cultures are due to the fact that they are connected to the same global mind. Thus, even if we sometimes find it hard to understand each other, especially if we come from different cultures, we can hardly imagine how difficult this would be without the common connection of all human beings to this global mind.

The global mind, however, is something that in a sense has an existence outside of ourselves, because it is independent of our individual minds. This fact would come as no surprise to a Hindu or a Buddhist, but may be quite shocking to someone wedded to a reductionist or materialist worldview. This relative independence of the global mind raises some interesting new perspectives. For instance, neurologists typically describe brain scans and show certain mental activities located to specific brain regions. From this, they automatically assume that our thinking or other mental processes take place exclusively in these locations. The findings presented here do not invalidate the locations determined in this way. Yet, it seems the data needs to be interpreted differently. Consequently, when an activity is discovered in a certain brain region, this should be taken to mean that this particular brain region is then engaged in a resonance with the Earth's inner core. This, in other words, means that thinking takes place through the resonance between the brain and the inner core.

So what is thinking, and where does it actually take place? As the resonance with the inner core is necessary for us to stay conscious, a fascinating prospect opens that thinking and memorizing actually take place, partially or even totally, through the interactions of our brains with the interior of the Earth. That memories are stored in the inner core would be consistent with the fact that they are often left intact even if parts of the brain are damaged or removed. In more practical terms the surgical procedure of hemispherectomy, removal of half the brain,[11] results in no long-term effects on memory, which makes you wonder where in the brain those memories would be stored. Arguably, the simplest answer is that they are not stored in the brain at all. A few specific regions of the brain have of course been suggested as being involved with memorizing, but this may simply mean that they have a special role for developing the resonance. No cellular or molecular mechanism has been provided as to how memories could be stored in the brain.

Moreover, is it not true that when we try to retrieve a memory we have a feeling that we are "going somewhere else" to search for it? Are we then searching our brains to find it, which is the established viewpoint, or are we searching crystal matrices in the Earth's inner core? If the latter were true, it would mean that all of our experiences of reality would depend on this relationship to the Earth and that this may influence them all. If all mental disorders with memory failures display abnormal gamma brain waves,[12] does this not strongly imply that the inner core also plays a critical role for memory storage? Even if it may not yet be possible to answer this question conclusively, memory remains a mystery to traditional brain research.

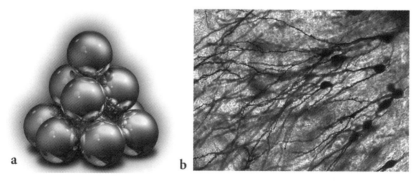

Figure 54. (a) Hexagonal closed packed spheres, each of which has twelve neighbors of the type assumed to exist in the inner core of the Earth. (b) Human brain neurons.

Is it possible then that our memories are instead being stored in the Earth's inner core? To answer this we may note that the memories we keep are usually experiences clearly defined in space and time. For this reason, when we revisit a place, memories from earlier visits to the same place are often activated. We also tend to store the memories from our lives in an essentially sequential order, in principle according to a time line. Both of these observations would immediately imply that linear coordinates in the dimensions of space and time would be crucial for memorizing. But then again, we have seen that the dimensions of space and time find their origins in the mind and not the brain. This by itself would disqualify the brain as a place for storing such coordinates.

However, since we know from the associated brain frequencies that memory retrieval and cognitive functions are associated with the crystalline inner core of the Earth, we may argue that the close packed hexagonal atoms there (Fig. 54a) are the most probable candidates for providing linear coordinates to our experiences in time and space. This would apply not only to memory storage in accordance with a time line of life, but also in relation to the places on Earth we have memories from. In fact, close packed atoms could conceivably serve to define linear coordinates on the level of the inner core, so that all memories could be unambiguously defined in space and time. Furthermore, because of their structured nature, they might serve as matrices for logical operations and information processing.

Of course, as no one has seen the Earth's inner core, all studies of this are indirect. To understand exactly how thinking and memory works we would need more detailed knowledge about the structure of the inner core. Yet, there is a consensus among geophysicists that chemically speaking the inner core is constituted by close packed iron atoms spiked with other metals. At the very least, as suggested above, such a crystalline, but not completely uniform, structure could be used for defining the coordinates in space and time of our memories.

Possibly, the inner core could also serve to store visual, auditory, or other experiences of the senses, such as taste and smell, associated with those coordinates. Just from looking at brain cells (Fig. 54b) it in fact seems almost inconceivable that these would be able to provide an unambiguously defined time line for our memories, spatial coordinates, or even the logical processing necessary for compartmentalized thinking. Moreover, based on its size and organized structure, the potential for memory storage in the inner core of the Earth would seem incomparably larger than that of the brain. Curiously, the origin of the common idea that "we only use a small part of our brain" (which regarding our individual biological brains clearly is not true) would then find its explanation. There is indeed more to the capacity of the brain than we have thought, but for this to be expressed we may need to recognize the larger Earthly context, which it is in resonance with.

NORMAL "PARANORMAL" PHENOMENA

Before closing, there are a few things of a more speculative nature that deserve to be looked at in the light of the explanatory potential of the discovery of the global mind. Hence, if it is true that memory, or at least a component of it, is stored in the underworld of the Earth, this opens up some additional new and interesting perspectives. For instance, most people in their daily lives have experienced either synchronicities or precognitions. Synchronicities are remarkable and seemingly unlikely coincidences that often have a deeper meaning. Examples are when someone calls just when you were about to call him or her, or when you run into your next-door neighbor at a market in a faraway land. Precognitions are hunches, when out of nowhere you get a strong sense that something is going to happen, which may also come to you in dreams. In fact, any new idea that later materializes may be looked upon as such a precognition. You may also experience remote viewing and guiding visions out of nowhere, and some people referred to as psychics may have a more developed ability to experience such things.

It seems obvious that no such experiences could be explained if our minds were created by our individual brains and so were isolated from the minds of the rest of humanity. From a materialist perspective they are thus regarded as anomalies. Yet, a range of such phenomena has given many people the insight that there are nonmaterial factors at work guiding them throughout their lives. But again, it depends on the kind of resonances we craft and make habits of, in relation to the inner core, to what extent they will be developed in a particular individual.

It would go too far to provide here detailed explanations to all such phenomena. What is emerging from the study in this volume is, however, a rational explanation to why such phenomena and synchronicities are possible in the first place. If all humans are connected to the same global mind, with its linear dimensions of time and space, then we can understand why we sometimes transcend the generally accepted constraints of space and time. Our lives, in other words, connect on a level that is not directly visible to us, and this is what gives rise to synchronicities. Maybe these occur when the time lines of different persons cross paths in the Earth's inner core. Regardless, in this new paradigm, where we all have part in the same global mind, "paranormal" phenomena must be looked upon as normal. The existence of the whole world of spirit, and all the interactions people have on this level, for instance in dreams, can be explained in this way.

More broadly, the fact that history is driven by a predetermined sequence of alternating mental states (chapter two) also means that it is sometimes possible to make predictions about, or even see, the future. An example of such a prediction is my own regarding the downturn of the world's economy in late 2007 featured prominently in *The Mayan Calendar and the Transformation of Consciousness*.[13] Some things are simply already set to happen in accordance with the Mayan calendar, and sometimes we are able to tune into those events. This is not to say that everything is predictable in its detail, or that anyone claiming psychic abilities is to be trusted completely, but it does imply that foretelling certain aspects of the future is, in principle, possible.

The new knowledge about the connection to the Earth may also have consequences for how we look at our everyday use of the mind, and especially the power of this. The power of the mind, incidentally is what this book took its beginning with. Why is the mind so powerful and why is it that setting our minds to something means we can move mountains? If we set our minds to a goal this will often manifest, at least eventually, and sometimes this happens in miraculous ways. What is the explanation to such everyday magic? Why does providence seem to move when we are committed?

I believe the power of the mind is related to the fact that almost everything we want to accomplish will depend on the consent and help of other people, and the only reason the mind is powerful is if others align with our own goals. Generally, a big project requires not only people that we already know, and can influence directly, to align with our goals. It also requires many other people to "mysteriously" turn up to support us. Then, amazing synchronicities will often pave the way for someone who has set his or her mind to something, as long as this is aligned with the prevailing global mind (so that it is what we would call "meant to happen"). What I am then suggesting here is that the power of our minds is derived from the connection we all share to the global mind through our common resonance with the Earth's inner core. On the level of the inner core a project may thus come to have a life of its own and, through the contacts established on this level, amazing synchronicities with others may come to support it.

However, I think we need to recognize that in reality we are not able to accomplish just anything that we set our minds to. Most people with some experience of life have failed to accomplish certain things they set their minds to. The reason there are certain things we are unable to do is that these may not be supported by the prevailing polarities of the global mind and the kind of behavior that this fosters. In order to be successful, a project that you set your mind to must not be behind or ahead of its time. The timing must be right for it and in accordance with the shifting polarities of the Mayan calendar. The building of the Egyptian pyramids may serve as a good example for this, since at the time of the downloading of the eight-partitioning this was an idea whose time had come. Everyone then experienced the reality of the primordial mound and wanted to contribute to the manifestation of its order on Earth. To have people do the same thing today would be much more difficult.

THE QUEST FOR IMMORTALITY

If our minds are connected to a time line defined by geometric structures of close-packed atoms in the Earth's inner core, the fascinating prospect opens up that it is by this time line that the duration of our whole lives, or at least the life spans of our individual minds, is defined. From a biological perspective aging has always been a mysterious phenomenon, and its connection to death may not be as clear-cut as many would spontaneously think. While the average life span of humanity has increased dramatically in the past few centuries, there still seems to be a maximum life span of 120 years that no amount of conveniences or modern health care has allowed us to surpass.

Why would this be? What I speculate here is that the human life span is defined by a finite length of time lines on the level of the Earth's inner core. As we come to the end of our time lines, we, or at least our bodies, die and our minds desert us. It would therefore be because of the connection of our minds and bodies to this finite length that we are mortal beings. Even if this insight might not give us physical immortality, as was the aspiration of some ancient cultures and spiritual traditions, it might at least help us understand our physical mortality and who knows what may come out of this over time?

This gives us reason to return to the ancient Egyptians, who believed that after death they would go to the realm of the so-called *duat*,[14] the underworld that existed in the interior of the Earth. There they would undergo a number of rites of passage, facing demons of different kinds, until eventually the god Anubis compared the weight of their hearts to that of a feather (Fig. 44). Those with souls whose hearts passed the test would become immortal and live in a paradise in the afterlife, whereas the souls of those that did not would vanish. These prospects undoubtedly influenced how they lived and prepared for the afterlife.

Maybe then, the pharaohs' quest for immortality and building pyramids as reflections of the primordial mound also had something to do with the time line of resonance with the Earth's inner core. There is much for everyone to speculate about here. On the one hand, the Egyptians distinguished between the so-called *ka*, which we may infer was what has here been called the mind sphere[15] (the ka was known to leave the body during sleep or unconsciousness), and, on the other hand, the *ba*, which was a formless cosmic energy animating all beings, what I have here called the spirit.

What I am speculating is that when entering the afterlife, the limiting and yet protective mind sphere, the ka, which the human soul was enveloped by throughout his or her lifetime, is dismantled. Only as the ka is dismantled in the duat would he or she have to go through the trials of the soul. Maybe in this way the ancient belief system of the Egyptians could make sense to us. Could the almost universal existence in ancient belief systems of an underworld, Duat, Hades, Xibalba, hell, or Hel then have some real foundation in the inner core of the Earth and be a name for a potential gateway to immortality?

We may further ask: "What happens with our memories when we die?" Are they somehow stored in the Earth's inner core in the "akashic records," as the accumulated memories of humanity in which everything, or at least significant things, are kept track of? This would certainly be consistent with the Eastern view that we reincarnate and accumulate karma over several lifetimes. If we share such a view, we may indeed ask where else our past actions, or at least the memories of them, would be recorded. Could it be that an incoming new soul would also retrieve some aspects of the memories stored in the inner core as it returns to a new life? Conceivably, this could generate memories from past lives. After all, we know that memories from earlier lifetimes or from the collective unconscious could not have been stored in our physical bodies or brains, since these obviously did not exist before we were reborn. It is a fact that a large part of the Earth's population holds reincarnation to be real, and maybe through the storage of memories in the inner core we would be able to make sense of this.

An even larger group of people believe they have destinies in the present lifetime that are not based on their genes or environment and that these destinies instead are connected to their souls. Could it be that we retrieve those destinies from the memory bank of the inner core as we enter life? Perhaps there is a soul part of us, with a certain encoding and destiny that is given to us at birth through the resonance established with specific memories or archetypes stored in the Earth's inner core. This is speculative, of course, but we no longer have to regard as speculative that human consciousness exists through resonance with the Earth's inner core.

THE QUANTUM FIELD OF THE MIND

As I said in the introduction, the idea that the mind does not originate in the brain is far from new, even if a contrary materialist paradigm has dominated science for the past two hundred years or so. Several researchers, like Mario Beauregard in *Brain Wars*, have also argued that the mind is independent of the brain. He, for instance, summarizes the extensive evidence within parapsychology that, not only telepathy, but also the abilities to remotely view into the past and the future are real phenomena as we touched upon earlier.

Such abilities would obviously not be possible if our minds were products of isolated brains, and so representatives of the materialist paradigm will strongly object to any hint of their existence. Nonetheless, such phenomena would be immediately understandable if it is recognized that all humans have a part in a common global mind, and even more so if the inner core of the Earth somehow serves as a common medium for the storage of information. The so-called sixth sense would then not really be a sense, but a sum of experiences generated by our connections to the global mind. On my own part, I for instance tend to believe that people in general display such a sixth sense to a much higher extent than they think and read each other's minds all the time even though this is not recognized as telepathy. There are certainly also psychics whose readings are more accurate than would be expected if they had been made randomly attesting to the existence of a "sixth sense".

With the present theory, everyone who has an interest in the mind or consciousness, has now gained a verified and very encompassing model to work from in order to address a whole range of related questions. Through the discoveries presented here, we now have the knowledge that a global "mind field" indeed exists. Such a claim, however, would matter little if it were not for the fact that we have here defined some of the *specific* properties of this field, especially its delineation in space and time. Thus, in the dimension of time, expressions of this mind field have varied according to the seven DAYS and six NIGHTS of the Mayan calendar waves. In the dimension of space, the mind field is defined by the eight-partitioning, including the primary separation between the Eastern and Western hemispheres along the 12th longitude East.

Arguably, we could call this field a quantum field for the very reason that it undergoes quantum shifts in accordance with the Mayan calendar. However, the point to realize is that no scientifically sounding name would make this field more meaningful without an exact delineation of its properties. Fields of a psychic nature have been postulated before, but it is only through an exact delineation of its properties that this field may become useful for understanding history, or for explaining such a phenomenon as remote viewing. The latter is indeed often based on geographical coordinates and thus practiced in relation to the inner core of the Earth.

The existence of a global mind field conforms very well to the view of many aboriginal peoples of our planet that have maintained there is a mental connection between the human beings and the Earth. For this, the quote of Chief Joseph, "The earth and myself are of one mind," may serve as an excellent example, and we can now see that he and many with him were literally right. This connection to the Earth is not even something we have a choice about. It is just part of what consciousness is. If we want to stay conscious, our minds and thought processes will be connected to the Earth whether we like it or not. The only question is if we are aware of this fact or not and how we choose to relate to it.

A PARADIGM FOR THE TRANSFORMATION OF OURSELVES AND OUR WORLD

As I pointed out introductorily, I will not present a full discussion about the future in this volume. We have yet hardly mentioned the Seventh, Eighth and

Ninth Waves, which carry crucial aspects of the current mental shift and explain what will be generated in the time to come. Yet, it seems in its place to end with a few notes about the future of the mind even if enough of a background to these higher waves is yet to come. It is natural if we now ask: "What will be the consequences for humanity that the mind of the 13ᵗʰ baktun of the Long Count has come to an end?" and "How does this new knowledge help us transform the world in a positive direction?"

To provide context to these questions I discuss in appendix one how the waveform of the Long Count (and incidentally all other creation waves as well) have continued after October 28, 2011. In Fig 55 we may see the three theoretically possible ways in which this might have happened. For reasons presented in this appendix I have concluded that among these model C is the right one and that so *we have now entered the fourteenth baktun of the Long Count*. This also means that some of the figures and diagrams in the present book, such as Fig 2 and Fig 10, may not have given the full picture to the extent they gave the impression the Long Count ended after its thirteenth baktun. In reality, the Long Count merely continues into eternity and no new Long Count of thirteen baktuns begins at the current or any other time in the future. Unlike the pre-Long Count, the Long Count is an endless wave.

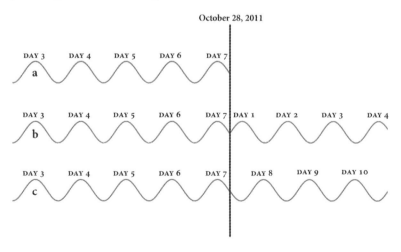

Figure 55. Three conceivable ways the Long Count could have continued after the end of Day 7 on October 28, 2011.

Model C means that at the shift point of October 28, 2011 the Long Count went into its NIGHT mode and that *the mind of the Sixth Wave will stay deactivated for a whole baktun*, that is to say until 2406 C.E. In fact, all the nine waves went into their NIGHT modes at the same date. One of the consequences of this is that the higher the frequency of a wave (Fig 21) the sooner it will return to its DAY mode. Thus, for instance, the Eighth Wave returned to its DAY mode after 360 days and the Ninth Wave already after 18 days. Our immediate future will thus primarily be shaped by the higher waves and those are the ones that we can now most easily download.

The shift is thus much more complex than anyone had probably expected. For this reason it is not very surprising that people were much divided beforehand in their expectations regarding "2012". Some believed, notably without any foundation in Mayan texts, that the world would come to an end, while others foresaw a time for a more positive transformation to unity consciousness. Those that were primarily in resonance with the Sixth Wave might because of its impending deactivation have expected an "end of the world" or at least an "end to civilization." The Old Order, represented for instance by the Big Media very actively gave space to the idea that the shift in the Mayan calendar would mean the end of the world. Those, on the other hand, that downloaded the Eighth or even Ninth Wave might have expected a "transformation into unity consciousness." Because of the combined effects of the different Waves both views probably hold some truth, which will manifest in the era to come.

Because what is currently beginning in the Sixth Wave is a NIGHT, the time ahead will clearly not be a straight continuation of the mentally based world that came out of its last DAY, when Protestantism, capitalism and science around 1617 began to spread all over the world from Europe. Instead, the world will now be shaped by the Seventh, Eighth and Ninth Waves, which in the time ahead will be activated according to a very interesting and complex pattern that will be discussed in the third volume of this trilogy. Yet, even if I believe that from this we can know some aspects of the future we should keep in mind that *the Mayan calendar does not really tell us what "will happen," but what frames of consciousness can be downloaded at any given time.* Moreover, as we have seen, we humans do not design the overall framework of our existence and have a more humble role in the big scheme of things. Rather, the freedom that we have is to choose what to download and I believe it is in this regard that in unity with the divine we may co-create the future according to the principle of As inside-So outside.

To download a new mind means a transformation of consciousness and as mentioned many had intuitively expected that the shift would amount to such a shift to unity consciousness. This is also happening and especially the Ninth Wave, activated as recently as March 9, 2011, indeed now facilitates the transformation of the old mind. Because of the nature of the Ninth Wave (Fig 26), new opportunities for spiritual awakening are becoming available that will unify us with our source so that we can be directly guided by this. Over the time period of a generation or so the result will be a complete reorganization of human civilization that from our current perspective may seem very surprising. Yet, paradoxically, the global mind will never become static, but continue to undergo change. Accordingly, the shift that we have gone through does not fit with the simple view that an old era ends and a new one begins. The future is far from understandable from a simplistic cyclical view of history. Instead, evolution has a linear direction forward and yet its waves will continue endlessly. The current thus seems to be a time when it may serve us to discard a whole range of outdated concepts of how history unfolds and to assimilate a new paradigm. Paradigm shifts always mean unexpected things and only if we can more deeply understand the nature of our existence and what make human beings human will we be able to deal wisely with our present and understand what kind of future that may be possible for us to co-create.

Currently we are thus presented with a choice as to what mental frames (Fig 26) to download and naturally also the question of how to do so. I hope the discussion presented in the present volume has served as a valuable background for this. This study of our minds has taught us:

1. Human civilization was the product of our ancestors themselves, who with the help of divine guidance in the form of spiritual imprints were inspired to build the world as we know it.

2. The universe evolves in accordance with a pre-set time plan. At any given point in time, only holograms from certain waves, with specific frames of consciousness, may be downloaded.

3. Our mental abilities, and by implication the way our civilization has been created, are not hardwired into our brains. Therefore, who we are and what we may become is not something immutable generated by our genes or our DNA. Instead, our mental abilities are created from the resonances we craft with the global mind. For recreating ourselves on this basis, I believe our intentions are of utmost importance. The downloading of holograms, geometric imprints or frames of consciousness emanating from the divine source may directly depend on these intentions, which in turn may depend on our own understanding of what the options are.

In this volume, we have also seen that the external manifestations in the world rarely occur exactly at the mental shift points in the Mayan calendar, but may be drawn-out processes. Part of contributing to the shift is then for us to be aware of the overall direction that the time plan points out and not give in to negative beliefs or cynicism about the future of the world. To contribute to the shift thus partly means right intention, right speech and right action, steps on the eight-folded path of Buddhism. But, and this is an important but, we are now living in a universe where the global mind is very different from in the time of Buddha or from any of the founders of the historical religions of humanity. New frames of consciousness now generate possibilities that never existed before and it may be exactly these new opportunities that we should now embrace. Consequently, each one of us is now very much able to contribute to the spread of unity consciousness. Many people have already started to do so, whether they have a theoretical understanding of the shift or not. Oneness University in India reports, for instance, that the number of people awakening spiritually worldwide has increased markedly since October 28, 2011.[17] Hence, the deactivation of the Sixth Wave mind does allow for a more authentic self-expression and a heart-centered way of living and we may look at this as a step on life's journey contributing to elevating the collective consciousness of humanity.

I believe that in the time ahead the downloading of unity consciousness will turn out to be a reward in itself because of the joy it gives. Making it real in the world may however sometimes require that we stay faithful to our intentions. *What is new is not that all obstacles for attaining unity consciousness have disappeared, but that this state is no longer totally blocked.* This truly represents a "first" in history and in this sense the evolution of the human mind has taken us to a place where we have never been before. What may have been impossible only a few years ago is now within reach. Ultimately, after what may become a difficult transition period, this will create a happier and certainly more peaceful world. We now all have the opportunity to participate in the creation of a divine age, by first generating an inner change, which secondarily results in new external manifestations. On a daily basis, everyone may be part of the transformation of the global mind into unity consciousness. In this, no one is powerless and everyone is able to contribute.

APPENDIX I:
THE 2011 MAYAN CALENDAR
SHIFT OF THE AGES

In the preface I stated that essentially nothing disruptive, either good or bad, occurred on the date October 28, 2011, marking the end of the thirteen first baktuns of the Long Count. This also applied to December 21, 2012, which many had come to believe was the end date. Why was there this apparent lack of drama? It would seem that we had reasons to expect that after such a long evolutionary process, involving nine different waves, something spectacular would immediately have happened. However, as mentioned earlier, the Plumed Serpent was in ancient times known to sometimes molt its skin and direct evolution in ways other than predicted. Such times, when we are forced to reappraise the calendar, may also be when we are given the chance to deepen our understanding of the creation process. What is presented in this appendix is a short form of an article of mine available free on the Internet.[1]

Some archaeologists believe the ancient Maya held great expectations of the baktun shift to take place in the year 829 CE. In a global perspective, and especially in Europe, where the Dark Ages then came to an end, this shift indeed meant a step forward for civilization. Yet, locally speaking—among the Classical Maya in Guatemala and Chiapas—it meant a collapse of their culture. Since this collapse presumably was unanticipated by the Maya, it may have been the very reason they abandoned the Long Count. This illustrates that the creation waves do not always have the effects that we as individuals or cultures may expect or desire. Regardless, a significant consequence of the abandonment of the Long Count is that our knowledge about this particular calendar today no longer comes from an unbroken living tradition among the Maya. Instead, this knowledge now comes from Mayanists and archaeologists.

Based on studies by such Mayan scholars, it has at least until recently generally been believed the Long Count is a calendar comprising thirteen baktun periods, each of 394 years, amounting to a total time of 5,125 years. This is also how it has been presented throughout this book, starting in the year 3115 BCE and ending in 2011. For understanding our past, no problem is associated with presenting it in this way. Yet, partly because of the lack of drama at its purported "end," the question may well be asked if this basic understanding is complete. What, for instance, happens after the thirteenth baktun of the Long Count comes to an end? In principle, there seems to have been three different, mutually exclusive ways in which the Long Count could have continued after this shift point (a, b, and c in Fig. 55).

Since the Long Count (the Fifth World) starting in 3115 BCE was preceded by a pre-Long Count of thirteen baktuns starting in 8240 BCE (the Fourth World), Mayanists have previously just assumed that the present Long Count similarly to the pre-Long Count would be limited to thirteen baktuns. This could conceivably have resulted in two different scenarios for the shift, either as I and other authors have earlier implied that, at the completion of the Long Count and the nine waves these would be frozen in their seventh DAYS (Fig. 55a), or as a repetition of a series of "Worlds" with the same duration of thirteen baktuns, following one upon another (Fig. 55b). However, the ancient Maya did not think of their calendar system either as alternative A or B. New research[2] shows that *the ancient Maya did not look at the thirteen baktuns as a recurring cycle. Instead, the present Long Count is the last creation and, for this reason, this is developed by an unending sequence of baktuns.* Therefore, the correct continuation of the Long Count wave of shifting DAYS and NIGHTS is presented in model C in Figure 55 meaning that we are now in the fourteenth baktun in an unending sequence.

From a modern perspective model C may, however, indeed seem quite remarkable. I cannot imagine it is something many people could easily accept as normal or regular. Hence, it deserves to be pondered more deeply by everyone. We know of no parallels to such a non-cyclicity in any other calendar system of the world, and certainly not from modern times where a period (in this case thirteen baktuns) would not be repeated. From a materialist perspective, this non-cyclicity makes the Mayan calendar system even more mysterious and again shows that the Long Count, unlike other calendars, needs to be understood in a metaphysical context.

Paradoxically, then, even if the Plumed Serpent of seven DAYS and six NIGHTS has now, as of October 28, 2011, run its course, the Long Count continues indefinitely as a wave movement. The current shift hence did not bring a "new sun" or a "Sixth World of Consciousness," but the one that mediated the eight-partitioning 5,125 years ago continues to reign. Parallel scenarios incidentally apply to all nine waves. This paradox is not fully expressed in the figures in this book, such as Figure 2 or 10, which give the impression the Long Count ends with the thirteenth baktun. This points to the complexity of the continuation of the Mayan calendar, which is also the reason this topic will be discussed in depth in volume three.

What there is especially to note is that model C is the only one of the alternatives in Figure 55 where the shift at October 28, 2011, would not present a discontinuity. This already explains an aspect from our own time, namely why the recent baktun shift was mostly experienced as lacking drama or immediate consequences. Many authors, including myself, have based their conclusions on models implying that this shift would be a discontinuity, but from model C, with a wave that simply continues, we can understand why it was not experienced in this way. Superficially, this new finding may seem to mean the baktun shift we experienced on October 28, 2011, would be without real consequence, as the Long Count is not even ending and no new Long Count is beginning. This is, however, far from the truth. The new finding merely explains why we did not experience a discontinuity at the baktun shift. In other regards, this shift was very important and no shift of a similar magnitude is visible on the horizon, especially since the Long Count should now be recognized as continuing indefinitely.

APPENDIX II:
SHORT SUMMARY OF
BIOLOGICAL EVOLUTION

In this appendix I will give a brief presentation of the four lowest waves, which are also the longer ones that play a role in the seeding and evolution of biological life. In Figure 23 significant events in the evolution of life, dated according to the estimates of modern science, were compared to the thirteen steps one by one to sustain such a model. In *The Purposeful Universe*, a completely new scientific theory of biological evolution was presented on this basis. It discusses biological evolution and its relationship to the wider context of the ongoing creation of the universe at large, as well as on the molecular level. This book also specifies the methodology, discusses uncertain points, and much else, which there is not space to go into here.

It is important to emphasize that while this is a theory of evolution, it is not a Darwinist theory of evolution. Thus, while Darwin may rightly be credited as the person who most strongly promoted the idea that biological species evolve, the mechanisms he proposed for this, natural selection (survival of the fittest), is in my view and that of a large number of people only a small part of the explanation to the evolution of the species. Understandably, many people doubt that life is an accident and that evolution does not have a direction, which are the basic premises of Darwinism.

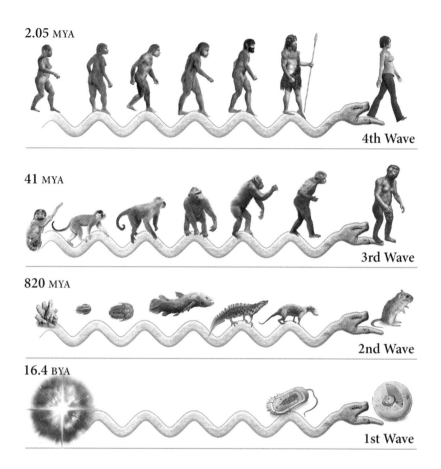

2.05 MYA

4th Wave

41 MYA

3rd Wave

820 MYA

2nd Wave

16.4 BYA

1st Wave

Figure 56. Biological evolution as created by the four lowest waves of evolution of the "Plumed Serpent." Each higher wave has a twenty-fold higher frequency than the one below. To the left are shown the times of activation of each of the waves of thirteen steps.

In the model presented here, in contrast, biological evolution is driven by four different waves. These four waves shown in Figure 56 play different roles in biological evolution. First, they have different frequencies (Fig. 21), and secondly, the kinds of phenomena they bring into existence are quite different (Fig. 22). Thus, each wave in its own particular way contributes to give evolution a direction. Biological evolution is consequently much more specific and directed than Darwin thought. Each of the four lowest waves, in fact, plays a unique and special role in the development of the living species. For instance, while the First Wave after the Big Bang develops a universe of some 100 billion galaxies, with cellular life in some, the Fourth Wave develops a human brain of about a 100 billion cells. The roles of these two waves are consequently quite different.

A very short description of the process of biological evolution based on these four waves reads like this: The activation of the First Wave gave rise to the Big Bang and the creation of the basics of the physical universe leading up to higher cells emerging on Earth when its seventh DAY began 1.3 billion years ago. The Second Wave was activated 820 million years ago—on the top of the First—and as this happened the higher cells created by the First Wave were transmuted to the first multicellular organisms. The latter are then stepwise developed into increasingly left-right polarized animals that, at its seventh DAY, 63 million years ago, gave rise to the higher mammals. As the Third Wave was activated 41 million years ago, some of these higher mammals transmute into primates that increasingly walk upright and have their hands free so that they can use tools. With the activation of the Fourth Wave, some of these erect primates 2.05 million years ago were transmuted into the first human species, *Homo habilis,* able to make tools. At the beginning of its seventh DAY, 158,000 years ago, the Fourth Wave finally gave rise to *Homo sapiens,*[1] our own species. None of these steps in evolution were random or accidental, and biological evolution, like mental, is very precisely timed.

This model accounts for an aspect of biological evolution that has never previously been given a satisfactory explanation, namely, why evolution accelerates. It has, for instance, been an enigma that it took about two billion years for the first cells to evolve into higher cells and only two million years for the brains of different human species to evolve from a volume of about 500 to 1,500 cubic centimeters.[2] Carl Sagan developed his so-called "cosmic clock"[3] to describe this acceleration of novelties from the Big Bang to the present time. This acceleration of biological evolution is inconsistent with the Darwinist view that changes should happen randomly and through slow and gradual changes. The acceleration of evolution is however well described by the metaphysical Mayan calendar. The Fourth Wave, in fact, has a frequency 20 x 20 x 20 = 8,000 times higher than the First Wave, which explains why evolution has accelerated.

The four lowest waves differ not only regarding their frequencies, but also fundamentally when it comes to their roles for developing the *geometry* of the body plans of the biological species. The First Wave is about developing spherical cells, the Second Wave develops animals with an increasing left-right polarity, the Third Wave makes these erect, and the Fourth Wave again concerns spherical expansion, this time of brain size. From this we can conclude that the body plans of biological species relate to an invisible three-dimensional coordinate system. However, the four waves play distinct roles for creating species aligned with this coordinate system (Figs. 23 and 56). The creation of biological species are then related to the geometry of the Tree of Life, and their body plans are organized around its three-dimensional coordinate system.

Incidentally, in this we have a parallel in the evolution of the human mind, which is also created through an invisible geometry. It is then because an interface between the biological and mental geometries exists, as shown in chapter five, that the human being is a whole, even though our nature is both physical and nonphysical.

Without repeating here the detailed analysis of the similarities between the different waves, we may, however, notice a few significant points. One is that (Figs. 23 and 56) the first step in each of them may qualify as a seeding of a distinct evolutionary process of life. The first matter, the first animals, the first monkeys,[4] and the first humans could all clearly qualify as starting phenomena for such processes. This indeed seems consistent with the role the Plumed Serpent has in the *Popol Vuh* as a seeder of life. From these initiatory phenomena in their first DAYS, the creation waves continue in such a way that new species often come into existence close to the beginning of DAYS.

Marked parallels between the four waves are also evident at the points in time that they are completed at the beginning of their sixth and seventh

DAYS. In all of these we can see, for instance, that at the beginning of the sixth DAY, some kind of proto-form is generated—prokaryotic cells, proto-mammals, *Australopithecus afar*, and archaic *Homo sapiens,* respectively. These prepare for what comes with the seventh DAY. In this, a new organization of life emerges in its highest form: eukaryotic cells, higher mammals, *Australopithecus afar*, and *Homo sapiens,* respectively. All of these are fruits of wave processes in thirteen steps. These fruits, in turn, will generate the seeds that will be developed by the next higher wave. The brain volumes of these species will also increase stepwise in the peaks of the Second, Third, and Fourth Waves, thus generating the organ in *Homo sapiens* that the mind acts upon in the higher waves. Each wave then takes life to a point from which a new and higher level of evolution can begin. Such observations are all consistent with the development in thirteen steps with distinct spiritual qualities as shown in Figure 24.

SUMMARY OF CONCLUSIONS AND AFTERWORD

At the current time we are at a point of a great paradigm shift. This volume aspires to outline certain aspects of this, especially in how it pertains to the evolution of the mind and the rise of human civilization. The main points that have been evidenced are:

1. The human soul manifested in *Homo sapiens* with the 5th Wave about 100,000 years ago, and the human mind with the 6th Wave 5,125 years ago. Civilization is a product of the evolution of the human mind, which is in resonance with the global mind. The pyramids, writing, and numbers of the early civilizations were, for instance, created by the new eight-partitioned, compartmentalized mind emerging at the beginning of the Long Count. Agriculture and some other phenomena preparing for civilization were instead the results already of the preparatory Long Count starting 10,250 years ago.

2. The mind is divine in nature and does not originate in the brain. It is not static, but follows a preset rhythm of evolution determined by the Mayan calendar. Human history is a function of mental shifts originating in imprints of basic sacred geometry generated by this divine mind. These imprints account for the power of metaphysical symbols.

3. The separation between the civilizations of the East and of the West, which is also at the origin of the separation of the left and right brain halves, reflects the hemispheric polarity of the Earth's inner core. The special role of Europe for exporting civilization during the thirteenth baktun (1617–2011) is explained by its location in between these hemispheres.

4. Consciousness is a state of "knowing with" something else and is not something that exists in isolation. Human consciousness, in particular, emerges in relation to the Earth's atmospheric-geophysical system created by the Tree of Life.

5. We are all one in the sense that we are connected to the same global mind, and yet we are diverse because we are individually connected to this.

6. The "collective consciousness" of humanity has a real existence and is mediated to us through our common connection to the Earth's inner core. The similarity in the myths, religions, and legends of cultures in different parts of the world finds its origin in this collectively held consciousness.

7. We are the fruits of an evolutionary wave that took its beginning with the Egyptian, Sumerian and Indus Valley cultures 5,125 years ago. Hence, human beings at all times are part of the same process and also connected with one another through their relationship to this wave.

8. Both individual and collective memory is accessible through our resonance with the inner core of the Earth, and logical reasoning depends on this entirely. Human thinking occurs in resonance with the inner core of the Earth, and disturbances in this resonance may generate mental disorders.

9. Many phenomena that are sometimes now called "paranormal," such as precognitions, synchronicities, remote viewing, and telepathy, find their explanation in the existence of a global mind, where we are all connected to a larger context. The chief parameters in space and time of this mind field have now been defined.

To some extent these matters will be further discussed in the forthcoming volumes of this trilogy. The second of these volumes is planned to focus on spirituality and altered states of consciousness and the third on the future. Yet, the reader may already now wonder what the tangible results of the above nine conclusions may be and to what extent we will be able to develop fruitful use of this knowledge. As many will know, such work is already going on in many places and will continue to do so. The primary purpose of the present book is to present a theory that may serve as a rationale for what many today intuitively sense. Hopefully, by providing further ground it will support the movement forward for such themes and their practical applications.

I think it should be pointed out that the Mayan calendar really describes long-term changes in human consciousness and that at this shift we are now only at the beginning of such a change. Only as the new paradigm becomes more established will those turning it into practice find the firm ground under their feet necessary for the practical applications to be developed, and it may be a little too early for us to see these clearly.

We are however now living at a time when a new theoretical framework for the changes later to come needs to be developed. Since we are now at a place in time when we can summarize all the previous evolution, including that of civilization, we may be in a position where we can recognize a much larger truth than previously. This truth is about the nature of consciousness and may be one that over time allows us to bridge conflicts between nations and religions and even between the positions of theists and atheists. Even if this may take some time and be the task of future generations, the work we do at the current time may in different ways prepare for such a unity later to come.

Hence, I believe we should strive for the truth even if we do not see its immediate consequences. Even if the world does not change overnight, we still have to continue to perform basic research and thinking about the nature of reality for the sake of preparing for what will come later. Most importantly we have to explore how we may transform our reality in a positive way and for this we need a theoretical foundation. If we are able to take some new steps at this shift, we do not know if this may profoundly impact, for instance, the health and longevity of future generations. We do not know if, by truly understanding brain-Earth interactions, we may be able to heal mental disorders and design our own future intelligence and its relationship to the heart. If we have now identified the reason for our mortality, could this at some, possibly remote, point in the future even give us immortality?

To take another example, we keep wondering about the existence of extraterrestrial civilizations and contacts with these. Yet, how can such a question even be discussed if we do not know the factors that led to the emergence of civilization on our own planet? Maybe in a more or less remote future such contacts with inhabitants of other solar systems will be an established reality, but maybe this will require that we have a profound understanding of why civilization emerged here on Earth so that we may also be able to understand others. Again, if at this shift we are now able to formulate a more inclusive truth than previously, this may have practical and far-reaching consequences further down the line and so it is very important how we act and think.

The point is, then, not only to see that the ancients were right in certain significant regards and that those aspects should be integrated in our modern worldview if we are to move forward. More importantly, it is with a broader and truer worldview that as a species, in due time we may also be able to attain longstanding goals that we can only imagine today. To what extent this will happen is impossible to foretell, but what seems certain is that it is less likely to happen if our basic assumptions about reality are flawed. For this reason, theoretical work remains just as important as ever for preparing future generations for the challenges and opportunities they will face.

Notes

CHAPTER 1

1 Wikipedia: Great Pyramid of Giza.

2 http://www.touregypt.net/featurestories/red.htm

3 The theory, which today seems the most promising regarding this is the "internal ramp" theory proposed by French Architect Jean-Pierre Houdin. YouTube: Khufu Reborn - Dassault Systemes.

4 The shape of Egyptian pyramids is thought to represent the primordial mound from which the Egyptians believed the Earth was created. Wikipedia: Egyptian Pyramids.

5 Most archeologists will give this beginning date according to the so-called GMT correlation as 11 August 3114 BC. There are however strong reasons to believe that this date was based on the *local* solstice in Izapa, Mexico. See M.J. Grofe, Measuring Deep Time: The Sidereal Year and the Tropical Year in Maya Inscriptions, Oxford IXth International Symposium on Archaeoastronomy, *Proceedings IAU Symposium*, 278, 2011. I am here instead using what seems to be the true global beginning date of the Long Count of June 17, 3115 BC. See also YouTube: Mark van Stone interviewed by Carl Johan Calleman on the Mayan calendar and the 2012 date.

6 Wikipedia: Pyramids. See also P. Coppens, *The New Pyramid Age*, Winchester, UK, 2007.

7 In a nearby site there is one rectangular structure dated to the second half of the 9th millennium BC. Wikipedia: Nevali Cori.

8   In the Syrian site Jerf el-Ahmar the evolution from round to rectangular dwellings in many layers could be followed and it was concluded that "Some 11,000 years ago in this bend of the Euphrates, people learned how to set stones together to form right angles." http://archive.archaeology.org/0011/abstracts/farmers.html

9   Round huts were replaced by rectangular houses in the late pre-dynastic era of Egypt: http://goo.gl/H78ec

10   http://archaeology.about.com/od/jterms/qt/jericho.htm

11   http://goo.gl/MSke0

12   http://www.archaeology.org/9909/abstracts/pyramids.html

13   http://www.ancient-egypt.org/index.html and Wikipedia: Early Dynastic Period of Egypt.

14   Egypt was unified, and pharaonic rule began, sometime around 3150 BCE. Wikipedia: History of ancient Egypt.

15   http://www.shsu.edu/~his_ncp/Egypt.html

16   D. Freidel, L. Schele, J. Parker, Maya Cosmos, pp. 59–122.

17   Wikipedia: Twin pyramid complex; Maya stelae.

18   The Sialk ziggurat, in Kashan, Iran, is the oldest known ziggurat, dating to the early 3rd millennium BCE. Wikipedia: Ziggurat.

19   The pyramid in Hellenikon has been dated to 3000 ± 250 BCE. Wikipedia: Greek Pyramids.

20   In the site of Caral in Peru pyramids have been carbon dated to 2627 BCE. Wikipedia: Caral.

21   http://goo.gl/8ze2n

22   http://goo.gl/b3taI

23   http://www.china.org.cn/english/15802.htm

24 Wikipedia: Pyramid.

25 Wikipedia: Stonehenge; Avebury.

26 See, for instance, http://www.european-pyramids.eu/wb/index.php for a number of suggested European pyramids.

27 "The Analyses of the Landscape and Topography", http://goo.gl/KUPcn

28 http://www.thebiggesthoaxinhistory.com/en/ is a good overview of the Bosnian pyramid controversy. Despite its name, it presents the views of both sides.

29 The enclosures are dated to 9600 to 8800 BC. Wikipedia: Göbekli Tepe.

30 http://gobeklitepe.info

31 J. Diamond, *Guns, Germs, and Steel*, pp. 99–100.

32 http://www.smithsonianmag.com/history-archaeology/gobekli-tepe.html

33 Wilkinson, Toby, *Genesis of the Pharaohs: Dramatic New Discoveries Rewrite the Origins of Ancient Egypt*, pp. 9–10.

34 D. Freidel, L. Schele, J. Parker, Maya Cosmos, pp. 71–75.

35 http://goo.gl/FQuSs

36 As I discuss in chapters eight and nine in The Purposeful Universe, the centrioles are straight and perpendicular units in cells. However, they are absent in brain cells.

37 For the eight-sidedness of the Great Pyramid, please watch YouTube: The Revelation of the Pyramids at 6:00 minutes or read at http://www.catchpenny.org/concave.html

38 http://world-pyramids.com/pyramid.html

39 Wikipedia: Ogdoad.

40 http://ancientegyptonline.co.uk/ogdoad.html

41 Wikipedia: Sumer.

42   The cuneiform is then also what is called a determinative, which is added to a name to indicate that it is divine. http://goo.gl/fo4vN

43   In Mesopotamia it was believed that pyramid temples served to connect heaven and Earth. Etemenankia, the ziggurat at Babylon, literally means "House of the Platform between Heaven and Earth."

44.   Wikipedia: Hittites; Hittite mythology

45.   Wikipedia: Indus Valley Civilization.

46   Wikipedia: Dendera Zodiac.

47.   Wikipedia: Aztec calendar Stone.

48   The eight-partitioned imprint, commonly visible on Mesopotamian seals, seems to have been what Zecharia Sitchin based his books about Planet X, Niburu and the Annunaki on. Wikipedia: Zecharia Sitchin. Scholars however maintain that Niburu is not mentioned in any Sumerian text as a planet in an orbit outside of Pluto (http://www.sitchiniswrong.com/nibirunew.pdf). If no one is able to find such a text there seems little reason to take these stories seriously.

49   Calculated based on Eckhart Schmitz, *The Great Pyramid of Giza: Decoding the Measure of a Monument*, p.17, 2010. http://goo.gl/cjyg8R

50   J. Grant, *Bogus Science or, Some People Really Believe These Things*, Facts, Figures and Fun, Wiley, UK, p. 156.

51   R. Bauval, A.G. Gilbert, *The Orion Mystery: Unlocking the Secrets of the Pyramids*.

52   YouTube: UFOTV® Presents: The Lost Caves of Giza.

53   The workers were fed well and had access to medical treatments. http://goo.gl/fXsRa

54   Robert N. Bellah, *Religion in human evolution*, From the Paleolithic to the Axial Age, Belknap Press, Cambridge, MA, 2011, p. 215. See also Wikipedia: City.

55 This is an idea proposed in *The Riddle of the Pyramids*, 1974.

56 You often hear it claimed that the Egyptian pyramids have never served as tombs. In reality, archaeologists have found quite a few artifacts showing that they indeed sometimes were tombs. See http://egyptian-mysteries.com/?q=node/18. See also http://news.nationalgeographic.com/news/2009/01/090114-mummyegypt-queen.html

57 See C.J. Calleman, *The Mayan Calendar and the Transformation of Consciousness*, pp. 50–62.

58 R. Bouckaert, P. Lemey, M. Dunn, S.J. Greenhill, A.V. Alekseyenko, A.J. Drummond, R.D. Gray, M.A. Suchard, Q.D. Atkinson, Mapping the Origins and Expansion of the Indo-European Language Family, *Science*, 337, 957-960, 2012.

59 Quirigua Stele C states that they were both ruled by the Six-Sky-Lord.

60 Wikipedia: Tower of Babel; Eridu; Etemenanki.

61 Tiamat's death by Marduk has sometimes been seen as evidence of the establishment of male dominance. I think it can also be seen as civilization's victory over the chaotic spirit world.

62 Ana Maria Hoys Vazquez, *Historia Antigua I. Proximo Oriente y Egipto*, Ed. Sanz y Torres, Madrid, 2007.

CHAPTER 2

1 http://goo.gl/MU71R

2 Wikipedia: Tiglath-Pileser III.

3 Wikipedia: Achaemenid Empire.

4 Wikipedia: Julius Nepos.

5 Wikipedia: Treaty of Verdun.

6   The concept of proto-nation is not generally an established one. Here it refers to the early forms of European nations organized around a monarch in early medieval times. In contrast to the mature nations they did not necessarily have one set capital and are characterized by a significant power of regional lords of the nobility.

7   Wikipedia: Siege of Osaka.

8   Wikipedia: List of emperors of the Qing Dynasty.

9   Wikipedia: Ogdoad.

10   A. Cho, A Singular Conundrum: How Odd Is Our Universe? *Science,* 317, 1848-50, 2007.

11   Peter H Wilson, *The Thirty Years War, Europe's tragedy,* the Belknap Press of Harvard University Press, Cambridge, MA 2009, p. 787. Wikipedia: Thirty Years' War.

12   Wikipedia: Babylonian numerals.

13   Wikipedia: Egyptian mathematics.

14   Sources: U.C. Merzbach, C.B. Boyer, *A History of Mathematics*, 3rd edition, John Wiley and Sons, Hoboken, NJ, 2011; E. Robson, *Mesopotamian Mathematics*, Clarendon Press, 1999: J. Höyrup, *History of Science,* 34, 1–32, 1996.

CHAPTER 3

1   The last inscriptional dates were, for instance, for Bonampak (795), Palenque (799), Yaxchilan (808), Quirigua (810), Copan (820), and Tikal (879). L. Schele and D. Freidel, *A Forest of Kings*, p. 381.

2   Chichen-Itza declined as the regional center between 1200 CE and 1250 CE. Wikipedia: Chichen Itza.

3   This is claimed in the so-called *Florentine Codex* written by Franciscan

friar Bernardino de Sahagún together with Aztec men about the culture, cosmology, and history of the Aztec people.

[4] R.W. Kimball (ed), *Quetzalcoatl: The Ancient Legend*.

[5] Wikipedia: Hernán Cortés.

[6] Wikipedia: Quetzalcoatl.

[7] *Popol Vuh*, p. 73.

[8] http://www.chichenitza.com/

[9] http://www.catchpenny.org/concave.html

[10] L. Schele, D. Freidel, *A Forest of Kings*, pp. 71–72.

[11] S.G. Morley, R.J. Sharer, *The Ancient Maya*, Stanford University Press, 1994, p. 531.

[12] The Six Sky Lord (Wak Chan Ahau) is sometimes considered by Mayanists as a mysterious god, but since it is stated at Stela C in Quirigua that the creation event at the beginning of the Long Count happened because of his involvement (L.V. Foster, P. Mathews, *Handbook to Life in the Ancient Maya World*, Oxford University Press, 2005, New York, NY, p. 172), it seems natural to look upon this deity as the initiator of the Sixth Wave.

[13] M. van Stone, *2012 Science & Prophecy of the Ancient Maya*, pp. 41–46.

[14] Wikipedia: Copan; Palenque.

[15] The last inscriptional dates were for instance for Bonampak (795), Palenque (799), Yaxchilan (808), Quirigua (810), Copan (820) and Tikal (879). L Schele and D Freidel, *A Forest of Kings*, p 381.

[16] In the year 1617, the Mayan King Kan Ek sent emissaries to Merida to inform the Spanish that the 12th bak'tun was near and that they were prepared for the change it would bring. http://mayan-calendar.com/ancient_longcount. html

[17]   Wikipedia: Ce Acatl Topiltzin.

[18]   Wikipedia: Aztec.

[19]   Wikipedia: Moctezuma II.

[20]   R. Thornton, Decline of Population in Mexico, In *American Indian Holocaust and Survival, A Population History Since 1492*, University of Oklahoma Press, 1987.

CHAPTER 4

[1]   http://goo.gl/Yv5GM

[2]   http://goo.gl/AUSIY

[3]   Wikipedia: Burial.

[4]   http://goo.gl/yZ2bL

[5]   Wikipedia: Shanidar Cave.

[6]   A. Newberg, M.R. Waldman, *How God Changes Your Brain: Breakthrough Findings from a Leading Neuroscientist*, Ballantine Books, New York, NY, 2010.

[7]   Wikipedia: Upper Paleolithic.

[8]   Wikipedia: Venus of Hohle Fels.

[9]   Wikipedia: Cave painting.

[10]   C.J. Calleman, *Solving the Greatest Mystery of Our Time*, p. 81.

[11]   A.W.G. Pike et al, U-Series Dating of Paleolithic Art in 11 Caves in Spain, *Science*, 336, 6087, 1409–1413.

[12]   There are now claims of Neanderthal art that is around 43,000 years old. http://goo.gl/VNvnA

[13]   Wikipedia: Paleolithic flutes.

[14]   http://goo.gl/eu9EW

15 Wikipedia: Cave painting.

16 Wikipedia: Marcelino Sanz de Sautuola.

17 See for instance Stela C at Quirigua. Wikipedia: Quirigua.

18 http://goo.gl/K4Hvi

19 http://www.telesterion.com/catal2.htm

20 G. von Petzinger, *Making the Abstract Concrete, The Place of Geometric Signs in French Upper Paleolithic Art*, Thesis, University of Victoria, B.C., 2005.

21 G. von Petzinger, personal communication.

22 Extinctions of fifteen genera of mammals can be reliably timed to the interval 11,500 to 10,000 radiocarbon years BP, shortly following the arrival of the Clovis people in North America. Yet, as usual, there are several different factors that have been suggested as causes for this extinction, and maybe it was caused by a combination of such factors. Wikipedia: Quaternary extinction event, note-3.

23 Small mammoths seem to have survived at Wrangel's Island outside of Siberia until 2000 BCE. Wikipedia: Mammoth

24 J. Diamond, *Guns, Germs, and Steel*, pp. 99–100.

25 I. Tattersall, *The World from Beginnings to 4000 BCE,* Oxford University Press, 2008, p. 113.

26 J. Diamond, *Guns, Germs, and Steel*, p. 167.

27 G. Cochran, H. Harpending, *The 10.000 Year Explosion*, NY, 2009.

28 http://goo.gl/05xgi

29 Wikipedia: Göbekli Tepe.

30 Wikipedia: Göbekli Tepe.

31 See YouTube: Ancient Aliens Debunked for an interesting documentary regarding this.

32   The Zep Tepi was the first occasion, when the sun rose for the first time, which I here interpret as the eight-partitioned sun rising for the first time. Wikipedia: Ancient Egyptian creation myths.

33   YouTube: The Mystery Of The Sphinx.

34   http://goo.gl/R7wXJ

35   YouTube: The Mystery of the Sphinx. 10:00 min.

36   Wikipedia: Wheel.

37   Wikipedia: Crossroads (hieroglyph).

38   http://goo.gl/CFJ6A

39   Wikipedia: Winged sun.

40   http://www.reshafim.org.il/ad/egypt/texts/horus_of_behutet.htm

41   http://firstlegend.info/3rivers/thewingedsolardisk.html

42   Wikipedia: Stonehenge.

43   Wikipedia: Avebury.

44   Wikipedia: Station stones. http://goo.gl/3Y3AD and http://goo.gl/Nv8eI

45   YouTube: Who built Stonehenge.

46   Simon Schama, *A History of Britain, At the edge of the world? 3000 BC–AD1603*, The Bodley Head, London, 2009. As Rome conquered Iron Age Britain they only found towns. Rectilinear house building is only visible from Roman times. Wikipedia: British Iron Age.

CHAPTER 5

1   Wikipedia: Lateralization of brain function.

2   Wikipedia: Pineal gland.

3 This does not necessarily mean that the direction the pineal points in is one of its axes. It only means that an axis can be unambiguously defined in relation to the direction the pineal is pointing.

4 B. Vígh, P. Röhlich, T. Görcs, M.J. Manzano e Silva, A. Szél, Z. Fejér, I. Vígh-Teichmann. The Pineal Organ as a Folded Retina: Immunocytochemical Localization of Opsins. *Biol Cell.* 90, 653–9, 1998.

5 http://goo.gl/EG6D

6 Wikipedia: Parietal Eye.

7 G.J.C. Lokhorst, T.T. Kaitaro, The Originality of Descartes' Theory About the Pineal Gland. *Journal for the History of the Neurosciences,* 10, 6–18, 2001. http://goo.gl/8ph90

8 http://saintpetersbasilica.org/index.htm

9 Wikipedia: Outer Core; Inner Core; Earth; Van Allen Belts. Note that the radiuses of the Van Allen Belts are estimates of their average extensions and not spherical radii in the strict sense. For the inner-inner core please see: http://goo.gl/703Aa

10 Wikipedia: Schumann resonance.

11 Wikipedia: Inner core.

12 There is some variation in how these ranges are defined. Wikipedia: Electroencephalography sets the lower level of gamma waves at 30 Hz. Yet, there is a whole literature, which focuses on 40 Hz gamma waves and this is why I am using it here.

13 E.J. Garnero, A.K. McNamara, Structure and Dynamics of Earth's Lower Mantle, *Science,* 320, 626–628, 2008.

14 Wikipedia: Gamma wave.

15 Crystal at the center of the Earth: http://www.psc.edu/science/Cohen_Stix/cohen_stix.html S Tateno, K Hirose, Y Ohishi, and Y Tatsumi, The Structure of Iron in Earth's Inner Core, *Science* 330: 359-361. http://goo.gl/VSqBW

[16] http://www.nhahealth.com/science.htm

[17] X. Sun, X. Song, Tomographic Inversion for Three-dimensional Anisotropy of Earth's Inner Core, *Physics of the Earth and Planetary Interiors*, 167, 53–70, 2008.

[18] A Lutz, LL Greischar, NB Rawlings, M Ricard and RJ Davidson, Long-term meditators self-induce high-amplitude gamma synchrony during mental practice, *Proc Natl Acad Sci USA* 101: 16369-16373, 2004.

[19] T. Alboussiere, R. Deguen, M. Melzani, Melting-induced Stratification above the Earth's Inner Core Due to Convective Translation. *Nature*, 466, 744–747, 2010. For a broader overview, see R. Deguen, Structure and Dynamics of Earth's inner core, *Earth and Planetary Science Letters*, 333–334, 211–225, 2012.

[20] L. Waszek, A. Deuss, Distinct Layering in the Hemispherical Seismic Velocity Structure of Earth's Upper Inner Core, *J Geophys Res*, 116, B12313, 1–14, 2011.

[21] C.J. Calleman, *The Mayan Calendar and the Transformation of Consciousness*, p. 45.

[22] YouTube: Secret Sacred Geometry of Washington DC.

[23] Wikipedia: Angkor Wat.

[24] Some of these estimates vary widely between different sources especially regarding China. Wikipedia: Buddhism by country.

[25] L Waszek and A Deuss, Distinct layering in the hemispherical seismic velocity structure of Earth's upper inner core, *J Geophys Res* 116: B12313, 1-14, 2011.

[26] http://www.quantumconsciousness.org/EEGmeditation.htm

[27] http://www.finerminds.com/mind-power/brain-waves/

[28] M.A. Elliott, H.J. Müller, Evidence for 40-Hz Oscillatory Short-term Visual Memory Revealed by Human Reaction-time Measurements. *J Exp Psychol Learn Mem Cogn*, 26, 703–718, 2000.

29 G. Plourde, A. Garcia-Asensi, S. Backman, A. Deschamps, D. Chartrand, P. Fiset, T.W. Picton. Attenuation of the 40-Hz Auditory Steady State Response by Propofol Involves the Cortical and Subcortical Generators. *Anesthesiology*, 108, 233–42, 2008.

30 K. Lehongre, F. Ramus, N. Villiermet, D. Schwartz, A.L. Giraud, Altered Low-Gamma Sampling in Auditory Cortex Accounts for the Three Main Facets of Dyslexia, *Neuron*, 72, 1080–1090, 2011.

31 A Widmann, E Schröger, M Tervaniemi, S Pakarinen and T Kujala, Mapping symbols to sounds: electrophysiological correlates of the impaired reading process in dyslexia, *Frontiers in Psychology* 2012. http://goo.gl/1U23a

32 T. Koenig, L. Prichep, T. Dierks, D. Hubl, L.O. Wahlund, E.R. John, V. Jelic, Decreased EEG Synchronization in Alzheimer's Disease and Mild Cognitive Impairment, *Neurobiol Aging*, 26, 165–171, 2005.

33 T.W. Wilson, D.C. Rojas, M.L. Reite, P.D. Teale, S.J. Rogers, Children and Adolescents with Autism Exhibit Reduced MEG Steady-State Gamma Responses, *Biol Psychiatry*, 62, 192–197, 2007.

34 G.P. Krishnan, J.L. Vohs, W.P. Hetrick, C.A. Carroll, A. Shekhar, M.A. Bockbrader, B.F. O'Donnell, Steady State Visual Evoked Potential Abnormalities in Schizophrenia. *Clin Neurophysiol*, 116, 614–24, 2005.

35 C.S. Herrmann, T. Demiralp, Human EEG Gamma Oscillations in Neuropsychiatric Disorders, *Clin Neurophysiol*, 116, 2719–2733, 2005.

36 http://goo.gl/2OPmm

CHAPTER 6

1 Toby Wilkinson, personal communication.

2 A frame around a mummy portrait from the 2nd century CE found in Hawara in Egypt is considered the oldest wooden frame of a painting. Wikipedia: Picture Frame.

3   The Egyptian Sothis calendar based on the heliacal rising of Sirius has been dated to 3000 BCE. Wikipedia: Egyptian calendar.

4   Wikipedia: Roman republic.

5   Wikipedia: Timeline of ancient Rome.

6   Wikipedia: Olympiad.

7   Wikipedia: Nabonassar.

8   M.J. Grofe, Measuring Deep Time: The Sidereal Year and the Tropical Year in Maya Inscriptions, Oxford IXth International Symposium on Archaeoastronomy, *Proceedings IAU Symposium*, 278, 2011, Ed. C.L.N. Ruggles.

9   http://history-world.org/mesopotamiancalander.htm.

10   Wikipedia: Anno Domini.

11   Sources: H. Haarman, *Universalgeschichte der Schrift*, Campus-Verlag, Frankfurt, 1990 and P.T. Daniels, W. Bright, *The World's Writing Systems*, Oxford University Press, New York, NY, 1996.

12   Wikipedia: Elamite language; Jiroft civilization; Minoan civilization.

13   The earliest confirmed Chinese writing is from the late Shang dynasty (c 1500-1100 BCE) but according to legend it was invented about a thousand years earlier. Wikipedia: Chinese characters.

14   Wikipedia: Cascajal Block; Maya script.

15   Wikipedia: Vinča culture.

16   Most anthropologists believe *Homo sapiens* have had the brain capacity to speak for about 100,000 years: S Schultz, E Nelson, RIM Dunbar, Hominin cognitive evolution: Identifying patterns and processes in the fossil and archaeological record, *Phil Trans Royal Soc B-Biol Sci*, 367: 2130-2140, 2012.

17   Wikipedia: Electroencephalography. M.A. Kisley, Z.M. Cornwell, Gamma and Beta Neural Activity Evoked During a Sensory Gating Paradigm: *Effects of Auditory, Somatosensory and Cross-modal Stimulation*, 2006.

18 Wikipedia: Metrology.

19 http://goo.gl/zPrZm

20 Wikipedia: Cubit.

21 Wikipedia: Indus Valley Civilization.

22 Wikipedia: History of Money.

23 In India coins were minted before the 5th century BCE. Wikipedia: Indian coinage.

24 C.J. Calleman, *The Mayan Calendar and the Transformation of Consciousness*, p. 221–233.

25 http://goo.gl/WxGu4 and http://www.europeanbraincouncil.org/projects/eyob/

CHAPTER 7

1 DE Wildman, M Uddin, G Liu, LI Grossman, and M Goodman, Implications of natural selection in shaping 99.4% nonsynonymous DNA identity between humans and chimpanzees: Enlarging genus *Homo*, *PNAS* 100, 7181-7188, 2003.

2 G von Petzinger, Personal communication.

3 Wikipedia: Mandala.

4 Wikipedia: Atlantis.

5 Wikipedia: Olaus Rudbeck.

6 Wikipedia: Troy; Schliemann.

7 Wikipedia: Sea Peoples.

8 Wikipedia: Athens.

9 http://goo.gl/U079U

10 YouTube: Secrets in Plain Sight 1-23.

11 Wikipedia: Hemispherectomy.

12 CS Herrmann and T Demiralp, Human EEG gamma oscillations in neuropsychiatric disorders, *Clin Neurophysiol* 116: 2719-2733, 2005.

13 C.J. Calleman, *The Mayan Calendar and the Transformation of Consciousness,* p. 233.

14 Wikipedia: Duat.

15 Wikipedia: Ancient Egyptian concept of the soul.

16 http://www.calleman.com/content/articles/The9thWaveContinues.htm

17 http://www.onenessuniversity.org/

APPENDIX I

1 http://www.calleman.com/content/articles/SomeNewReflections.htm

2 This is the work of Mark van Stone reported in *2012: Science and Prophecy of the Ancient Maya.*

APPENDIX II

1 T.D. White, et al, Pleistocene Homo Sapiens from Middle Awash, Ethiopia, *Nature,* 423, 742, 2003.

2 http://goo.gl/288X5

3 http://goo.gl/Fx9N4

4 We usually think of monkeys as just another animal, but the Maya looked upon them differently. They saw them as being of a separate creation. D. Freidel, L. Schele, J. Parker, *Maya Cosmos,* color plate 21.

BIBLIOGRAPHY

Argüelles, José, *The Mayan Factor: Path Beyond Technology*, Bear and Co, Santa Fe, NM; 1987.

Bauval, Robert and Gilbert, Adrian Geoffrey, *The Orion Mystery: Unlocking the Secrets of the Pyramids,* William Heinemann Ltd, London, UK; 1994.

Beauregard, Mario, *Brain Wars: The Scientific Battle over the Existence of the Mind and the Proof That Will Change the Way We Live Our Lives,* HarperOne, New York, NY; 2012.

Calleman, Carl Johan, *Solving the Greatest Mystery of Our Time: The Mayan Calendar,* Garev, London and Coral Springs, FL; 2001.

Calleman, Carl Johan, *The Mayan Calendar and the Transformation of Consciousness,* Inner Traditions, Rochester, VT; 2004.

Calleman, Carl Johan, *The Purposeful Universe: How Quantum Theory and Mayan Cosmology Explain the Origin and Evolution of Life,* Inner Traditions, Rochester, VT; 2009.

Cochran, Gregory and Harpending, Henry, *The 10,000 Year Explosion: How Civilization Accelerated Human Evolution,* Basic Books, New York, NY; 2009.

Coppens, Philip, *The New Pyramid Age,* O Books, Winchester, UK; 2007.

Crick, Francis, *The Astonishing Hypothesis: The Scientific Search for the Soul,* Simon and Schuster, New York, NY; 1994.

Curtis, Gregory, *The Cave Painters: Probing the Mysteries of the World's First Artists,* Anchor Books, New York, NY; 2007.

Diamond, Jared, *Guns, Germs, and Steel: The Fates of Human Societies,* WW

Norton, New York, NY; 1999.

Freidel, David, Schele, Linda and Parker, Joy, *Maya Cosmos: Three Thousand Years on the Shaman's Path*, Morrow and Co, New York, NY; 1993.

Goodman, Felicita D., *Where the Spirits Ride the Wind: Trance Journeys and Other Ecstatic Experiences*, Indiana University Press, Bloomington, IN; 1990.

Hancock, Graham, *Fingerprints of the Gods,* Three Rivers Press, New York, NY; 1996.

Hand Clow, Barbara, *Awakening the Planetary Mind: Beyond the Trauma of the Past to a New Era of Creativity,* Bear and Co, Rochester, VT; 2011.

Jaynes, Julian, *The Origin of Consciousness in the Breakdown of the Bicameral Mind,* Mariner Books, Boston, MA and New York, NY; 2000.

Kimball, Richard W. (ed.), *Quetzalcoatl: The Ancient Legend*, Tiguex Books, Albuquerque, NM; 1985.

Lewis-Williams, David, *The Mind in the Cave: Consciousness and the Origins of Art,* Thames & Hudson, New York, NY; 2004.

Mattsson, Carl-Anton, *Forntidens Pyramider*, Nyköpings Tvärvetenskapliga Förening, Parthenon, Nyköping, Sweden; 1994.

Mendelssohn, Kurt, *The Riddle of the Pyramids,* Thames and Hudson, London, 1974.

Nisbett, Richard, *The Geography of Thought: How Asians and Westerners Think Differently...and Why,* The Free Press, New York, NY; 2003.

von Petzinger, Genevieve, *Making the Abstract Concrete: The Place of Geometric Signs in French Upper Paleolithic Art*, Thesis, University of Victoria, BC; 2005.

Popol Vuh: The Mayan Book about the Dawn of Life, translated by Dennis Tedlock, Simon and Schuster, NY; 1985.

Richards, E.G., *Mapping Time: The Calendar and Its History*, Oxford University Press, Oxford, UK; 1998.

Roys, Ralph, *The Book of Chilam Balam of Chumayel*, University of Oklahoma Press, Oklahoma City, OK; 1967.

Schele, Linda and Freidel, David, *A Forest of Kings: The Untold Story of the Ancient Maya*, William Morrow and Co, New York, NY; 1990.

Sitchin, Zecharia, *Twelfth Planet: Book I of the Earth Chronicles*, Skin and Day Publishers, New York, NY; 1976.

Van Stone, Mark, *2012: Science & Prophecy of the Ancient Maya*, Tlacaelel Press, San Diego, CA; 2010.

Waters, Frank, *Mexico Mystique: The Coming Sixth World of Consciousness*, Swallow Press, Chicago, IL; 1975.

Wilkinson, Toby, *Genesis of the Pharaohs: Dramatic New Discoveries Rewrite the Origins of Ancient Egypt*, Thames and Hudson, London, UK; 2003.

ILLUSTRATION SOURCES

Cover. Satellite photo of the Giza pyramids from Apollo Mapping and DigitalGlobe. With permission by Ikonos.

Figure 1. All Giza Pyramids in one shot. Photograph by Ricardo Liberato.

Figure 3a. From the Mayan *Codex Madrid*, pages 75–76. Courtesy of Famsi.org.

Figure 3b. From the Nahuatl-Puebla or Mixtec-Puebla *Codex Feyervary-Mayer*, page 1. Courtesy of Famsi.org.

Figure 4. Satellite photo of the Great Pyramid from Apollo Mapping and DigitalGlobe. With permission from Ikonos.

Figure 5a. Ur III (Middle Bronze Age) form of the cuneiform character Dingir (An), meaning "heavens" or "deity" (Unicode character U+1202D, Cuneiform Sign An). Courtesy of Geoff Richards.

Figure 5b. Bronze religious standard symbolizing the universe, used by Hittite priests; height: 34 cm; found at Alacahöyük; 2100-2000 BC; Product of Hattian art; Museum of Anatolian Civilizations, Ankara, Turkey. Courtesy of Georges Jansoone.

Figure 6. Relief of the Babylonian sun god Shamash. Twentieth or nineteenth century BCE. The Louvre, Paris.

Figure 7. The diversification of the Indo-European languages. Adapted from R. Bouckaert, P. Lemey, M. Dunn, S.J. Greenhill, A.V. Alekseyenko, A.J. Drummond, R.D. Gray, M.A. Suchard, Q.D. Atkinson, Mapping the Origins and Expansion of the Indo-European Language Family, *Science 337*: 957-960, 2012.

Figure 8. The evolution of the Mesopotamian symbol of god/heaven. *Historia Antigua I. Próximo Oriente y Egipto*. Ed. Sanz y Torres, Madrid 2007. Used with permission from Dr. Ana Maria Vazquez Hoys.

Figure 9. 18-Rabbit dressed up as the World Tree, from page 67 in *A Forest of Kings* by Linda Schele and David Freidel. Courtesy of Linda Schele.

Figure 14c. The four directions of the Maya, from page 67 in *A Forest of Kings* by Linda Schele and David Freidel. Courtesy of Linda Schele.

Figure 19. Quetzalcoatl from page 123 in *Codex Maglibechiano*. Courtesy of Famsi.org.

Figure 20. The spring equinox descent of the Plumed Serpent on the Central pyramid in Chichen-Itza. Photograph by the Author.

Figure 25. Lady Wak Tuun (6 Tun), one of the wives of king Bird-Jaguar IV during a bloodletting rite, Lintel 15 of Structure 21, 755 CE, Yaxchilan, Mexico. Courtesy of Linda Schele.

Figure 27a. Original Venus from Hohle Fels, mammoth ivory, Aurignacian, age about 35–40,000 years. Discovered in September 2008 in the cave "Hohler Fels" in the Ach Valley near Schelklingen, Germany. Picture was taken at Urgeschichtliches Museum, 89143 Blaubeuren, Germany, on July 18, 2010. Courtesy of Silosarg.de.

Figure 27b. Lion-headed figurine from Stadel im Hohlenstein cave in Germany carved out of mammoth ivory using a flint stone knife. Courtesy of J. Duckeck.

Figure 29. The cave in Altamira, Spain. From the hall of polychromes published by M. Sanz de Sautuola in 1880; after Cartailhac, 1902.

Figure 30. The Sorcerer of the Trois-Frères Sanctuary, France. Drawing by Henri Breuil.

Figure 31. Non-figurative signs from the Paleolithic cave in Niaux, France. Courtesy of Jean Clottes.

Figure 32. Detail from Chumash art on the walls of painted cave in the mountains above Santa Barbara. Courtesy of Doc Searls.

Figure 33. The sculpture of an animal (fox?) at Göbekli Tepe, close to Sanliurfa. Wikimedia commons. Photographer unknown.

Figure 34. Stonehenge phase one. Copied from en: Image: Stonehenge phase one.jpg from Wikimedia Commons. The plan shows the first of the three Stonehenge construction phases archaeologists think took place. Drawing by adamsan.

Figure 35a. From stele to Assurnasiripal II at Nimrud (ninth century BC). Originally from en.wikipedia uploaded by Dbachmann.

Figure 35b. Wikimedia Commons. File: Ancient Egypt Wings.

Figure 37a. The Pigna in Cortile Belvedere. Courtesy of Manfred Heyde.

Figure 37b. Saint Peter's Square from the Saint Peter's Basilica dome in Vatican City. Architect: Gian Lorenzo Bernini. Courtesy of valyag.

Figure 41. A schematic representation of the translational convective mode. From T. Alboussiere, R. Deguen, and M. Melzani, Melting-induced stratification above the Earth's inner core due to convective translation, *Nature 466*, 744-747, 2010. With permission.

Figure 42. Modified from R. Nisbett, *The Geography of Thought*. An illustration of the ideal Black Java rooster in the American Standard of Perfection cir. 1905. The American Standard of Perfection, the American Poultry Association and line art drawing of a Holstein cow. Courtesy of Pearson Scott Foresman.

Figure 44. Weighing of the heart scene, with Ammit sitting, from the book of the dead of Hunefer. The fourteen gods of Egypt are shown seated above, in the order of judges. Unknown Egyptian artist. Photograph courtesy of Jon Bodsworth.

Figure 45a. The Baker and His Wife. Painting from Pompeii. Anonymous Roman artist.

Figure 52. Clockwise from upper left hand corner:

- The Dharmachakra, "Wheel of Dharma", a symbol for Bodhi Dharma or Buddhism in the West.

- Ba Gua, yin-yang symbol surrounded by signs from the I Ching.

- Nordic Sun Wheel

- Ur III (Middle Bronze Age) form of the cuneiform character Dingir (An) meaning "heavens" or "deity" (Unicode character U+1202D, Cuneiform Sign An). Geoff Richards.

- Celtic cross. Courtesy of LordShadowblade.

- Islamic eight-pointed star.

- Buddhist lotus flower.

- Hunab-Ku, Meaning One God; Photoshopped image from *Codex Magliabechiano*.

- Center, Hindu Yantra.

Figure 53. So-called Camunian rose with human figure. Rock 24, Foppe, Nadro, Val Camonica, Italy. Photograph by Luca Giarelli.

Figure 54a. Hexagonal close-packed unit cell. Wikimedia Commons.

Figure 54b. Image of Golgi stained neurons in the dentate gyrus of an epilepsy patient. Cells though to play a role in memory formation. 40 times magnification. Courtesy of MethoxyRoxy.

Figures 2, 3, 11, 12, 13, 14, 15, 16, 18, 26, 36, 38 courtesy of Bengt Sundin.

All other images and tables are the copyright of Carl Johan Calleman.

INDEX

Page numbers in **bold** indicate illustrations or charts.

ABOUT THE AUTHOR

Carl Johan Calleman was born in Stockholm, Sweden. He holds a Ph.D. from the University of Stockholm in Physical Biology from 1984. He has also been a Senior Researcher at the Department of Environmental Health at the University of Washington in Seattle. He has served as an expert on cancer for the World Health Organization and has authored or coauthored articles that have been quoted more than 1,500 times in the scientific literature proper. He is recognized as the main proponent of the idea that the Mayan calendar reflects the evolution of consciousness and has developed a complete theory around this. He has previously written three books on this topic: *Solving the Greatest Mystery of Our Time: The Mayan Calendar* (Garev, 2001), *The Mayan Calendar and the Transformation of Consciousness* (Inner Traditions, 2004, translated to thirteen different languages), and *The Purposeful Universe* (Inner Traditions, 2009). His website is www.calleman.com.